# there's
# been
# an *a novel*
# accident

BESTSELLING AUTHOR OF *CALL ME TUESDAY*

# LEIGH BYRNE

It happened at the Snake Shadow Crossing
where nothing is as it seems,
where there are no snakes, only snake shadows,
and blood rains from the sky.

—Addison Quinn, age 11

## PROLOGUE
# ADDISON

T wo days after the accident, I lay in a hospital bed, exhausted from fighting sleep. Every time I dozed off, I was in the car again, and in front of me—stark against the pale November sky—was a blood splatter that covered half the windshield of our '98 Taurus. What happened after the blood came back in rapid-fire fragments: Mom's shrill scream in unison with screeching tires; Dad's white knuckles clenching the steering wheel; an explosion of glass, and me on the ground, slipping out of consciousness as my perfect childhood rolls into a ditch and bursts into flames.

"Nine-Year-Old Survives Fiery Crash That Killed Her Parents" was the front-page headline of *The Driftwood Daily Herald*. The article described how a young girl's life was miraculously spared when she was ejected from a vehicle before it caught fire. Although the story made for sensational, compelling news, it was not entirely true. Yes, my body somehow survived with minor injuries, but I did not escape the wreck with my life. An essential part of me—the part that makes you feel alive—was destroyed in the fire with my parents.

A routine investigation determined a slick spot in the road made my dad lose control of the car—an unfortunate yet common-as-dirt accident—and the blood I'd seen on the windshield came from one of my parents.

But they had it all wrong.

The blood couldn't have been from the wreck because it was there before.

And on the outside of the car.

When I tried to explain what I remembered to a policeman, he patted my arm dismissively. "The poor girl's confused," he whispered to another officer. "It must be the head injury."

My concussion was mild; my memory fine, and I was sure of what I'd seen. The police didn't believe me because what I said made no sense.

Blood doesn't appear before wounds.

Blood doesn't fall from the sky.

It must have come from someone—some*thing.*

The unimaginable truth was more than thirteen years beyond my reach. But this much I knew without a doubt: The wreck that killed my mom and dad was no common accident, and whatever caused that blood splatter was responsible for their deaths.

# CHAPTER 1
# ADDISON

We knew we could never be an ordinary family, but that didn't stop us from pretending. We woke up early, put the turkey in the oven, and then started making the stuffing, mashed potatoes, cranberry sauce, and everything ordinary people eat on Thanksgiving Day. Everything except a green bean casserole, the holiday dish that had once been my grandmother's favorite. There hadn't been greens in our house for thirteen years; we'd banished them from our lives because they reminded us of that day. But the truth was we could've removed all the green beans from the world, and the memory would have found us, the sorrow claimed us because Thanksgiving would still be there. Thanksgiving would always be there.

We stood in the dining room doorway admiring all we had done. The table was set with gold-rimmed plates, and at each setting were two sparkling crystal goblets, one for our water and another for iced tea. The antique silverware was polished; the linens ironed crisp, and scattered about were items from the china cabinet reserved for special occasions: the porcelain-handled pie server, the rose glass butter dish, the sterling gravy boat. We knew all the fuss we'd gone through, the elaboration, was over the top for just the two of us. But we needed the distraction; it was no day for free time or idle minds.

We lingered for a while, hoping to find something we'd missed, some small detail we'd overlooked, anything to keep us from sitting at that long mahogany table and trying to fill the silence with something other than the forbidden subject.

"Well, I guess we should eat before the food gets cold," Gama finally said.

We took our seats, joined hands, and bowed our heads as Gama ran down the list of everything for which we were thankful. The same things as any other family: the food, our health, each other.

Through all she'd lost, the one thing Gama had held onto was her faith. To her, God was the answer to everything. The wreck was God's will. The deaths were God's will. It was somehow consoling for her to let a superior being take responsibility for what had happened. What could she have done? It had been out of her control, *God's will.* But I refused to believe that a compassionate God would single out certain people for hell on earth while allowing others to breeze through life unscathed by tragedy. It was less painful to view my existence as a crapshoot, a game in which I was an unlucky player than to think God hated me that much.

As soon as Gama had said *Amen,* she sprang back up, rushed across the room, and got the brass candelabra out of the china cabinet. "I almost forgot the ambiance," she said as she placed it in the center of the table and lit the fresh wicks.

Even the forgiving candlelight wasn't enough to blur the deep lines of anguish etched into her face. Gama had been lost in the murk of her gloom so long I'd almost forgotten the playful sound of her laughter, could barely remember when her features were soft, and her eyes sparkled with true joy. She was fifty-five at the time of the wreck and had looked younger than her age by at least five years. Now she looked older by five. Shiny, chestnut hair had once grazed her shoulders; now, it was almost solid white, cropped short, and tapered at the neck. All her church friends who'd lost their husbands wore the same unobtrusive hairstyle; it was seemingly a rite of passage for the widows of Driftwood approaching seventy.

When Gama saw me looking, she managed a smile that was out of place with the woe deep in her eyes as if she'd cut it from a photograph of herself during an earlier, more cheerful chapter of her life and tried to patch it over her sadness. "There," she said and took a step back from the glowing candles. "I think that's everything."

She sat at the table, and immediately picked up a knife and carved five thin slices from the turkey breast. After she'd placed one slice on my plate and another on hers, she cut two more and left them on the platter so there would again be five. There *had* to be five. Five knocks on a door. Five cracks of an egg on the edge of a bowl. Dishes, laundry, and mail had to be arranged in stacks of five. She got up at five in the morning and settled on the couch for a nap at ten. Without exception, she had dinner on the table at five o'clock in the evening, and at ten p.m., no matter what she was doing or who was visiting, she excused herself and turned in for the night.

Watching Gama fill her plate with small, rounded servings of stuffing, peas, cranberry sauce, and a yeast roll had comforting predictability, like watching a beloved movie you've seen so many times you could recite every word. There was more food she could've added—mashed potatoes, yams, squash casserole—but that would have thrown off the delicate balance she worked so hard to maintain.

Despite my best effort, I could not avoid looking at the empty chairs; two across from me where Mom and Dad had once sat, one beside me for the brother or sister I never had, and, of course, Grampa's place at the head of the table.

My grandfather's passing came without warning early one morning, three weeks before his sixtieth birthday. Gama was in the kitchen making breakfast when she noticed he was taking too long to get dressed. It wasn't like him not to be already at the table with a cup of coffee in one hand, the morning paper in the other. When she called out to let him know his food was ready, he didn't respond. This was also unlike Grampa, who would've come back with something sassy like, "Don't get your panties in a wad, old gal. I'll be there when I get there." When Gama went to investigate the holdup, she found him slumped over the end of the bed, face down between his knees. He'd been trying to tie his shoes; his fingers were still entwined in the laces.

Gama blamed Grampa's heart attack on the butcher shop he ran for thirty-some-odd years. Fatty meat every day: bacon or sausage for breakfast, roast beef or ham sandwiches for lunch, and for dinner, steaks or pork chops. "Back then, nobody knew too much red meat was bad for you," she'd said, in a defensive tone, as if she somehow felt at fault for cooking it for him.

Grampa's sudden death was both alarming and confusing to me. He seemed vibrant when I'd seen him on Easter Sunday less than a month earlier. He'd romped around our front lawn with me like a kid hunting the hardboiled eggs we'd stayed up late decorating together the night before. Losing him made me realize that someone I loved could be snatched away in an instant, but even that crash course in loss would not prepare me for what would happen six months later.

After Grampa's funeral, Mom tried to talk Gama into coming to live with us in Indianapolis. Adjusting to the move would've been easy since Gama had spent most of her life there teaching for the public school system. When Mom was grown and out of the house, Gama and Grampa decided they needed a change, sold the butcher shop, and moved to Driftwood, Indiana, the everybody-knows-everybody town on the Ohio river where Grampa was born. "The place has a way of getting under your skin," he'd once told me. "Most people don't leave, and the ones who do usually end up finding their way back."

There must've been some truth to what he'd said because, despite Mom's pleading, Gama wouldn't even consider leaving Driftwood. She had grown to love the warmth of the townspeople and the simplicity of her life, substituting at the grade school whenever she felt like it, and doing volunteer work for the food bank.

Looking at Mom's empty chair, I thought of when she'd jokingly called us a skeleton family. "It means there aren't many of us," she'd explained, seeing the puzzled expression on my face. "You know, like a skeleton work crew."

We were never a big family, even before the deaths. Like Mom, Dad was an only child. His parents were older when they had him, a change of life baby, and by the time Dad reached his late twenties, they'd both passed away. His father lost a long battle with pancreatic cancer at age 76, and his mother, who suffered from dementia, died two years later in a nursing home.

I wondered what Mom would have said if she could've seen what was left of our family. Gama and me, seated side by side, our solemn eyes, our fake smiles, pushing our food around on our plates. We weren't even a skeleton anymore, just two lonely bones.

Three bones, including Hero. He lay sullenly under the table at my feet. He knew what day it was;

he'd been there since the beginning and had suffered through it with us every year. I plucked a piece of turkey from my plate and extended it to him. He sniffed my offering, turned up his nose, and looked at me beseechingly through dusky eyes.

"Gama, I'm worried about Hero. He's completely lost his appetite."

"Oh, honey, he's just old. Take it from someone who knows; as you age, you eat less."

"No, it's more than that," I said.

"Then maybe you should take him to the vet."

"I've already made an appointment for in the morning."

"Good. Dr. Jacobs will know what to do." With her fork, Gama tidied the edges of the piles of food on her plate, trying to make them appear smaller. "The stuffing seems a bit dry," she said. "What do you think, Addy? Does the stuffing seem dry to you?"

The stuffing was perfect, as always; she just wanted an excuse to go into the kitchen for some broth to pour over it. "Everything's delicious, Gama."

"You sure? You've barely touched yours." She offered me the gravy boat. "Here, put gravy on it."

"No, thank you, Gama."

"This probably isn't helping my cholesterol problem," she said, drizzling the gravy over her food. "But it's Thanksgiving, right?"

"Yes, it is."

"Hey, that reminds me. Guess who I bumped into at the drugstore the other day while filling my prescription?"

"Who?"

"Kevin Winslow."

It was the second time Gama had mentioned the name within a month. A couple of weeks earlier, we were coming out of church, and from out of nowhere, she'd said, "Isn't Kevin Winslow a handsome young man?"

Kevin Winslow, what little I knew of him, was a nice guy, polite and soft-spoken. As a kid, he had the misfortune of kinky, pumpkin-orange hair with freckles to match. He wasn't ugly, nerdy-cute, maybe, but handsome? Not so much. That day at church, I'd brushed off Gama's remark about Kevin— she always saw the best in everyone—but now it was clear she was up to something.

"Oh, really?" I said, playing along.

"He's the new pharmacist, you know."

"Good to hear he's doing well."

"Say, didn't the two of you go to school together?"

"He was a couple of grades ahead of me."

"Well, he asked about you."

"He did?"

There was no reason for Kevin Winslow to ask about me. I remembered him, that hair, those fluorescent freckles, and he most likely knew of me —everyone in town knew the kid whose parents were killed in the worst car wreck Driftwood had ever seen—but we'd never spoken more than a couple of words to each other.

"He wanted to know why you weren't at church

last week."

Church. The never-ending debate. When I was younger, I'd gone with Gama every Sunday, but recently I'd grown disinterested. It broke her heart, and she didn't hesitate to let me know whenever she had the chance.

"Would you pass me the rolls?" I asked.

She raised an eyebrow. "I told him you'd be there this Sunday. It's your week, you know."

"Yes, Gama, I know." We had come to a compromise. I'd promised to go to church with her every other Sunday if she'd stop bugging me about going.

"He said it'd be good to see you. Such a nice young man, Kevin Winslow. Don't you think?"

"Very nice." *Please don't ask me if I think he's handsome.*

"And handsome too, don't you agree?"

"The rolls?"

In her mind, Gama had married me to Kevin Winslow. She could see our orange-haired kids running around the house. This is where I felt the pressure. I knew it was all up to me to flesh out our skeleton family and give her some great-grandchildren before she was too old to enjoy them. And I wanted to—nothing thrilled me more than seeing Gama happy—but having babies would have required me to be intimate with someone, and I had a problem with that. My last attempt at a relationship didn't end well, and I was in no hurry to fail again.

*

After dinner, we cleared the table, washed the dishes, and put away the abundance of leftover food. When the work was all done, the pretending was over. We could no longer pull it off because we were about to do something ordinary people never do on Thanksgiving, something we'd done every year since the wreck—drive to the cemetery to be with the rest of our family.

When we arrived at the gravesites, Gama popped the trunk and took out a shopping bag with fifteen plastic, yellow mums, five for each grave. During the spring and summer, we put fresh flowers in the vases on the headstones, but artificial ones had to do when it was cold. She started with Grampa's site, clearing away the debris, and tossing out the old flowers to make room for the new.

After arranging the mums in the vase, she patted Grampa's headstone five times. "You would've loved the feast we had today, Papa," she said. It was not unusual for her to speak directly to the graves as if what was left of the bodies inside them could hear her.

Next, she moved on to Mom's site, then finally to Dad's, which she treated with equal love and attention. After careful consideration, Gama had decided to bury Dad beside Mom instead of his parents because she thought that was where he would've wanted to be, and there was no one else to say otherwise.

As she was finishing up, it started to rain. She fished her compact umbrella out of her purse, and we huddled beneath it in hushed reverence, watching the raindrops prick at the mums; our grief mingled with the gray clouds above us.

\*

That night, I went to my room early, telling Gama I was tired from all the cooking and sleepy from the turkey. But really, it was the pretending that had worn me down.

Gama was in the kitchen, gently rattling dishes, and opening and closing drawers. She was making herself some tea to help her relax. Soon she would sit at the table with her cup of chamomile and, in the dim light of the range hood, worry that I might have slipped back to that dark day, all the while slipping back there herself. But how could we not? It was that time of the year again. And it was raining.

The rain always got me. As I lay listening to the steady drizzle on the tin roof, it slowly morphed into the intermittent fat droplets that pelted the car hood that day. My window became the blood-splattered windshield, my bed, the cold, wet ground, and once again, I was catapulted back to the seven seconds of my life that had come to define me. In the years since the wreck, I'd relived those seconds hundreds of times; it was beyond my control. But the memories I clung to were the last precious hours of love and safety before when the horror of what lay ahead was inconceivable.

The day it happened, there was a downpour. Mom, all dressed up in a black skirt and blue cardigan sweater, stood at the kitchen window, twirling her hair around her index finger. Dad and I were seated behind her, a cold casserole and two tin-foiled pies stacked on the table in front of us. Gama was expecting us for dinner around noon, but we weren't going to make it. The drive from our Indianapolis suburb to her house took about three hours, and it was already 10:30. Mom, who'd always been afraid of traveling in bad weather, refused to leave until the rain had stopped. She was adamant and unapologetic about her set-in-stone decision, and Dad and I knew better than to question her.

Early afternoon, when the rain slowed to a sprinkle, Mom announced it was okay for us to get on the road. Dad and I promptly took the food to the car before she changed her mind and waited for her to join us. We were accustomed to Mom being the last one to leave the house. Had she turned off the oven? Locked the back door? She checked again to ensure she hadn't forgotten anything and then came out with her arms loaded: an umbrella, extra napkins, a package of brown and serve rolls, just in case.

As soon as she was in the car, she fastened her seatbelt and then looked back over her shoulder at me. "Everybody buckled up?"

I hated seatbelts. They grabbed me from behind and forced me to sit down, be still. "But Mom," I groaned in protest. "I don't want to crush the ruffles on my blouse."

She frowned at me. "It's better to have wrinkled clothes than to be injured if we were to have an accident."

"Besides," Dad chimed in. "It's against the law not to wear seatbelts. If the police catch us, they'll put on their siren and pull us over."

My heartbeat fluttered in suspense. "What will the policemen do to us then, Dad?"

"Put us in handcuffs and throw us in jail, that's what."

All I knew about jail was what I'd seen on TV: dank, concrete rooms filled with filthy, sweaty men, tattooed and toothless, a place I was sure I didn't want to go. With a long dramatic sigh, I gave in and buckled up.

As we made our way to Gama's house, an annoying stop-and-start rain continued, which made Mom uneasy and forced Dad to keep flipping the windshield wipers on. Lulled by the rhythm of the wipers and with nothing to look at but endless power lines that, as we got closer to Driftwood, would turn into equally boring stretches of farmland peppered with rundown barns, fifteen minutes into the trip, I fell asleep counting light poles.

When I woke up, we were almost there. The sky was still overcast, but the rain was gone, and so were the stress lines on Mom's forehead. The song "Don't Worry Be Happy" came on the radio, and she cranked up the volume. "I haven't heard this in forever," she squealed and then turned to me. "This is the song that was playing when I told your dad we were having a baby."

Mom raised her arms and began singing and clapping her hands to the rhythm of the choppy tune. She was thirty-two then, but she looked like a teenager when she danced, with her flush cheeks and long brown hair swishing across her face. I started singing with her—I'd heard the song so much I knew the words by heart—and soon Dad joined in, tapping out the beat on the steering wheel with his fingers. Whenever he sang the words, *be happy,* he turned to me in the back seat and made a goofy face. Mom, always the worry wart, told him to keep his eyes on the road, but he just laughed and continued singing.

Before I knew it, we were entering Driftwood. I could see the Snake Shadow Crossing, an old stone pedestrian bridge we passed under to get to Gama's house. According to Gama, the crossing, which was part of Driftwood's scenic river trail, was initially known as the River Walk Bridge. But the locals unofficially renamed it when they began noticing, if the sun's angle was right, twisty shadows on the road that resembled dangling snakes. Gama said there weren't really any snakes on the crossing and that although no one knew for sure, it was believed the shadows were from the gnarled branches of the ancient oak trees that stood at each end.

As we approached the Snake Shadow Crossing, I got excited because I knew the jokes were coming.

Dad would point in front of us and say something like, "Hey Addy, there they are, see?" And, as always, I'd quickly search the road for shadows and find none. "Too late, munchkin," he'd say when the crossing was behind us. "You missed them again."

The whistle of Gama's teakettle brought me back to the present just in time; the sound lasted only a split second before she removed the kettle from the burner to keep it from disturbing me. Now that the rain had stopped, her every movement was amplified by the still of the night: the hot water gurgling as she poured it into her teacup, her chair sliding across the floor when she pulled it out from the table.

I wondered what she thought as she sipped her tea, how she remembered that day, what she'd been doing while she waited for us to show up. I'd always imagined her pacing from the kitchen to the dining room, fretting over the food, wondering what was keeping us, and hoping we'd walk in the door any minute. And when she heard the tragic news, what did she do then? Did she collapse to the floor and cry, or did she remain calm and stoic as I'd always known her to be?

After the wreck, Gama had no choice but to be strong enough for us both. When I was released from the hospital, she did her best to make the transition to my new life in Driftwood as seamless as possible. To love me enough to compensate for my two dead parents while processing her own pain. And what did I give her in return? More pain.

The inevitable damage to my developing psyche, an unavoidable side effect of becoming an orphan in the worst possible way, began to manifest in the months after the wreck.

I wasn't a bad kid in terms of acting out, but I wasn't good either. I was nothing at all, a non-participant. I couldn't shake the feeling that I was supposed to have died with Mom and Dad, and I thought it wouldn't be long before I joined them. Every morning I woke up prepared to step in front of a car or stumble upon a serial child killer. For weeks, I wandered from day to day, stuck in this purgatory I'd created for myself, straddling a line between life and death, unable to cross over or return fully.

The nightmares were relentless and gory: Mom and Dad trapped in the car, surrounded by flames, their skin melting from their bones, their bloody palms slapping at the windows, begging me to help, but all I could do was lie on the ground, unable to move, and watch them burn to death.

I had questions. Morbid questions. Did my parents die before the car caught fire? Or were they trapped inside, watching the flames, terrified of the agony they knew was coming? Gama denied the gruesome possibility that Mom and Dad had burned alive. How could she have been so sure? "It's what the police told me," she said. But how could they have known?

I became obsessed with making sense of the blood I'd seen on the windshield before the wreck. The most logical explanation I could conjure, given its high placement on the car, was that we hit a bird. But there was a problem with that theory. The splatter had a dense, dark center the size of a large egg's yolk, and its scattered perimeter and surrounding droplets covered a good portion of the windshield. Something as light and porous as a bird would've left nothing more than a feathered smudge.

A big bird then, I reasoned further, a buzzard. A buzzard with a belly full of blood. Or better still, a rabbit or a squirrel. A squirrel darted in front of the car, ricocheted off the front bumper, then landed on the windshield. A squirrel caused the wreck. A squirrel killed my parents. There, done.

Just as I would almost have myself convinced, an image of the splatter would pop into my head and shoot that theory down too. An animal hitting a moving car with enough force to draw blood would have likely left behind something more: a bit of brain matter, a tuft of fur. At the very least, the blood would've been smeared across the glass.

My frustration led to more nightmares. An endless stream of animals smacking into a windshield: a splayed squirrel, one eyeball attached only by a tendon; a twitching bird with a broken neck, blood spewing from its mouth. And snakes, lots and lots of snakes, their half-shattered bodies slithering through their own guts.

Again, I turned to Gama, hoping for an answer. "Oh, honey, it wasn't blood you saw." She swept away the notion with a wave of her hand. "It must've been a splash of mud from all the rain."

Finally, after weeks of being badgered with the same questions every day, Gama put the wreck away in a box that she would never open again. "I'd rather not discuss depressing matters," she said whenever I brought up the subject. "Can we please talk about something positive?"

During that tumultuous time, Gama became so focused on tending to my needs and dealing with my erratic emotions that there was no room for her grief, but inside, where no one could see, the loss of her husband and only child had mutilated her. Since I'd become older and less demanding of her attention, the despair she'd suppressed for so long was inching its way to the surface. In recent years, I'd walked in on her more than once with her face buried in her hands.

Gama was now stirring sugar into her second cup of tea. I counted as she tapped her spoon on the saucer: one...two...three...four-five.

The fives began shortly after the deaths and had become progressively worse over the years. We never talked about her peculiar habit, and I had no room to judge, given all the crazy stuff in my head. I figured it was her way of trying to bring order to a world that had become cruelly chaotic. But sometimes, I worried that Gama's mind was in a state of constant unrest because, no matter how hard she tried, she would never make us the family of five we'd once been.

## CHAPTER 2
# ZANE

"**W**hat kind of man eats Thanksgiving dinner alone?" Zane asked out loud as if someone else was in the room to answer him. As he peeled back the plastic film from his Hungry-Man tray, he reminded himself that it was by choice he was alone. He'd turned down invitations from his brother Zach, his Uncle Brady, and Reenie, the receptionist at his work.

Zane knew he wouldn't have been good company but he didn't want to hurt anyone's feelings, so he'd told Uncle Brady he was going to Reenie's for dinner, and told Reenie he was going to his Uncle Brady's. Zach didn't need an explanation. His brother was the only living person who knew why Thanksgiving was Zane's most difficult time of the year.

Zane hated that he'd had to lie, not so much to Brady, who'd most likely acted out of familial obligation, but Reenie had invited him from a place of sincere concern. She didn't want him spending his first Thanksgiving without his ma alone. Reenie and her husband Rex were like family to Zane, but he could never tell them the real reason he wanted to spend a day meant for gathering in solitude.

He took a little solace in knowing that if his ma had been alive, she would have approved. She would've told him his lies were *necessary*. Legal lies, she'd called them. "Fibbing is allowed when the truth would hurt someone you care about."

Zane glared at the compartmentalized food in front of him. There was a slice of turkey on top of a bed of soggy stuffing, a triangular section of strangely bright green beans, and another containing something red and congealed that he assumed, given the Thanksgiving theme, was some sort of cranberry concoction. *At least it resembles a Thanksgiving dinner.* He chuckled, thinking how his ma would've cringed if she could have seen what he was about to eat. She'd insisted on making a huge Thanksgiving meal for the three of them every year, even when it became the anniversary of "that day."

Zane ate the turkey, picked at the stuffing, and realized—after tasting it—that the red stuff was a cherry cobbler. He left the green beans in their compartment untouched, put his napkin on top of them, and pushed the tray away. He had an aversion to green beans. He had his reasons.

After he'd eaten, he began to get restless. He was not one to waste a day off work doing nothing. He went into the living room and gathered up the stack of cardboard boxes he'd picked up at the grocery store on his way home from work the day before. He was going to be moving soon, so he decided to get a head start by packing some of his ma's things.

He was so ready to get out of Driftwood. When he moved to Florida for college, he had no intention of ever living in the area again. He planned on getting his degree in veterinary medicine and setting up a practice somewhere interesting, like Maine or Colorado—anywhere but Driftwood. Run and never look behind him. That was the plan. What he didn't plan on was his ma's cancer.

Zane's ma didn't ask him to move back home to take care of her. She would've never done that, being as fiercely independent as she was, the single mother who raised twins all on her own. No, she didn't ask for his help, but she needed it nevertheless, and he would be there for her. It was the least he could do after all she'd done for him, all she'd sacrificed.

Zach had offered to help, but he lived in North Carolina and was in no position in his life to make a move. He and his wife, Michelle, had recently opened a bed and breakfast, plus they had a baby on the way. On the other hand, Zane had just graduated and didn't have any ties to Florida, except for a couple of college buddies. And Jesse.

I-don't-do-long-distance-relationships-Jesse. I'm-not-good-with-sick-people-Jesse. Zane knew from the jump that their relationship would not be long term and he was pretty sure she'd known it too. In the beginning, it had been all good. Attending a school like the University of Florida was, in a way, a social status equalizer. The students like him, riding on grants, scholarships, and loans, rubbed shoulders with the ones whose parents were rich enough to pay for their college tuition, like Jesse. But after they graduated, their differences were laid bare. For all their sexual chemistry, he and Jesse were not in the same league. He would've never been accepted by her old money parents or fit in with her country club friends, her big city plans. They'd had fun together partying and living the college life, but she wasn't someone he wanted to settle down with.

As soon as he told Jesse about his ma's illness, he saw signs she wanted to bolt. The cancer was like a rotten tomato hurled into her pristine world. The look on her face had said it all: How dare this ugly, messy *intruder* invade my perfect life? She hung in there for around three months, longer than Zane had expected.

After he found out about his ma's cancer, it made sense for him to move back to Driftwood to care for her. There was even a job waiting for him. Dean Jacobs, his ma's former employer, and a long-time family friend heard of their misfortune and offered Zane a position in his veterinary practice. It was a generous offer, a good opportunity for Zane, fresh out of veterinary school, and the experience would've been valuable since he planned on opening his own practice someday. He certainly needed the income—medical bills had eaten through most of his ma's savings—but a big problem was holding him back: the job was in Driftwood, the last place Zane wanted to be.

He knew it would be hard to say no to Dr. Jacobs,

the man who'd taken a chance on Zane's pregnant, unskilled mother and hired her as his receptionist when she was new to town and desperate for work. The closest thing Zane had to a father figure and the one who'd encouraged him to follow his dream of becoming a vet. But he was resolute in his decision to remain in Florida and hire an in-home nurse to care for his ma.

Still, he needed money, so he looked around for a decent-paying job. Zane realized if he couldn't find work in Florida fast, he would have no choice but to move in with his ma, and he'd still need a job, but one that would be easy to walk away from, not tether him to Driftwood.

When he was about to decline Dr. Jacobs' offer, something made him rethink his decision: his ma got worse. Time was running out. He needed to step up and take care of his dying mother; it was the right thing to do, and Zane was the kind of guy who always did the right thing. At least he'd turned into that guy. But his ma's cancer was in the advanced stages, and he hated to take the job at Dr. Jacobs' clinic, not knowing how long he'd be staying in town. "Doesn't matter," Dr. Jacobs assured him. "Besides, you'd be doing me a favor. I could really use the help." With no other choice, Zane accepted the offer.

His ma lived only seven more months after he moved back home.

Now that she was gone, there was nothing to keep him in Driftwood, and he couldn't wait to leave. He planned to give his notice at work Monday morning and then go ahead and put the house up for sale. As soon as it sold—and it would sell fast because it was a stone's throw from the riverfront— he was leaving town to start over somewhere else.

Zach had suggested he stay in North Carolina for a while, maybe even consider moving there permanently and setting up a practice. It wasn't an out-of-the-question option. Why not? Lake Lure was as good a place as any to begin a new life. The more Zane thought about living close to Zach, the more he liked the idea, especially with a niece or nephew on the way. He could stay at the B&B for a while, see how things went, then decide if he wanted to put down stakes. There was no reason not to at least give it a try, and no other offers were on the table. It was settled; he would call his brother later with the good news.

Zane stood in the living room holding an empty box, overwhelmed by all his ma's tchotchkes. Packing up her things was a task he'd been putting off and putting off; going through a lifetime of someone's personal belongings was daunting, and in this instance, it was sure to be stressful, as well.

The curio cabinet seemed like a good place to start; it held several faceless, wooden figurines, something his ma had collected over the years. He and Zach had given her a few for Mother's Day and her birthday because it was an easy gift, but Zane had never fully understood their purpose and why they had no faces. Weird.

He opened the curio and took out a woman figurine embracing a heart. On the bottom, it read *Always.* He wondered who'd given it to her; she'd allowed so few people into her life. He carefully placed the figurine in the box and reached for what looked like the same woman—they had no faces—holding a bird; that one was marked *Soar*. He moved on to yet another woman with a bouquet of flowers in her hands, then to a grouping of several wire-winged angels, then twin children—he and Zach had given her that one—more angels, and finally a faceless dog. He wasn't sure which of their pets it represented; there had been so many.

Once he had emptied the curio, he started on the fireplace mantel lined with family photographs. There was a photo of his ma, fresh-faced and captivating, Zach, and him standing in front of her. He couldn't remember who had taken the picture —he'd been only around five years old—but he wondered if it was the same person who'd given her the angel holding the heart.

Now, looking through a grown man's eyes, Zane could appreciate what a striking woman his ma had been, something he'd been oblivious to as a boy. The constant wolf whistles from guys on the streets who'd probably assumed she was his sister, and the frequent phone calls from local men trying to get her to go out with them suddenly made sense. He'd been almost fifteen when his friends started making sleazy comments. He'd overheard one of the raunchier ones come right out and say he'd do her in a heartbeat. Back then, even though Zane had been guilty of making similar remarks about girls he knew in school, hearing his friends' crude overtures directed toward his ma had made him feel angry and protective.

She could've had any man she wanted, and yet, to his recollection, she'd never been in a serious relationship. The only person he remembered her dating with any consistency was Mack Sterling, a Driftwood police officer. After a few months, things seemed to fizzle out, for his ma anyway. Zane suspected the relationship had been pitifully one-sided after seeing Mack's open display of emotion at her funeral.

Once, he, or Zach, had asked her why she didn't go out more often. "Because I've got my hands full enough with the two of you," she'd said. But he often wondered if maybe his dad had been her one true love, and that's why she'd never been involved with anyone else. He recalled how she'd broken down when she told him his dad was dead. It was the closest he had ever seen her to depression. These were all things that had never occurred to Zane before and made him realize how little he knew about his ma in that area.

Zane could hardly believe the youthful, vibrant woman he was looking at in the photograph was the same frail creature he'd seen in her final days at the hospital. He knew seeing anyone succumb to cancer was tragic, but watching it devour such beauty had been particularly heartbreaking.

She'd found the lump in her breast months before she told him she had cancer. He and Zach flew in for her surgery, which confirmed the advanced stage. He had been alarmed by the news, but being a man of science, he was hopeful and eager to discuss the next steps with the oncologist. Then his ma informed him that no such discussion would be necessary. She'd done her research and had decided what her course of action would be. She knew she had two, two, and a half years with chemotherapy, six to nine months without it. She'd already made up her mind: she was refusing treatment.

The three of them were seated at the kitchen table when she told them. They had always been a kitchen table family. Not only was it where they'd eaten all their meals, but it was also their conference table, their game table, where every tragedy had been discussed and every critical decision had been made. Where they'd cried over the Snake Shadow accident.

When his ma told him she'd decided against the chemo treatments, he put his hand on hers. "Please at least try, Ma," he pleaded. "If not for yourself, then do it for Zach and me."

"I am thinking of the two of you. I don't want to waste a second I have left with my bald head hanging over the toilet."

"But if you have the treatment, you might buy more time with us later after you get to feeling better."

"Might; I *might* buy more time. There's no

guarantee. I know my odds, and my chance of recovery is not enough for me to spend my final months puking my guts out."

Zane pulled his hand away. "So, you're just going to give up?"

"I need the two of you to respect my decision. It's final, and there's no point continuing a futile argument."

He'd been furious with her then and thought she was being selfish. But now, thinking back on their conversation, he realized he was the one who'd been selfish, desperately trying to hold on to her for as long as he could. He returned the photograph to the mantel. He wasn't ready to pack it away.

He taped up the box, marked it *Ma's Figurines*, and took it into her bedroom. It was the first time he'd been in there since her death. He flipped on the overhead light and looked around. Being amongst her most personal belongings, he could feel her presence. The phone rang and Zane, thankful for the diversion, put down the box to go answer it.

It was Trudy Bishop. She was all in a panic because her two-year-old German Shepard, Kaiser, had gotten into a Waldorf salad and eaten three, maybe four grapes before anyone could stop him. She was in tears on the phone because she'd read online that grapes could be toxic to dogs, and she was sure her Kaiser would keel over at any minute.

Zane knew Trudy's concern was valid. Although rare, there were documented cases of dogs dying after eating grapes or raisins. But if his memory was correct, Kaiser was a big boy—ninety pounds or so —and Zane was confident it would take more than a few grapes to kill a dog of that size. He told Trudy to watch Kaiser closely for the rest of the evening for symptoms of poisoning, such as vomiting, diarrhea, and lethargy. In that case, she should bring him to the clinic for an emergency exam; otherwise, Zane would see them first thing the following morning.

After he hung up the phone, Zane returned to his ma's bedroom to turn off the light and shut the door. He knew he'd have to go through everything when the house sold, but he couldn't bring himself to do it yet. Just looking at her pictures had left him feeling drained. He would tackle the rest of her stuff another day.

*

As Zane drove to the clinic, blood suddenly splattered his thoughts just as it had splattered the car windshield thirteen years earlier. Of all the terror of that day, more than the fire, even more than the wreck itself, the splatter haunted him most. The blood made what happened real.

*Why didn't we just stay home?* It was a question he'd asked himself many times over the years. A pointless game of "if only" he often found himself playing. *If only* the rain hadn't stopped, they would have been forced indoors to watch TV or play board games.

*If only.*

He came upon the ditch where the car crashed

and tried to keep his eyes straight ahead on the road in front of him. *Don'tlookdon'tlookdamnitdon'tlook!* But somehow, his sight always found the place where the car had burned away to a pile of rubble. He was disturbed that he still knew exactly where it was after so many years. He could've taken spray paint and drawn a precise outline where the ground had once been blackened from the fire.

His ma had been wise to move the family away from Driftwood when she did. He could see that more clearly now than when he was a boy. He remembered how heartbroken he and Zach had been when they found out they were leaving. They loved living in Driftwood, riding their bikes on the river trail, the long summer days swimming, fishing, and skipping rocks, or simply hanging out with their friends, doing nothing at all.

She'd told them they were moving to Braxton, Indiana so she could take a job working in real estate with her brother, Brady—more money. But even then, that didn't make sense to Zane. His Uncle Brady's office was only a fifteen-minute drive away. Many people lived in Driftwood for the charm and safety of the close-knit town but worked in nearby Braxton, where the better-paying jobs were. She could've easily commuted to work like nearly one-third of the residents of Driftwood did. No, she didn't want to leave; she loved Driftwood as much as he did, especially their rental near the riverfront. She'd always said it was the ideal place to raise her boys. She was settled there, content, and she would've never left unless she had to.

She had to.

Zane knew why his ma had moved them away from a place they all loved; she'd done it for Zach and him. Everything she had done, she'd done for them. Moving to Braxton distanced the family from the constant reminder of what happened that day at the Snake Shadow Crossing. Kept them from slipping and saying something they shouldn't. Letting the secret out. He'd had his suspicions of her true motive then, but the proof that he'd been right didn't surface until after he and Zach had left home when the house in Driftwood, which had always been a rental, went up for sale and his ma, without hesitation, bought it and moved back—and commuted to work in Braxton.

His ma had always been stronger than him. He couldn't get far enough away from Driftwood now. When he was in college, the space between him and the crossing had worked for a while, an out-of-sight, out-of-mind sort of thing. He became so preoccupied with his studies that he rarely had a chance to think about anything else. All the work almost buried the past. Almost. There were times, deep into the night, when thoughts of that grim day crept back in. The memory was a burden he would bear for the rest of his life. The best he could do was to try to keep it at bay by staying busy.

Driftwood was the last place on earth Zane wanted to be, yet there he was. And to make matters worse, his plan to sell the house and go to North

Carolina had been shot to hell by some unsettling news he'd received earlier that morning: Dr. Jacobs had suffered a stroke and had to be admitted to the hospital. Zane couldn't leave now; he needed to stay and pick up the slack at the clinic while Dr. Jacobs recovered. He was looking at possibly another two or three more months in Driftwood.

He couldn't help but wonder if Karma had finally caught up with him to even the score, and his penance was passing the wreck's site twice every day and reliving the worst minutes of his life over and over.

But all things considered, he knew he'd gotten off easy.

As he hit a stretch of the open road, clear of all visual reminders of the accident, Zane tried to think about something else. Work; it's what he'd always relied on to occupy his thoughts whenever his mind began to wander back to that rough patch of his life. He expected the clinic to be busy; the day after Thanksgiving always was. No matter how much he warned people not to give their pets table scraps— particularly rich holiday foods—they never heeded his advice.

When he pulled into the clinic parking lot, he noticed  someone was in a car waiting for them to open. Upon closer inspection, he recognized Trudy and remembered the phone call he'd received from her on Thanksgiving. He hadn't heard anything more from her, so he assumed all was well with Kaiser. He threw his hand up and waved as he drove to the back of the building where he parked.

When he walked into the clinic, he could hear the familiar sounds of drawers opening and shutting, paper rustling. He went to the front desk, where Reenie was bent over a file cabinet. "Good morning," he said.

She turned around and faced him, holding a yellow folder. She wasn't her usual chipper self. No smile, which wasn't at all like Reenie. She peered at him over the top of her reading glasses. He could tell from her red-rimmed eyes she'd been crying. "Morning, hon," she said.

"Hear anything else?"

"No. He's stable; that's all I know."

"That's good."

Tears welled in her eyes. "Why do these things always happen around Thanksgiving or Christmas?"

Zane had often wondered himself. "It does seem that way, but I think bad things happen every day; we simply notice them more around the holidays." He pulled his American Express card from his wallet and extended it to Reenie. "Would you mind ordering something nice from the florist to send to the hospital?"

"Already did that first thing this morning. We'll split the cost later."

"You're the best, Reenie."

"And don't you ever forget it." She handed him his appointment files. "No time for chit-chat. You've got a busy morning ahead of you, young man."

"I figured as much. I see Trudy is already here

waiting in the parking lot."

"Kaiser's file is on top. He's the first patient like you said."

"Good. Anything else I should know?"

"Nope, just the usual after Thanksgiving stuff." She turned back to her files. "Oh, except your girlfriend is coming in."

"My girlfriend?"

"You know, Kim Webber."

"Again? Wasn't she here a couple of weeks ago?"

"It's been over a month; I think it may be a record."

"What's wrong with Sam now?"

"Same thing that's always wrong with him."

"Oh, yeah, the mysterious rash."

"You may as well ask the poor woman out before she goes broke paying vet bills. It's obvious she's got a thing for you."

"You don't know that. Maybe she's a hypochondriac."

"Trust me; she likes you."

"If she does, I'm flattered but not interested."

"Why not? Is it because of that cute blonde who came to see you last spring?"

"Jesse?"

"She seemed nice, but I haven't seen her around since then."

"Yeah, we're kind of…not together anymore."

Zane could pinpoint the minute he knew it was over between Jesse and him. They were at the River View Diner, during one of her few visits to

Driftwood. They'd left his ma's house because Jesse "needed to get away for a while." She kept shifting in her seat from one butt cheek to the other as if the booth was too dirty for her designer jeans.

"I feel so bad about your mother," she said. "Really, I do. It's just that I'm not used to being around sick people." She picked a speck of something out of her iced tea, wrinkled her nose, and then wiped it on a napkin. "I mean, I never know what to say to her. We have no history between us, and I don't feel right talking about the future...or anything cheerful. That would seem disrespectful since she's, you know...dying and all."

It was the single most superficial thing Zane had ever heard anyone say. But in a way, he got it. Spending her days sitting with a terminally ill woman she barely knew was more than Jesse had signed up for. More than she could handle. She needed a way out of the relationship, an easy reason to walk, and he was happy to provide her with one. He remembered the relief that dawned in her eyes when he suggested they take what he'd called "a break from each other." He knew then—they both knew—the break would be permanent.

"Long distance relationships are tough." Reenie patted his arm in a motherly way. "Well, you shouldn't have trouble finding someone to date. That is if you'd get out and mingle every once and a while."

"Get out and go where? Besides I'd rather be alone if I can't have the girl I want."

Reenie fluffed her salt-and-pepper curls, then took off her glasses and batted her blue-shadowed eyes. "And what girl would that be?"

"You know my heart's always been in the palm of your hand."

She put her glasses back on. "Sorry, my Rex doesn't share his toys."

"Can't say that I blame him."

He went into his office and sat at his desk to look over the files for his morning appointments. At first glance, everything appeared to be routine except for a couple of post-Thanksgiving ailments—Kaiser and a puppy with diarrhea. A few vaccinations, then Sam, the cat with the rash he could never find. His last appointment before he broke for lunch was with a thirteen-year-old mixed-breed dog named Hero who was having trouble walking, probably a classic case of arthritis.

As Zane readied himself for his first appointment, he was confident his morning would be smooth and uneventful, but he could not have been more wrong.

## CHAPTER 3
# CORINNE

*1986*

Corinne stood in the living room of her apartment, trying to figure out the color of the carpet that seemed to change depending on the time of day. It was almost four in the afternoon, and in the indirect light from the east-facing window, the carpet looked greenish-brown. That morning, she could've sworn it was gold. Goldish-brown. After some studying, she concluded it had once been either green or gold, and the brown part was from years of grime. She debated whether it would be worth the trouble to lug a steam machine up the steep flight of stairs to find out.

Not long after she moved in, Corinne realized she probably shouldn't have rented a walk-up. Her reasoning had been that the exercise might help keep her weight in check. So much for that idea; her last weigh-in at the doctor's office, she was at 182, fifty-two pounds over her previous weight of 130, which was thin for her 5'8" frame.

Corinne missed being thin. There were many things she missed about her pre-pregnant self.

Still, with all her maladies—unrelenting morning sickness that often lasted well into the night, wicked ugly stretch marks, and bulging varicose veins—not once had Corinne regretted her decision to keep her babies. The closest she'd ever come was right after the doctor had told her she was having twins. It was a brief panic, a moment of self-doubt that lasted a nanosecond at best, and then it was gone.

After it was too late, Corinne also realized that she shouldn't have selected a place above a pizza restaurant. At first, waking up to the spicy aroma had been nice, but a couple of months into her pregnancy, when the morning sickness kicked in, it became nauseating. However, judging by the dingy carpet, she was pretty sure the apartment would've smelled even worse if it hadn't been for the pizza place. She gagged at the thought. Odors were particularly bothersome to her and, oddly, had worsened in her third trimester, opposite of how her doctor said it was supposed to be. But then, nothing about Corinne Isaac fit neatly into a slot.

Looking around at the dim, outdated space, it was evident she'd been so busy working on the babies' room that she'd neglected the rest of the apartment. Walking into the nursery was like entering an alternate universe. It was bright, with freshly-painted pale gray walls, and the faint, powdery scent of disposable diapers lingered in the air.

She was proud of what she'd accomplished in the nursery with her budget. She had found two cribs at two different garage sales that almost looked identical, painted them soft blue, and unless you inspected them closely, you couldn't tell they weren't the same. She'd picked up a Bentwood rocker for cheap at the Salvation Army, which she'd also painted to match the cribs, and splurged on a couple of mobiles from K-Mart. Stocked with baby supplies, laundered garage sale blankets, and onesies in excellent condition, she was confident the nursery was ready for her newborns.

She'd spent so much time working on the nursery it hadn't occurred to her that when the babies began crawling, they'd be venturing into other areas of the apartment. And if she was going to redecorate, she had to do it now because she would not have the opportunity after they were born. She was having twins; she wouldn't have time to do anything but tend to them and go to work for the next eighteen years.

Corinne knew her apartment was not the ideal place for her babies, but she would have to work with what she had because it was all she could afford for now. She looked around her for inspiration. New curtains would help. The existing ones were gaudy orange floral and so busy they made her head spin whenever she looked at them. She decided she would walk downtown to the Dollar Store to buy new ones, along with a few area rugs to throw on top of the dirty carpet, and maybe a couple of scented candles to cover the smell of the pizza that covered the stink of the apartment.

Stepping into her stretched-out sneakers—she had to keep them tied because she could no longer reach her feet—she reminded herself that the exercise, according to her obstetrician, would do her good. But really, she didn't need the incentive. Since spring had set in, she'd found herself looking for excuses to be outside, strolling the brick streets of the square downtown or the winding tree-lined river trail.

Corinne knew the instant she entered the tiny town with its quaint mom-and-pop shops and old-fashioned wrought iron street lights that Driftwood was where she wanted to raise her twins. At the time, she was staying with her older brother, Brady, in a neighboring city. She'd packed up and moved from her home in Indianapolis when her mother's relentless urging to make adoption arrangements became unbearable.

Brady had been generous to take her in, but he lived in a small, one-bedroom apartment with his fiancée, who took up a lot of space. Corinne had been camping out in his living room for two months, her belongings stuffed into a couple of duffle bags behind the couch. She had outstayed her welcome, and she needed to support herself. She came to Driftwood to interview for a receptionist position at a veterinary clinic. The job was perfect for her; she adored animals, and the pay was decent, but most importantly, it came with medical insurance. Three months into her pregnancy, she needed insurance as much as she needed the job.

Even as Corinne had been charmed by the town, she'd been nervous about the job interview. It took everything she had to keep her hands steady on the steering wheel long enough to drive to the clinic. Pulling into the parking lot, she fought the impulse to turn around and go back out. She sat in her car for almost half an hour, trying to muster her courage until she had to go inside or home.

Once she'd met Dr. Jacobs, she realized she'd been worried for nothing. He immediately put her at ease with his laid-back attitude and small-town hospitality. He got to the point and told her the receptionist position had only three requirements: she must be an animal lover, well organized, and good with people. If the description fit her, the job was hers. She could not believe her luck; she was all those things and was willing to work hard too. Still, she knew she couldn't celebrate yet; there was one more thing they needed to discuss. Dr. Jacobs had been so kind; the least she could do was be upfront with him about her pregnancy. She took a deep breath and spat out the truth.

Suddenly, Dr. Jacobs became reserved. He really didn't have to say anything; his hesitance said enough. Just as Corinne was ready to thank him for the opportunity and then head to the Dairy Queen for a chocolate Sunday to make herself feel better, he smiled at her. "Did I not mention that there was a fourth requirement? You must really, *really* need the job."

Corinne had to climb a steep hill to get to the

Dollar Store. It took a while because of the extra weight she was carrying, not to mention the chafing on her inner thighs. She stopped in front of Bridget's Snip Stop, the salon where she got her hair trimmed once every two months, to rest for a minute. She tapped on the window and waved at Bridget, who was inside teasing an elderly lady's hair. Corinne liked Bridget, one of the few people she'd met in Driftwood who was close to her own age.

Bridget put down the comb she was holding and jogged to the front of the salon. She stuck her head out the door. "Hey girl, where are you headed?"

"To the Dollar Store to get some curtains."

"Why didn't you drive? That's a lot of weight to haul on foot."

Corinne giggled. "Are you saying I'm fat?"

"Yes, I am."

"Well, it's because I'm fat that my doctor said I should walk as much as possible."

"When's your due date again?"

"Twelve days from now."

"Holy shit, you look like you're about to explode!"

"I feel like it too."

Bridget, who had two kids of her own, one still in diapers, rested her hand on the top of Corinne's belly. "Wow, you've really dropped since I last saw you."

Corinne's heart leaped. "You think so?"

"Oh yeah; it shouldn't be too much longer now."

"I hope you're right; I don't know how much more of this I can take."

Bridget took a step back into the shop. "Listen, I

need to finish up Mrs. Mitchel before she falls asleep on me. Good luck with the curtains."

Standing in the curtain aisle of the Dollar Store, Corinne was stumped as to what color would go best with a carpet that had no distinguishable color. *Yellow?* Yellow goes with greenish-brown; it goes with goldish-brown. She liked yellow. A bright color would lighten the place up. But what size? She'd forgotten to measure the living room window before she left. There was no going back to the apartment—she'd come too far, and the journey had not been easy—and she was not leaving that store without curtains either. She took a chance and decided on a size in the middle. It was not a large window, so she figured she could probably make them work by adjusting the rod. She tossed them into her shopping cart.

She was putting everything back that she'd pulled off the racks when she felt a slight twinge in her left side, right below the ribcage. Nothing intolerable—she'd had worse menstrual cramps— but it was enough to get her attention. She was, after all, toward the end of her pregnancy. But even so, she was not alarmed. Corinne had learned from two previous emergency room trips not to panic at every discomfort. "You'll know when you're in labor," the ER nurse had told her the last time. "There's a reason they're called *pains.*" The idea of facing that snarky nurse with another false alarm was more unbearable than the twinge, so, curtains in tow, she shook off the discomfort and headed to the other end of the store to shop for candles.

In the candle aisle, she began the tedious but necessary task of popping the lids and smelling the candles one by one. Some of them made her feel woozy when she sniffed them, which was the case with many scents, particularly musky ones. While smelling a coconut-vanilla candle, she felt another twinge, same side, same intensity. No big deal, she figured it was probably gas and went on with her shopping. After eliminating fifteen or more candles, she settled on a crisp lemon one that also matched her new yellow color scheme. This gave her the idea to browse the store to look for more matching accessories to spruce up her apartment.

When Corinne was at the checkout counter paying for her finds that now included two yellow throw rugs and a cheerful daisy floral arrangement, she felt a third twinge, this one sharp enough to make her bend at the waist.

"Are you okay?" the clerk at the checkout asked.

She regained her stature. "Oh, yes, I'm fine."

"Are you sure? You look a bit pale." He walked around to Corinne's side of the counter. "Here, why don't you sit down for a minute?" He helped her to a plastic lawn chair on display by the door.

"Maybe for a second," she said. "I am a little tired."

The clerk, an elderly man in his seventies, stood in front of her scratching his knuckles nervously. This was something he didn't expect to encounter when he decided to take a minimum wage job to supplement his Medicare insurance. "How far along are you?" he asked.

"I'm due in about two weeks."

"Oh my, maybe you should call someone."

"No need for that." Corinne touched him on the arm. "No worries, I'm not in labor."

"So, this isn't your first baby then."

"Well, yes, it is, but...."

"Then how do you know you're not in labor?"

"Cause I went to the hospital twice last month with similar pains, and it was gas both times."

He grinned. "I see. Still, you can't be too careful. At least let me call your husband."

Corinne shifted her weight in the chair. *Why do older people always assume all pregnant women are married?* "There is no husband."

"Oh," the store clerk said, dropping his head.

Corinne looked out the door to avoid eye contact. She didn't have to see the clerk's face to know his expression—judgmental, with a trace of pity. It was the same response she'd gotten from many people of his generation when they found out she was unwed.

"What about your mother?" he asked. "I know you have one of those."

Her thoughts flashed back to the disappointment on her parents' faces as she stood before them right after she told them she was pregnant. "What will you do for money?" her mother had asked. Her way of saying she had no intention of offering Corinne monetary support.

"I'll get a job," Corinne shot back.

"How can you possibly take care of a baby?" Of

course, her mother had no way of knowing Corinne was having twins. "You're just a baby yourself."

Her dad, a man of few words, who'd been silent until then, finally spoke up. "But sweetheart, what about your education?" he asked.

She was in her second year of junior college, intending to transfer her credits somewhere else as soon as she decided on a major. "I can always go back to school later."

He looked away and shook his head, a gesture that had hurt her worse than anything he could've said.

The clerk returned to the checkout counter and picked up the phone receiver. "Here, do you want to use the phone to call your mother?"

Corinne scooted to the front edge of the chair. "You know, there's no need to call anyone. I'm feeling much better now." She pushed herself to her feet, both hands firmly on the armrests. As soon as she straightened up, another twinge pulled her back into the chair again.

The clerk rushed to her side and took her arm. "Whoa, easy there."

The fourth twinge was much stronger than the others; it ripped through her side and radiated to her back. Corinne was sure she was now in labor. "Maybe I should call someone after all," she said.

"Here, let me get you the phone." He darted back behind the counter—surprisingly fast, Corinne noted, for an elderly man—picked up the receiver and tried to walk toward her, but the cord wouldn't reach. "I'll have to dial it for you. What's the number?"

Corinne didn't know the number; she didn't even know who to call. She considered calling Brady but promptly dismissed the idea. She needed someone who would understand what she was going through. "Bridget. You can call Bridget Harlow," she said.

"You mean Bridget from the beauty parlor?"

"Yes...I'm not sure of the number, though."

"Heck, I can run and get her. You stay here and watch the store; I'll be right back."

"Oh, I'm not going anywhere."

When the clerk returned to the store, Bridget was with him. "I told you it wouldn't be long, she said. "Now, let's go have a baby!"

"What about the salon?" Corinne asked.

"I've already locked up for the day." Bridget winked. "You can do that when you run the place." She helped Corinne to her feet. "Come on...we'd better go *now*."

*

Corinne was sitting up in a hospital bed, her back ridged against the pillow behind her, waiting for the nurse to bring in her twin boys. Suddenly a wave of fear and self-doubt washed over her as reality set in: she now had two tiny humans counting on her to take care of them. She thought of something her mom had said during their last conversation before Corinne left home. "It's too difficult to raise a child yourself, and you can forget about the boy helping you. He hasn't even graduated high school yet."

How could Corinne have known Danny was barely seventeen? He'd told her he was eighteen, and she had no reason not to believe him. He acted older and certainly had the body of a man. She recalled when she'd first seen him, pushing a mower up and down the next-door neighbors' lawn, his muscles rippling across his shoulders and chest when he made a turn. Corinne lay on a lounger in her back yard watching him from behind dark sunglasses. She was interested in him, not so much because he was cute—he was cute, no doubt about that, with his disheveled sun-streaked hair against tanned skin— but because she was curious about who he was. The Bakers—the couple whose yard he was mowing— were the kind of neighbors who kept to themselves. But she had noticed they didn't have many visitors, and Corinne was sure she'd never seen the guy there before; she would've remembered him. He looked too young to be the Bakers' son—they were probably in their sixties. Maybe a grandson? Or perhaps he was of no relation, just some random guy they'd hired to mow their grass.

While she was pondering all this, he spotted her looking at him and stopped the mower. With a snap of his head, he flipped his hair out of his face, wiped his sweaty brow with a t-shirt hanging out of the back pocket of his cut-off jean shorts, then started walking her way. As he approached, Corinne turned a page of the book she was pretending to read as if to be oblivious to his presence. He introduced himself in a mannerly, older guy way, said he was from Canada and was spending the summer with his grandparents to see what it was like in the United States.

The conversation took off, and before she knew it, he was sitting on the lawn chair beside her. Time got away from them, and soon, they'd made plans for the evening. All she'd initially intended to do was be neighborly and show him around town, but they got along so well they spent the next day together, the next, and every day for the rest of the summer. That's how it got started, two people curious about each other. The sex, as it often does when you're young, full of hormones, and with too much free time, just happened.

At the end of the summer, before Danny returned home, they exchanged addresses and phone numbers, neither expecting the other to call. It was a fling. She never thought anything would come of the relationship, certainly not this.

When Corinne found out she was pregnant, Danny was back in school in Canada. She wrote to tell him because she thought he had the right to know but made it clear that she wasn't asking him for anything. A couple of weeks later, she got a response. Inside the envelope addressed to her was a check for $5,000 and a note:

*Dear Corinne,*

*We have been in contact with your parents, and we all*

*agree that it would be best for everyone involved if you put the baby up for adoption. At seventeen, Danny is in no way equipped to raise a child. We hope you will take this money and do the right thing. We wish you the best of luck pursuing your dreams. We just want our son to have a chance in life, the same thing your parents want for you.*

*Most sincerely,*

*James and Patricia Belanger*

Brady walked into the room, snapping her out of deep thought. "Hey there, wide load," he said. "I just saw the boys, and I've got to say, I don't know how such good-looking babies came out of you."

She took one look at her brother and burst into tears.

"Hey, hey, what's the matter?" He walked to her bed like he wanted to comfort her but didn't know how. He had never been good at that sort of thing. When they were kids, his way of showing affection was to give her a sock on the arm. But that wouldn't have been appropriate in this instance, so he stood there looking lost. "I'm sorry, Cori; I was only teasing." He put his hand on her blanketed leg, then retracted it as if he was embarrassed by his sensitivity. "You've got no reason to cry. You should be happy; you just dropped about fifteen pounds."

A wet, gurgling laugh erupted through Corinne's tears. Brady had always had that effect on her. Without even trying, he knew what to do, what to say. She straightened up and wiped her face with the bed sheet. "Only thirty more to go," she said, and they laughed together.

"Tell me, how did you come up with the baby's names? They're...umm...unusual."

"Well, I knew I wanted the first one born to be named Zachary. It's Danny's middle name, and I thought I should give him a tribute since he had a hand in all this."

"A hand?"

"You know what I mean. And I thought another *Z* name would be cool, something twin-*ish*, and there aren't many of those to choose from. It's like Zeke, Zander, or Zane, and I like Zane the best."

"Zach and Zane Isaac...hmm, it'll take some getting used to." He sat on the side of the bed. "So, what were you all upset about a few minutes ago?"

Corinne felt her throat tighten. "Maybe it's the hormones, but I'm scared."

"Of what? The Cori I remember has never been afraid of anything."

"Brady, I don't know if I can do this."

He chuckled. "Seems to me you've already done the hardest part."

"What if Mom was right? What if I can't care for a baby, let alone two?" She covered her face with her hands. "My God, there are two of them!"

"First off, you're not alone. You've got me, Dr. Jacobs, and Bridget, and you know Mom and Dad will come around sooner or later." She turned her face away so he wouldn't see the tears bound to spill. "Hey, look at me. You got this. Remember when I climbed out of the treehouse and missed the ladder's last rung?"

"Yeah, I laughed my ass off until I found out you'd cut your hand on a piece of broken glass."

"Who pulled the ribbon from her hair and tied it around my arm as a tourniquet?"

"I'd seen somebody do it on one of those doctor shows on TV."

"What happened to that Cori?"

"The wound wasn't bad enough for stitches, much less a tourniquet. Mom slapped a couple of butterfly Band-Aids on it, and you were good to go."

"That's not the point. The point is you kept your head and knew what to do. And you were only eleven. You can handle this. I have no doubt."

"I hope you're right."

"Hey, I've got some good news that might cheer you up. I think I found a house for you to rent so you can move out of that crappy apartment."

"Where?"

"In Driftwood, close to the riverfront, it's only a two-bedroom, but plenty of space for the three of you."

"If it's near the riverfront, I already know I can't afford it."

"That's the best part. The owners are an older couple who are more interested in having a good tenant they know will take care of the house than making money. They might agree to a reduced rent if you would be willing to do some work...cleaning, painting, stuff like that. Apparently, the previous renters were not kind to the place."

"I'll do whatever they want. When can we move in?"

"It's vacant, so whenever."

Corinne threw her arms around Brady's neck. "Thank you, thank you, thank you!"

"You're welcome. See, it pays to have a realtor for a brother."

A nurse entered the room, holding one of the newborns tightly cocooned in a blue blanket. "This is Zane," she said and handed the baby to Corinne, who carefully supported his head in the crook of her arm.

Another nurse was not far behind carrying Zach. "Can you handle them both at once?"

Corinne hesitated, so Brady answered for her. "Sure, she can. This girl can do anything."

Cradling her babies, Corinne looked down at their tiny crinkled faces and felt the strength from deep within her soar to the surface. It was a moment she would reflect upon years later when faced with impossible decisions. She would summon the unconditional love she'd felt when she first held her sons to find the courage to do what a good mother does: protects her children at any cost.

**CHAPTER 4**

# ADDISON

A cross the room, my silenced cell phone was vibrating on the dresser. Through slit eyes, I looked at the clock on my nightstand; it was 10:25. That's when it hit me: *Hero has an appointment with the vet!*

I flung back the covers, slapped both feet on the hardwood floor, and lunged for the phone. I didn't have to see the caller ID to know it was Lily. A few days earlier, I'd asked her to drive Hero and me to the vet clinic, and she was calling to tell me she was on her way over.

I could've gone to the clinic alone—I had a car and a license—but Lily always drove me places where I had to pass under the Snake Shadow Crossing to get there. It was something unspoken but understood between us.

Holding the phone on my shoulder, I picked up a crumpled pair of jeans from the floor by my bed and hobbled on one foot as I struggled to step into them.

"Hey, it's me," Lily said. "Just wanted to make sure you're ready. I tried texting first, but we both know how you are about checking your messages."

"Of course, I'm ready."

She laughed. "Sure, you are. I can hear you putting your clothes on, you know."

I grabbed a hoodie from the closet. "Don't worry about it; I'll be ready when you get here."

"I'll see you in about ten minutes then."

I never could fool Lily. She'd had my number since fourth grade.

While waiting for class to begin, I felt a tap on my shoulder from behind and turned around to a skinny, doe-eyed girl with big hair. She leaned into me and whispered, "Just so you know, I'm not buying this I-can't-talk bull you're selling to everybody else. But hey, if it works for you, keeps people from bugging you, I get it."

I hadn't spoken a word to anyone in over a month. Gama didn't want to discuss the wreck or the splatter, and I didn't want to talk about anything else. So, one Saturday morning, I was sitting at the kitchen table when she asked me what I wanted for breakfast, waffles or French toast, and I simply didn't answer.

At first, Gama thought I was mad about something—I was like that, pouty, stubborn—but after three days, she knew there was a problem and took me to our family doctor to see if I was having some sort of delayed reaction to my head injury. The doctor assured her there was nothing wrong with me, at least not physically, and suggested I see a psychologist.

Dr. Louise Conway was a deliberately plain

middle-aged woman who spoke in a calm, controlled monotone. She had mastered the quintessential psychologist persona—placid, carefully-measured smile, compassionate yet unbiased head tilt. Unlike Gama, Dr. Conway was more than willing to discuss the wreck, but not how I wanted to. She wanted to talk about my feelings. How losing my parents and being the only survivor made me feel. "Has someone hurt you or made you angry, and now you're using silence to punish them?" "If you could wave a magic wand and make anything happen, what changes would you make to your life?"

She continued with her formulaic questions, hoping to trigger tears or rage—any emotion at all —and I continued not answering. There was no need for me to talk; my silence had become my voice. A couple of sessions in, even though I hadn't said anything, she announced a diagnosis to Gama: survivor's guilt. Of course, I had survivor's guilt. I didn't need a psychologist to tell me I hated myself because I came out of the wreck alive, and my parents didn't.

After almost a month of getting nowhere, Dr. Conway told Gama there was no reason to continue my therapy because she couldn't help me if I refused to communicate with her. In time, almost everybody grew to accept the mute Addison with surprising cooperation. My teachers stopped asking me questions in class, and the kids at school even left me alone, until the know-it-all new girl showed up.

Every morning, Lily gave me a mischievous we-share-a-secret grin. On our breaks, she always sat beside me. She didn't seem to mind that I didn't talk; she was perfectly content with one-sided conversations. "It sucks that your parents are dead," she said during our first lunch together. "If it makes you feel any better, my dad's an alcoholic and doesn't want anything to do with me." She didn't even stop to take a breath before hitting the next subject. "Cool scars. How'd you get them? You probably ran through a glass door. I once knew a boy who did that. Well, he didn't *run* through it; his brother pushed him. His scars were a lot like yours. That's what happened, isn't it? Yeah, that's how it happened; you ran through a door...."

In the coming weeks, I learned that she and her mother lived on the south side of town in a trailer park Lily called a subdivision. They'd moved from somewhere in rural Kentucky, fleeing from her abusive father. Traveling north up the Ohio River, they'd stopped in random towns, searching for one that felt right. When they got to Driftwood, her mother did a Tarot card reading, and all signs pointed to it being a safe place for them to settle.

Soon, I got to where I looked forward to seeing Lily and hearing her funny monologues, and we became best friends. Not much had changed between us since fourth grade. She still talked nonstop, I still loved listening to her, and we remained inseparable. We'd even gone to the same college. Indiana State was only a two-hour drive from Driftwood, but because Lily wanted the full college experience, we rented an off-campus house that allowed pets, so Hero could live with us.

In the corner of my room, Hero was still asleep in his bed. I got down on my hands and knees and crawled over to him. After the wreck, he'd been the one who dutifully got me up every day—a cool, wet snort in my ear, a long lap of his tongue across my cheek—to let me know he was ready for his morning walk. Now, he barely stirred when I softly touched his back. "Hey boy, you up for a ride this morning?" When Hero was younger, he'd pounced to the door when I said the word *ride*. Now he looked up at me, his eyes yearning but his body unable to act. "That's okay, baby; take your time."

Stroking the top of his head, peppered with gray, I thought of how much he had changed over the years. When he was a puppy, he started out a tawny color, and his ears were pricked—or at least one of them was—the other one bent, ever so slightly, at the tip, and he had a faint mask that came to a point at his forehead and wrapped around his eyes. Gama thought he looked like a Shepard mix. But as months passed, his coat began to change to light gold, his mask gradually faded until it had almost disappeared, and his pricked ear started to fold over. One day he got up and was pale yellow with flop ears. Dr. Jacobs said he was "your garden variety mutt," which, as he pointed out, was a good thing because mutts tend to live longer.

I went over to my dresser, found an elastic band

and pulled my hair up into a high ponytail. Then, as I did every morning, I examined my scars in the mirror. Only two were on my face—the rest were on my neck and strewn across my back—but they were long and as jagged as the broken glass that had created them. One started about three inches under the outer corner of my right eye and ran down my cheek to my jawline. The other jutted from under my right earlobe and continued to my collarbone.

When I was younger, I went through a stage where I combed my hair over one side of my face to conceal my scars; later, I tried make-up. But I'd abandoned all that by the time I graduated high school. Now I wanted them to be seen, and I wanted to see them. Hero and the scars were all I had left from the last day I was with my parents.

"Come on, boy; we've got to go now." I slipped into some moccasins and then went back to try again to get Hero out of bed. Obediently, he planted his front paws on the floor and then waited for me to get behind him to help with the rest. As I lifted his rear end, he straightened his back legs, and together we brought him to a standing position. This had become part of our morning routine since he could no longer get up on his own after he'd been sedentary for a while.

Gama had been awake since five and had long finished her usual breakfast of tea and toast. She was now seated at the table, pretending to be engrossed in a crossword puzzle, an eye on the clock waiting for me to come out of my room.

When I walked into the kitchen, she looked up from the paper. "I was wondering if you would ever get out of bed today."

"Morning, Gama."

"Did you sleep well?"

"Yes. You?"

I'd slept maybe four hours, on and off. "Yes, fine," I lied.

"So, what are your plans for the day?"

Really, she wanted to know what my plans were for the rest of my life. It was a question she'd been asking me a lot lately in thinly-veiled ways. Like we'd be at the bank, and she'd say, "Look, Addy, they're hiring tellers. Why don't you put in an application while we're here?" Or we'd be watching TV, and an advertisement would come on about a job fair, and she'd say, "We should go check it out, just for fun."

It wasn't that she was trying to get me to move out; Gama would've happily let me live with her for the rest of my life. She wanted me to find a direction, have a purpose, and most of all, she was trying to keep me from slipping back into the black hole I'd lived in after the wreck.

I realized I would eventually have to do something with my life, and I was working on it... in my mind. At least I'd gone to college; that was a start. My degree was in business, which had seemed practical, even sounded practical, and I thought it would cast a wide net. I needed a wide net. The problem was I had no interest in business and felt no sense of urgency to get a job. Gama was partly to blame. After my graduation, she told me to take some time to think about what I wanted to do. "The answer will come to you," she'd said. I'd been out of school for six months, and nothing had come to me yet.

"Don't you remember? I have to take Hero to the vet." I opened the back door and watched him hobble across the room and go outside.

"Oh, that's right," Gama said. "Poor boy, he seems worse this morning."

"I know. I hope it's nothing serious."

"Oh honey, he's okay. He's merely slowing down." She got up from the table and went over to the counter. "Sit. I'll fix you something to eat."

"I can't. Lily should be here to pick me up any second."

"But you have to eat something."

"I'll grab a Pop Tart on my way out."

"Nonsense; it's almost lunchtime. I'll make a sandwich; you can eat it on the way." She pulled the leftover turkey out of the refrigerator. "So, what are your plans after you return from the vet?"

"I'll probably work down in the basement for a while."

She stopped unwrapping the turkey. "Addy, I know you enjoy your stained glass, but...."

I was sixteen when I fell in love with stained glass. Gama and I were shopping downtown when I saw a dragonfly sun catcher hanging in the front window of a craft shop and became transfixed by the way the sunlight reflected in the colorful wings.

Gama was pleased; it was the first thing I'd shown the slightest interest in since the wreck. That day, she took me inside the shop and bought me my first stained glass kit. I started out making sun catchers from simple patterns of birds and flowers. As I became more adept, I worked my way up to intricate designs, many of which I created myself. The detailed work of cutting, grinding, and then soldering together the glass fragments kept me distracted from my reality. Soon, I'd accumulated so many sheets of glass, sketches, and tools I ran out of space in my room and had to move my workstation down to the basement.

"But what?" I said. "My stained glass makes me happy. You do want me to be happy, don't you?"

"Of course, I do, but you're in that basement too much for a young girl."

"Gama, please don't start."

"I'm only saying you need to get out of the house more, get some fresh air."

"I'll get my fresh air on the ride to the vet."

The back door opened, and Lily stepped inside. "Hero's appointment's at eleven, right?"

"Right," I said.

"Well, get a move on then; it's a quarter till."

I grabbed the leash from a hook by the door. "I'll get Hero."

"He's already in the car," Lily said.

"How'd you get him in there?"

"I lifted his butt just like you do."

"Wait a minute." Gama stuffed some sandwiches

into a brown paper bag and extended it to me. "There's one for each of you."

"We don't need sandwiches," I said. "We'll be home in an hour or so."

Lily took the bag. "Speak for yourself."

*

About halfway to the clinic, Lily reached over and poked my leg. "You're awfully quiet this morning. Is something wrong?"

"I'm worried about Hero. And you know, it's that time of the year again."

"Oh, crap!" She hit the steering wheel with the palm of her hand. "Of course, it is. So, how'd it go yesterday?"

"As well as can be expected, I guess. You know Gama and all her food. What about you? Did you drive to your mom's?"

"Yeah, I had dinner with her and Aunt Winnie."

Lily's mom, Ava was a fortune teller—psychic adviser, she liked to be called—who'd recently moved to Nashville to live with her sister, Winnie, also a psychic. They did readings from their home and, according to Lily, did not accept payment for their services, but if somebody wanted to give a "donation," they were more than welcome to.

"How is your mom doing?"

"Well, she's still a nutcase. But I love her anyway," Lily said. "So, was it rough for you and Gama yesterday?"

"We did okay, but it seemed worse this year, at

least for me. It must've been the rain that brought everything back."

"Yeah, I can understand that." She paused a minute or two. "Hey Addy, you don't think about that blood splatter anymore, do you?"

Besides Gama and a couple of policemen, Lily was the only person who knew about the splatter. When I first told her, she was cynical but sympathetic. "Is there any way you could've been dreaming?" she'd asked. "I know I fall asleep in the car a lot." A few years later, "Could the concussion have messed with your memory?" Finally, in our senior year of high school, weary from being my sounding board for so long, she came to me with the answer. "Conversion disorder." She'd learned about it in psychology class. "It's when someone creates a problem to distract them from a tragedy."

Now, because she seemed so frustrated whenever we talked about the splatter, I tried to avoid the subject whenever we were together.

Lily took my reticence as an answer to her question. "You're kidding me. Still, after all these years?"

"I would've forgotten about it long ago if I only knew where it came from."

"I thought we decided it was from a bird."

"But Lily, there's no way a bird or any other animal smacking against a windshield could've produced an undisturbed splatter like the one I saw."

"Maybe something fell off of the crossing then."

"What, a giant glob of blood? Look, we've been

over this and every other possible scenario, and none of them make sense."

"I'm sticking with the bird. Bird blood and a slippery road caused the wreck. End of story." There again was the frustration. She wanted to fix this for me, make it go away, but she didn't know how. "Addy, let's be real; you're never going to know where the blood came from because your information is limited, so you keep going over and over the same things, hoping for a different outcome."

"Isn't that the definition of insanity?"

"You said it; I didn't."

Lily and I were incredibly in tune with each other. We knew when to let silence reconcile our differences. We dropped the subject there, the same place we had dropped it before, but we both knew it wouldn't be the last time we talked about the splatter. There would never be a last time until the mystery was solved.

We were now on Riverbend Road, close to where the wreck had happened. As we neared the Snake Shadow Crossing, I felt the tension in the car thicken.

"Have you ever seen the shadows?" I asked.

I could tell from Lily's expression she was surprised by my question. "Sure, when I was younger."

When we were kids, it was considered cool to have seen the shadows, and no one ever admitted it if they couldn't.

"Are you just saying that, or have you actually

seen them?"

"I've really seen them."

"How come I haven't?"

"Do you look toward the ends where the big trees are? They say that's how the shadows are cast."

"I know, and yes, I've looked there; I've looked everywhere."

"The sun has to be at a certain angle, and the trees bare."

"You'd think, of all the times I've been under it, I'd have caught that angle at least once."

"Don't worry; nobody can see them anymore now that they keep the trees trimmed."

The Snake Shadow Crossing was once the closest thing Driftwood had to a tourist attraction. People would come from surrounding areas to drive under it, hoping to see the shadows. But all the searching took eyes off the road and caused too many wrecks, so the city started trimming back the trees to do away with the shadows.

We came upon the ditch where the ground had remained charred for weeks after the wreck. As we passed the area where I'd landed when I was thrown from the car, I could see myself as a little girl lying on the ground motionless, bleeding; about ten feet away was Mom's green bean casserole still sealed in the Corning Ware dish. "Hold on tight," she'd said earlier that afternoon when she handed me the casserole to take to the car. "If you joggle it around, the topping will get soggy, and then you'll have to answer to Gama."

When we pulled up to the clinic, I opened one of the car's back doors to get Hero. "C'mon, boy, let's go." I attached the leash to his collar and gave it a tug. Although he could get out of the car without help, he wouldn't budge. I'd had this trouble with him before. He liked Dr. Jacobs, but he knew going to the vet usually involved shots or the violation of one or more of his orifices, which he did not enjoy. "Hero, you've got to do this," I said sternly. With an old dog groan, he stumbled out onto the parking lot.

Reenie Cooper, the receptionist at the clinic, addressed us immediately. "Good morning, Addison. It's been a while since I've seen you."

"Hello, Reenie."

"Well, tell me, how have you been?"

I liked Reenie, always had, but I hated her small talk; a simple hello was never enough. Whenever I saw her, she insisted on discussing the weather and other trivial matters before we got to the important stuff. Seemed like a waste of energy to me, but I went along with it. "Fine, thanks," I said.

"And Kathleen?"

Reenie saw Gama every Sunday at church. "She's fine, too."

"Did you have a nice Thanksgiving?"

"Yes, we did. Thanks for asking."

"Good to hear. I see you've brought your partner in crime with you. Hey there, Lily. How are you?"

"Mean as ever. What about you, Reenie?"

"Can't complain, and if I did, nobody would listen anyway."

Lily laughed. "How's Rex?" she asked, cutting her eyes at me. She knew the small talk was driving me crazy, and she was getting a kick out of it.

"Talk about mean...his hair's not red for nothing."

Finally, when I thought all relatives had been inquired about, I felt it was safe to get down to business. But as I opened my mouth to speak, Reenie started up again. "How's your mom, Lily?"

"Crazy."

"Well, aren't we all just a bit?"

Lily looked at me. "Some of us, more than others."

I gave her a smirk and then turned back to Reenie. "Hero has an eleven o'clock appointment."

Reenie pulled a manila folder from an accordion file on her desk. "I know, honey. The doctor's ready for him; you can go on back now."

Lily sat in the lobby while Hero and I went into the exam room to wait for Dr. Jacobs. After less than five minutes, I heard footsteps coming up the hallway. Hero heard them too and began wagging his tail in anticipation. We both looked at the door, expecting Dr. Jacobs to open it and greet us in his usual jovial manner. But instead, a young man I'd never seen before, dressed in jeans and a light blue button-down, walked into the room.

"Hello, Miss Quinn," he said. As he approached me, I first noticed that he was over six feet tall and thin for a man of his height.

"Where's Dr. Jacobs?"

"Reenie didn't tell you?"

I shook my head.

"Dr. Jacobs is in the hospital."

"Why? What happened to him?"

"He had a stroke yesterday."

"Oh, no; that's terrible!"

"Thankfully, there was no permanent damage, paralysis, or anything like that."

"That's good news."

"But no worries; my name is Dr. Isaac, and I'll be treating Hero today."

He looked too young to have finished veterinary school, and his shaggy blond hair and shadow of a beard struck me as unprofessional. "You will?"

He smiled and offered me his hand. "I've got a degree and everything," he said as if he'd read my mind.

He seemed nice enough, and I figured he must be okay if Dr. Jacobs had hired him. When I looked down to take his hand, I noticed a tattoo on his forearm—a single red balloon with a trailing string. Suddenly I felt lightheaded, and my heartbeat became rapid. I looked up at Dr. Isaac's face and saw that he had no color, nor did anything else in the room around us, except for the balloon tattoo, which was still bright red.

I retracted my hand. "I'm sorry; I just remembered I have to be somewhere."

"Right now?"

"Yes, it's important." I dashed for the door, pulling Hero along beside me.

When I reached the waiting room, Lily looked up

from her magazine. "Done already?"

"Lily, we need to leave."

"Leave? Why?"

"I'll explain later."

"What's the matter with you?"

I started for the exit. "Come on, please; let's go!"

"What about Hero's appointment?"

"I'll have to come back another day."

"Why? What's going on?"

"I just got a warning."

The warnings, red warnings, as I called them, began on a Sunday morning not long after I turned eleven. Gama and I were making our way up the long sidewalk that led to the church, chatting as we went. A few feet ahead of us, two elderly ladies, arms entwined, were cautiously taking the steps to the entrance. One of the ladies was carrying a red patent leather handbag that caught my attention. While I was gazing at the bag, Gama commented about some buttercups that had sprouted up near the church's front door. When I looked at the flowers, they turned gray, as if they'd died right before me. Gradually, everything else within my sight—the trees, the church, the sky, even the people—faded to black and white and shades of gray.

Everything but the red handbag.

I stood there on the sidewalk, frozen in my colorless world, all kinds of frantic thoughts racing through my head: *What's happening to me? Am I going blind?* I could hear Gama talking, but she sounded far away, even though she was standing beside me.

Right about then, the elderly lady carrying the red handbag plunged forward, her bag tumbling down the steps beside her, spilling its contents along the way. Gama, and some other people who'd been walking behind us, rushed to the fallen lady's side. As I watched them lift her to her feet, the color slowly started coming back around me until everything had returned to the way it was.

The lady banged up her shins, and the wrist she'd used to break her fall was swelling fast. Someone called 911, an ambulance came, and the EMTs put her on a stretcher and took her to the hospital emergency room. We later found out that, although she'd broken her wrist, she would be okay. However, I wasn't so sure about myself. I was baffled and terrified by the bizarre episode I'd had at the church. I didn't want to upset Gama—since the wreck, she panicked easily—so I tried to put the incident out of my mind, hoping it would never happen again.

But it did. Happen again.

A month or so later, on a Friday afternoon, I was in English class at school, and the teacher was reading aloud from a book of poetry. I wasn't paying much attention to what she was saying, but I found myself drawn to the book like I'd been drawn to the handbag that day at the church, specifically the color, which was also red. Like with the bag, I stared at the book, unable to look away, while everything else in the classroom lost color.

The following Monday, my English teacher didn't show up for class. While visiting her mother in

Chicago over the weekend, she'd been mugged and brutally beaten for her cash and credit cards while attempting to withdraw money from a bank ATM. She was in the hospital in serious condition.

After the second episode, it was clear something was seriously wrong with me, like a brain tumor, or even worse, I was going insane. I knew if I told Gama, she would take me to the doctor; if I didn't have a brain tumor, the doctor would most likely send me back to the psychologist, and I didn't want to go through that again.

The next couple of months went by with no more episodes. I was beginning to think whatever caused them had passed until one afternoon when our next-door neighbor, Moira was at our house for a visit. Being the colorful and fashion-forward lady she was, she had painted her fingernails a bright shade of red that complemented her pink floral blouse. She and Gama were having tea and enjoying one another's company while I, transfixed by those red fingernails, had another episode.

That night Moira suffered a fatal stroke.

After Moira's death, I recognized the pattern unfolding before me. All three episodes involved people possessing red items, and, all three times, something unfortunate happened to each of them. This was when I began to believe there was a connection between my episodes and the incidents that followed.

In the years ahead, the red warnings continued randomly. I could go months with no warnings at all, and then, out of nowhere, I'd see something as familiar as a stop sign, a fire truck, or a red ribbon in a classmate's hair, and my world would fade to gray. Sometimes the warnings foretold grave circumstances, like Moira's death or my teacher's mugging. Other times, it was something less serious, like a broken wrist. There were even a few instances when nothing at all happened after a warning, at least not anything I was aware of. But then, I had no way of knowing what tragedies unfolded in the strangers' private lives once they were out of my sight. This was the confusing part, the frightening part. Not knowing what the bad luck would be, or when it would occur, immediately after the warning, or days, even weeks later, rendered my "premonitions" useless.

Now I stood in the waiting room of the veterinary clinic in the wake of the most potent red warning I'd ever experienced. I was trembling and lightheaded, and all I wanted to do was get out of there, but, for some reason, I couldn't get Lily to go.

"Exactly what happened in the exam room?" she asked.

"Dr. Jacobs had a stroke yesterday; he's in the hospital."

"Yeah, I know; Reenie told me."

"I wish she'd said something to me before I took Hero to the exam room."

"She might have if you'd taken a few minutes to talk to her instead of rushing things along."

"Another vet is filling in for Dr. Jacobs," I said,

ignoring her comment.

"You mean Zane Isaac?"

"How did you know?"

"There are only two veterinary practices in the area; I took a wild guess."

"But how do you know him?"

"He brought some suit pants into the cleaners to be hemmed."

"Lily, I can't believe you didn't tell me about this!"

"What, am I supposed to run everything that happens at my work past you?"

"You could have mentioned he might be here, and then at least I would've been prepared."

"Prepared for what?"

"For his tattoo."

"His what?"

"He's got this odd tattoo on his arm. Have you seen it?"

"No, I haven't. But why does it matter?"

"The tattoo is of a balloon."

"So?"

"A *red* balloon."

"Oh, so that's what caused the warning."

"The feeling was stronger than it's ever been."

"But nothing happened afterward, did it?"

"No, not yet, but it's going to. You know how my warnings are; something bad always happens."

"Do you think running away will stop it from happening?"

"Maybe not." I continued toward the door. "All I know is I need to get out of here. Are you driving me, or do I have to walk?"

"Wait a minute. Don't you think you should at least tell Reenie you're leaving?"

"Can you tell her for me?"

"I could, but I'm not. This is all you."

"Fine, I'll do it myself." I stomped up to the counter. "Reenie, I need to cancel Hero's appointment for today."

Reenie looked puzzled. "Okay...mind if I ask why?"

"I remembered I have to be somewhere else."

"So, do you want to reschedule?"

"Yes, please."

"Sure." Reenie sat down at her computer. "Let me see what's available."

"I want the appointment to be with Dr. Jacobs."

She peered up at me over the top of her reading glasses. "Honey, Dr. Jacobs had a stroke. It's going to be a while before he can work again."

*Now she tells me.* "Then I guess I'll have to wait."

"What about Hero?" Lily asked. "Are you willing to let him continue to suffer for weeks, maybe longer, while Dr. Jacobs recovers?"

With all the distractions, I'd forgotten why I'd come to the clinic in the first place. I looked down at Hero sitting beside me. "I'll have to take him to the other vet."

"Why won't you see Dr. Isaac?" Reenie asked. "Did something happen?"

"Yes...well, no, not really. It's just that Hero is used to Dr. Jacobs."

Lily tugged my arm. "Addy, this is silly. You've got to go back in there...for Hero."

"Why can't we take him to the other vet clinic?"

"Because we're already here." She snatched Hero's leash out of my hand. "If you won't do it, I will."

"Okay, okay." I took back the leash.

Lily turned to Reenie. "Mind if we try again?"

"Of course; I'll let Dr. Isaac know." Seconds later, she returned to the reception desk and gave us the go-ahead.

Lily latched onto my wrist. "This time, I'm going in there with you."

Dr. Isaac was jotting something down in a folder when we got to the exam room.

"Hello there, Zane," Lily said like they were old friends.

Dr. Isaac smiled when he recognized her. "Lily, right? From the dry cleaners."

"Good memory," she said, smiling back at him.

He looked at me and nodded. "Miss Quinn."

Lily giggled. "I can't believe you remembered my name."

"You remembered mine."

"It's my job to know my customers."

*Oh no,* I thought. *Here we go with the small talk.*

Again, as if he knew what I was thinking, Dr. Isaac looked down at Hero. "Okay, now tell me about this guy."

"First, I should warn you, he doesn't like strange men and gets aggressive whenever one comes near me."

"Why only men?" Dr. Isaac asked.

"He had a bad experience once."

Thinking of how Hero had raised his hackles and exposed his teeth that night still made me shudder. It was around midnight, and Cole had stopped by our off-campus apartment; he'd been drinking and was looking to get laid. He'd no more than walked inside when he started groping me and planting sloppy, beer-drenched kisses on the side of my neck. "Get off me; you're disgusting." I shoved him away, and he stumbled backward.

When he'd regained his balance, he went to the fridge, took out a beer, and popped the tab. "Maybe I wouldn't drink so much if you weren't so damn boring."

"Not all of us want to get drunk every day, Cole."

"That may be, but you never want to do *anything*."

"Nobody asked you to come here tonight. I'm sure plenty of party girls out there would be more than happy to get you off."

He took a gulp of his beer. "I should have listened to my friends when they told me you were off in the head."

"Okay, that's enough." I pointed to the door. "Go. ...get out of here...now!"

"Gladly," he said. When he got to the door, he turned around and hurled his can of beer in my direction; it whizzed within inches of my head before smashing against the wall.

Having heard the commotion, Hero came

charging out of my bedroom, positioned himself between Cole and me, and began barking viciously.

Lily was right behind Hero, arm extended in front of her, finger heavy on the nozzle of her new pepper spray. She moved toward Cole, Hero by her side. "Look here, you drunken loser, I've been itching for a reason to see if this stuff works. So you better get out that door before I use this on you and enjoy every second of your suffering."

"You're both psycho bitches!" He kicked at Hero and missed. "Good riddance, scar face!" he said as he walked out and slammed the door behind him.

Dr. Isaac moved closer to Hero, and I choked up on the leash, preparing for the worst. "Careful. I'm not promising he'll be cooperative."

He crouched down to Hero's level. "Mind if I check you out, buddy?" As Dr. Isaac cautiously extended his hand, instead of the low growl and bristled hair I was expecting, Hero began wagging his tail.

My face got hot. "Wow, that's a surprise." I looked over at Lily for support; she was trying to stifle a grin.

"Dogs have good instincts about people. He knows I'm not going to hurt him...or you, for that matter," Dr. Isaac said. "So, you say he's been lethargic and having trouble getting around?"

"Yes, and he has no appetite."

"He's thirteen, right?"

"Approximately."

Dr. Isaac glanced at me quizzically. "Is he a rescue?"

"Sort of; I found him on the side of the road when he was a puppy."

"Actually, he found you," Lily interjected but stopped there because she knew I didn't like to talk about the details of the wreck with strangers.

"So, the two of you grew up together then," Dr. Isaac said.

"I guess you could say that. What do you think is wrong with Hero?" I asked, trying to steer the subject back to the present.

"Sounds like he might have some bad arthritis, but you can't be too careful with a dog his age. Let me look him over to make sure."

As I watched Dr. Isaac listen to Hero's heart and check his ears, I couldn't keep my eyes off the tattoo. *Why a balloon?* He lifted one of Hero's hind legs and carefully bent the knee joint. Hero responded with a whimper. "Feeling stiff, are you, buddy?"

I stroked Hero's back to comfort him. "So, what do you think it is?"

Dr. Isaac stood and faced me. "Yeah, it's like I thought; he has arthritis. He doesn't want to get up and move around because it hurts when he does, and you don't feel much like eating when you're in pain. Besides that, considering his age, he seems to be in good health."

"Is there anything you can do to make him feel better?"

"I'll give him something to ease the pain. We'll start with a shot of an anti-inflammatory now, and I'll send you home with some medication. He should be back up moving around in a few days."

"That would be great."

"The challenge will be getting him to take the pills since you say he's lost his appetite. What about treats? Is he still excited to get them?"

"Not lately."

"Then you may have to get creative and try special treats like peanut butter. I suggest sticking a pill inside some peanut butter on a cracker. If that doesn't work, put it in a chunk of hotdog or a cube of cheese. I've never met a dog that turned down a cube of cheese."

We made it out of the clinic without incident, with a month's supply of anti-inflammatory medicine for Hero's arthritis. As soon as we got into the car, Lily turned to me. "Well, that almost went off the rail."

"Sorry to inconvenience you, but I have no control over my warnings. Trust me, if I could, I'd make them stop in a heartbeat."

"I know you can't help it, Addy, but Zane's such a nice guy."

"For God's sake Lily, you just hemmed the man's pants. You don't know him."

"Well, I've met enough assholes to know he's not one."

"Did you see the tattoo?"

"Yeah, what about it?"

"Well, don't you think it's a bit odd?"

"No. Lots of people have tattoos."

"But it's not a normal *guy* tattoo."

"Maybe he likes red balloons."

"Or maybe he's a psycho who chops up people and leaves a balloon behind as a calling card."

"Somebody's been watching too many crime documentaries."

"And the balloon's drifting down instead of up like balloons are supposed to."

"Not from his point of view. Personally, I think it's unique and expressive."

"I wonder what it means."

"Does it have to mean anything?"

"Most tattoos do."

"When I see a single balloon, particularly a red one, I think of letting something go, you know, metaphorically."

"Wonder what awful thing he did that he had to let go?"

"That's mean."

"Look, I know you like this guy, but I'm telling you, there's something off about him."

Lily started the car engine and began backing out of the parking lot. "I can't see it, myself," she said. "He has a peaceful aura."

I rolled my eyes. "You and your auras and crystals and crap. Exactly what is an aura anyway?"

"It's the energy a person emits. It presents itself in colors, mostly around the head."

"How come I can't see auras? I can't see snake shadows; I can't see auras. What the hell's wrong with me?"

"Not everyone can, or maybe it's because you're

not looking for them."

"Tell me, what does Dr. Isaac's aura look like?"

"Bright green…like his eyes.

"And what does that mean?"

"I think it means he's a healer."

"Oh, that one was hard to figure out. What color is my aura?"

"I don't know. I've never been able to see yours."

"Maybe I don't have one."

"Everybody's got one; it's nothing but energy. There are a lot of people whose auras I can't see."

"Why can you see Dr. Isaac's then?"

"I'm not sure; maybe because it's strong."

I rolled my eyes again. "If you say so."

"Hey, you've got a lot of room to talk with your warnings."

Lily had been skeptical of my warnings from the beginning. The day I told her she'd just gotten her first car, a red Volkswagen Beetle. She pulled into my driveway, honking the horn, wanting me to take a ride. I stepped outside to greet her, and the instant I laid eyes on her new car, I got a warning. Lily could tell something was wrong, so she shut off the motor and joined me on the front porch. After I explained everything, I begged her to take the Beetle back to the dealership and choose another color, but she refused. "I'm keeping it," she said. "I like red. Besides, it was the only one on the lot my mom could afford." A week later, something flew off the back of a truck and cracked her windshield. She insisted it had nothing to do with the red warning, but decided to trade the Beetle for a blue Mazda.

Even though Lily had never come out and said so, I knew she still thought the incidents that followed my warnings were purely coincidental.

I chuckled under my breath.

"What?" she asked.

"I think it's funny how you have no problem planning your days around horoscopes and Tarot card readings but find it difficult to believe in my warnings."

"Auras and omens aside, no one has ever said anything but good about Zane Isaac. And believe me, the way people gossip around here, if he had so much as farted in church, I'd have heard about it."

"Well, maybe he hasn't done anything yet. Maybe it's what he's going to do."

"Have you considered that your warning could mean something bad might happen *to* Zane? That's the way it was with that teacher, right? And what about poor Moira?"

"But it's different this time. It feels like it did with Cole." On our first date, Cole showed up at my door with a red rose that turned gray the second I saw it.

"Oh, so your warnings have different feelings attached to them."

"It's like your auras, hard to explain, but somehow I can tell the difference."

"Okay, whatever." Lily reached into Gama's lunch bag and pulled out one of the turkey sandwiches.

"It doesn't matter anyway because I have Hero's medicine now," I said. "Hopefully, I'll never have to deal with Dr. Isaac again."

She dropped her jaw. "So, you're not going to take Hero back in a month for a check-up like you're supposed to?"

"Not a chance, unless Dr. Jacobs is there." I took out the other sandwich, broke a piece off, and offered it to Hero in the back seat. He still wasn't hungry.

"So, what will you do when Hero needs more medicine?"

"I'll call the clinic and see if I can get more."

"And if you can't?"

"Guess I'll have to take him to the other vet until Dr. Jacobs gets better."

"Don't you think that's a bit extreme? You've been going to that clinic for years. Honestly, Addy, what could go wrong?"

"Something might happen to Hero, that's what."

"And what on earth could happen that couldn't be fixed at a veterinary clinic?"

"I don't know. All I know for sure is I have the same feeling about Zane Isaac that I did with Cole. I ignored my instincts then, even though I knew something was not right in my gut, and look where that got me."

"You shouldn't have needed a warning to know Cole was a jerk."

Lily had never liked Cole, but he wasn't always a despicable person. In the beginning, he was charming and quick-witted. We met while in college, at a party Lily had dragged me to. I was sitting alone nursing a solo cup of cheap

Chardonnay while Lily was off somewhere being Lily. I spotted Cole across the room in a group of mostly girls. He had soft, smoky eyes and smiled often; his teeth were piano key perfect. When he caught me looking, he made his way through the crowd, walked straight up to me, and asked, "How did you get those hideous scars on your gorgeous face?" *Now there's a guy with balls,* I thought. I decided right then I was going to at least sleep with him.

"Okay, Lily, I screwed up, but at least I learned a lesson from my experience, and that's to never ignore my warnings."

"But what if you're wrong?"

"I'm not; you're just going to have to trust me on this one."

She took a bite of her sandwich. "Did Gama pack any napkins?"

"Yes, I think so." I pulled one out of the paper bag and gave it to her.

She wiped a bit of mayo from the corner of her mouth. "How many napkins are in there?"

"Um, let's see…looks like three."

"What? Not five?"

"Three napkins and *two* sandwiches."

Lily laughed. "Gama and her fives; she never slips up."

## CHAPTER 5
# ZANE

Zane and Reenie stood dumbfounded behind the clinic's front desk, watching Addison Quinn rush across the parking lot, pulling her old, arthritic dog beside her.

Zane turned to Reenie. "What was that about?"

"Beats me," she said. "All I know is that girl sure was in a hurry to get out of here. What on earth did you do to her?"

"Nothing; she just ran out of the exam room, claiming she had another appointment."

"Well, *something* sure spooked her. She started to reschedule and insisted on seeing Dr. Jacobs until Lily talked some sense into her."

"What's she got against me? We've never even met."

"I don't have a clue."

"She didn't say anything to you?"

"Addison's not a big talker."

"Yeah, I got that."

"She's been bringing Hero in since before I started working here. I've always known her to be timid and reserved, until today."

"What else do you know about her?"

"Not much, except she's from Indianapolis and moved to Driftwood to live with her grandmother. You know Kathleen Baker, don't you?"

"Can't say that I've met her either."

"Sweetest lady I've ever known."

"How long has Addison lived with Kathleen?"

"I believe since she was around nine."

"Nine? I thought you meant recently. How come she didn't live with her parents?"

"Because they're dead."

"Both of them?"

"Killed in the same car accident."

"Poor girl."

"And poor Kathleen too; she lost her daughter, you know."

"So sad."

"Kathleen's the one who told me about the wreck. You should've seen the sorrow on her face when she talked about it, still after all these years."

"How did it happen?"

"Not sure. Kathleen didn't offer the details, and I didn't push her to."

"Wow. I guess Addison has good reason to be temperamental."

"And the scars might make her a bit standoffish."

"What scars?"

"You didn't notice them? They're on one side of her face and neck."

"I couldn't get past her eyes," Zane said. "How did she get the scars?"

"I don't know, but it's not from lack of trying."

"What do you mean?"

"Do you know Lily, the girl who was with Addison today?"

"Now her, I know. We met at the dry cleaners where she works. Why do you ask?"

"Well, once, when I was at the cleaners, I casually mentioned something to her about Addison's scars. Just curious, and I figured Lily would know what happened because she and Addison are close."

"So, what did she say?"

"Nothing. Usually, Lily will talk your head off about most anything, but she skirted around the subject like it was some big secret. And you know me; that made me even more determined to find out. So, finally, I came right out and asked her."

"And what did she tell you?"

"That Addison got the scars from a bar fight. A *bar* fight! Can you imagine?"

Zane chuckled. "Surely Lily was joking."

"Of course, she was, but you'd have never known by her deadpan expression."

"That's too funny. You've got to love her sense of humor."

"But wonder why it's such a secret?"

"Maybe it's not. It could be Lily doesn't even know. You said yourself, Addison doesn't talk much."

"Oh, Lily knows, all right. Those two are practically joined at the hip. Besides, if she didn't know, why didn't she just say so? Why did she have to make a joke of it?"

"Maybe she was trying to tell you it's none of your business."

Reenie gathered some files from her desk. "Well, I guess it *is* none of my business."

"Or mine, for that matter."

"This is only speculation." Reenie lowered her voice even though no one was in the clinic but the two of them. "I can't help but wonder if Addison was in the wreck with her parents."

"Possibly, but don't you think if the wreck was bad enough to kill her mom and dad, her injuries would've been worse."

"Yeah, you're probably right."

"So, what are you doing for lunch? I'm starving."

"I brought leftovers. There should be enough for both of us."

"I was hoping you'd say that. Let me tie up some loose ends back in my office, and I'll meet you in the breakroom in five minutes."

*

"Something sure smells good," Zane said when he walked into the breakroom.

"It won't be much longer," Reenie said. "Go ahead and pour yourself some sweet tea from that pitcher there."

"You brought tea too? Reenie, what would I do without you?"

"Hey, I meant to ask. How was your girlfriend today?"

"Would you please stop calling her that?"

"Why won't you give Kim a chance? She's a nice lady and pretty too."

Zane knew Reenie meant well, but he was not in the least bit attracted to Kim Webber. "Because I don't want to start seeing someone right now."

"What are you waiting for?"

"Besides, you know I have a policy about having personal relationships with the patients' owners."

"Maybe you should share your policy with Kim, so she'll quit making appointments to see you." The microwave beeped and saved him from continuing a conversation he'd rather not have. Reenie took the food out and began dishing it onto a paper plate. "By the way, how was dinner with your uncle yesterday?"

For a second, Zane had forgotten he'd fibbed to Reenie about his Thanksgiving plans. "I had a nice visit," he lied again.

"Tell me all about it."

"Nothing much to tell." He scrambled for a new subject to keep from telling more lies to cover for the first one. "I can't figure out why I haven't met Addison Quinn if she's lived in Driftwood for so long."

Reenie handed Zane a plate full of steamy food and began filling a second plate for herself. "Well, assuming she's in her early twenties, that'd put her coming to Driftwood around the time you moved away."

"That explains why we never met when we were

kids, but I've been back for several months. You'd think I'd have run into her in a town this size."

"Not necessarily. Seems like Kathleen told me Addison's been away at college."

"So, Reenie, what do you think it is about me she doesn't like?"

"You don't know that she doesn't like you."

"Why else would she have run out the way she did?"

Reenie fanned the question away. "Oh, you're just used to women running to you. I swear you men always want what you can't have."

"There's something different about this girl."

"You can say that again."

"But in a good way, you know?"

"Wait a minute." Reenie stopped a forkful of stuffing short of her mouth. "Are you *interested* in Addison?"

"I don't know, maybe."

"I thought you said you didn't want to start seeing anyone right now, and what about your policy?"

Zane grinned. "For her, I might make an exception. I would at least like to get to know her better. But how can I possibly do that? You saw the look on her face."

"She was expecting Dr. Jacobs, and seeing you instead probably startled her."

"Maybe I should call her, set things straight. What do you think?"

"Oh, I don't know about that. Give her a while.

She'll warm to you." Reenie winked. "You've got a way of growing on people."

"But how will she get the chance to?"

"She's supposed to bring Hero in for a check-up in a month, right?"

"Yes, but the way she shot out of here, I wouldn't be surprised if she takes him somewhere else."

"Surely she won't go that far."

"And even if she does return in a month, I might not be able to wait that long."

"What do you mean you might not be able to wait?"

He picked up his tea and took a long gulp, trying to buy some time. "Reenie, I've been dreading having to tell you this, but as soon as Dean is well enough to work again, I'm thinking about putting the house up for sale."

"You're moving? Where?"

"If I can find a buyer, I might go to North Carolina and stay with Zach for a while."

"For a while? What do you mean by that?"

"He says Lake Lure would be an excellent place to set up a practice."

Reenie put down her fork and scooted her chair back from the table. "Oh, so you're leaving for good."

"Thinking about it."

"But this is where you belong; it's your hometown."

"I know, but it doesn't feel right here anymore."

"Maybe you're missing your mother, and living in that house with all those memories in your face every day probably doesn't help matters. Why don't you sell the house and move somewhere else in Driftwood? Those new riverfront condos are nice."

"It's not the house, Reenie. I would miss Ma no matter where I lived."

"What is it then?"

Zane wanted to tell her, purge himself of the secret he'd been carrying for many years. But Reenie would've never understood the real reason he wanted to move away from Driftwood. No, he couldn't tell her, but there was one thing he knew she would appreciate, something that may help her to accept his decision. "Zach and his wife are expecting a baby soon," he said. "Since I'm going to be an uncle, I thought it might be nice to live closer to them."

Reenie clammed up for a minute, tears filling her eyes. She and Zane had grown close since his ma's death. He was more than a co-worker to her; she considered him family. "It's been such an emotional day," she said. "First Dean, and now this."

"I know. I'm sorry. Maybe I should've waited...."

"No, no, I'm glad you told me. Family is important, and I want you to be happy, but that doesn't mean I'm not going to miss you like hell."

"I'm not gone yet, and when I move, we'll keep in touch, I promise."

"Yeah, that's what everybody says."

*

That afternoon, Zane sat at his desk, struggling to

finish his paperwork. He couldn't get the mysterious Addison Quinn off his mind. Over the years, he'd been guilty of indulging in self-pity because he had grown up without a father. But now, thinking of how lonely Addison must have been, must still be, made him thankful that at least he'd had his ma. Even with all that had happened, his childhood had probably been a picnic compared to hers.

Everything about Addison intrigued him, starting with the way she looked. Those eyes, sea glass translucent against her otherwise dark features. She didn't have on a speck of makeup when he saw her—not that she needed any—except maybe a smear of lip gloss. He pictured her jumping out of bed, finger combing her hair into a loose ponytail, allowing a few wispy strands to escape around her face, getting dressed in the first thing she saw in her closet, and running out of the house. This alone fascinated him. He'd never known a girl who put so little effort into her appearance and still managed to look stunning. Jesse, for instance, wouldn't even walk out for the morning paper without makeup.

Yes, Addison was beautiful, but he'd known plenty of beautiful girls, and none of them had ever captured his attention in the way she had. Not even Jesse. He'd been more infatuated with the idea of Jesse than Jesse herself, her flawless skin, her eighteen percent body fat.

What bothered Zane about Addison was that she seemed afraid of him for some unknown reason. And what concerned him, even more, was that he cared what she thought. He'd never been bent out of shape over other people's opinions. What was different this time? *Maybe she's the one,* he thought, and then laughed at himself for thinking it.

He remembered when his brother said he knew the second he laid eyes on his wife, Michelle, that they would be together forever. Zane told him he was full of it and that there was no such thing as love at first sight, no way of knowing the person with whom you will spend the rest of your life. But now that he'd met Addison, the notion seemed plausible. What if it turned out Zach had been right after all? What if Addison was his soulmate, his one chance at true love?

A sudden rush of urgency brought him to his feet. He couldn't let her slip out of his life without a fight. He couldn't let a minor thing like her hating him stand in his way. He took a deep breath and sat back down. He was getting ahead of himself. Way ahead. Really all he wanted was the chance to prove to her he wasn't such a bad guy. But how was he supposed to do that when she'd made it clear she wanted nothing to do with him?

Reenie knocked on the door and stuck her head into Zane's office. "You know you were talking about calling Addison Quinn earlier?"

"Yes?"

"I've been mulling it over, and I think you should do it."

"You do? What made you change your mind?"

"If Addison will keep you here for a while longer,

then I'm all for it."

Zane smiled. "So, what should I say to her when I call?"

"Well, I've been thinking about that too, and I believe I have an idea that might help you break the ice."

"Oh, yeah, what's that?"

"You could do a phone follow-up on Hero. Dean does them frequently."

A light came on in Zane's eyes. "To check on how his medication is working, see if maybe it needs to be stronger."

"Of course; that's a valid excuse to call."

"Then I could ease into a coffee invitation."

"Exactly."

Zane got up and walked around to the front of his desk. "Reenie, you're a genius. So, does this mean you're not mad at me anymore?"

"I wouldn't go that far...."

"Hey, would you mind pulling Addison's number up so I can add it to my phone contacts?"

"I thought you might ask." She took out a slip of paper from the pocket of her scrubs and gave it to him.

He stared at the numbers on the paper. "I should probably wait a few days before I call, right?"

"Yeah, I doubt Hero has made much progress in four hours."

## CHAPTER 6
# ADDISON

H ero was under the kitchen table watching me as I took a hotdog out of the refrigerator and began slicing it into hefty chunks. When I got his arthritis pills from the cabinet, he recognized the bottle and immediately pinned his ears back. I turned away from him, opened the pills, and quickly embedded one into a chunk of hotdog. It's time for your special treat," I said with an exaggerated lilt in my voice.

Getting Hero to take his arthritis medication had been challenging since day one. First, I tried to hide it inside a cube of cheese; but that didn't work because the cheese kept crumbling apart. Then I moved on to peanut butter. Like Dr. Isaac had suggested, I put the medicine on a cracker and piled peanut butter on top. Hero took the cracker from me, no problem, but instead of gobbling the whole thing down like he was supposed to, he put it on the floor in front of him, licked the peanut butter off, and then spat out the pill like a bird spits out a seed hull. When I got to the hotdog, which proved to be the best vessel, he'd caught on to the game and become leery of the new "special treats."

When Hero's first dose of medicine was finally inside him, I breathed a sigh of relief, but because of the red warning I'd had at the clinic, I was then worried he might have a bad reaction to the drug. That morning I watched him sleep for hours, waking him every so often to make sure he was still alive.

After a couple of days, he seemed to feel better, and his appetite increased, but he still needed help getting up. It wasn't until the fifth day that I really noticed a difference. I was down in the basement working when I heard a *pat, pat, pat* on the stairs. It was a sound I knew well but hadn't heard for a while. I looked up from what I was doing, and there was Hero, walking toward me, wagging his tail like a puppy.

Hero had been on the medication for over a week and was almost back to his old self, but coaxing him into taking it had not become easier. He could smell the medicine inside the hotdog, so I'd learned to feed him several clean chunks first, hoping he'd forget about the one with the pill in it.

"Here you go, boy." I bent down to him under the table and offered him a chunk without the medicine; as usual, he sniffed before he ate it. Then I fed him five more dummy chunks before the one containing the pill, which he also gobbled down. I was pretty sure he knew his medicine was in that last chunk, and it made me wonder if he'd been wise to the ruse all along and was just playing me to get more hotdog.

While tidying the kitchen, I noticed Hero standing by the back door.

"Need to go out, boy?"

He looked up at his leash hanging on the wall, then at me.

"You want to go for a walk?"

He wagged his tail.

"You do, don't you?"

He lifted both his front paws slightly off the floor, no more than an inch, an abbreviated form of his puppy pounce.

"Let's go then!" As I was heading to my bedroom to grab a jacket and put on shoes, the landline rang, startling me. I never answered the landline because it was almost always someone calling for Gama, but I was right there, so as a reflex, I picked up.

"Is this Addison?" asked a male voice I didn't recognize.

"Yes?"

"This is Zane Isaac." The red balloon tattoo popped into my head. "You know, from the vet clinic."

"Oh, hello, Dr. Isaac."

"Zane, please call me Zane."

After an uncomfortable pause, I realized he was waiting for me to respond. "Okay?"

"I didn't wake you, did I?"

It was a Monday morning around nine. "No, you're fine."

"I'm calling to see how Hero's doing."

Even though I'd had a bad feeling about Dr. Isaac, still, it was nice of him to call, and the least I could do in return was be polite. "He's feeling much better, and his appetite's back as well."

"Does he seem to be getting around okay?"

"Yes, as a matter of fact, I was about to take him for a walk when you called."

"That's fantastic news!"

"The medicine you gave him is working."

"Great. Just drop by the clinic when you need a refill."

"Will do," I lied. "How is Dr. Jacobs doing?"

"He's better and plans to return to work after New Year's."

"That's good." Hero was now at my feet, looking up at me impatiently. "I need to go now and take Hero for that walk. Thank you so much for calling."

"Wait, Addison; don't hang up yet."

"Yes?"

"Actually, there's one more thing I wanted to talk to you about." He paused again, and I wondered if he was expecting me to say something. "I feel like we got off to a bad start the first time we met."

"Yeah, about that; I should apologize for how I acted."

"No apology's necessary. I know you were expecting to see Dr. Jacobs when you walked into the exam room, and being met with a strange face probably caught you off guard."

"I'm kind of picky when it comes to Hero."

"That's understandable."

"Dr. Isaac...Zane, I appreciate your calling, but I really should go."

"Wait a minute; before you hang up, I was wondering if maybe you'd like to have coffee with me. Start all over. I'm not nearly as scary once you get to know me."

"Oh, there's no need for that," I said, as sweetly as I could manage to a man I didn't trust. "I appreciate the offer, though, and thanks for calling. Bye." This time I completed the hang-up.

I stood there for a few seconds, staring at the phone. *Did Dr. Isaac just ask me out?* I looked at Hero. "Give me five more minutes." He stretched out on the floor, and I picked the receiver back up and dialed Lily's number.

"You'll never guess who called and—I think— asked me for a date."

"What? Who?"

"Well, technically, he didn't ask me out, not to dinner or anything, only coffee. Does that count?"

"Depends on who's asking. Who was it?"

"Take a guess."

"Let's see, considering you hardly ever leave the house, I'm going to say the cable guy."

"No, it wasn't the cable guy."

"The mailman."

"It wasn't the mailman either."

"Just tell me. Unless you want me to keep going... the UPS man, the guy who reads the meters...."

"Dr. Isaac."

"Zane? Well, it's about time."

"You're not surprised?"

"Not even a little."

"Really?"

"Come on; it was obvious he was interested in you."

"Not to me." I'd never been good at reading people like Lily was.

"So, when are you guys going out?"

"We're not."

"Oh, Addy, do *not* say you turned him down."

"Okay, I won't say it then."

"I swear, you're so strange."

"Me? What about you?"

"I'm eccentric. There's a difference."

"That's nothing but a fancy word for weird."

"Maybe, but my weird and your weird are not the same."

"Why are you so intent on getting me to go out with Zane Isaac anyway?"

"Because I like him and think he'd be a good match for you."

"Have you forgotten about what happened at the clinic?"

"What, the thing with the tattoo?"

"You may not take my warnings seriously, but I do, and as I said before, I'm not about to make the same mistake I made with Cole."

"Addy, I really think you're wrong. Zane's nothing like Cole."

"You don't know that for sure."

"Let me ask you something. What if Zane didn't

have that tattoo on his arm? How would you feel about him then?"

"It doesn't matter; he does have it."

"Sometimes, you're impossible to reason with. I've got to get to work."

"Well, I have to take Hero for a walk."

"Fine. Bye."

*Click.*

Gama walked by as I was hanging up. "Who was that?"

"Lily."

"On the house phone?"

"I called her."

"On the house phone?"

"It was handy." To avoid explaining everything, I continued to my room, got my coat and shoes, then went straight to the back door and grabbed Hero's leash. "C'mon, boy, let's do this."

"Where are you off to?" Gama asked.

"We're going for a walk."

"A walk? It's been a while since you've done that."

"It was Hero's idea."

"Wow, that medicine is working wonders!"

"My walking buddy's finally back."

"Well, don't push him too much. Remember, he's still an old dog."

"I won't; we'll take it slow today."

When we got on the road, I realized how much I missed walking Hero. After the wreck, the daily responsibility had given me a reason to get up, kept me moving forward. I found peace in those early mornings when the only sound was our feet against the pavement—me stumbling behind Hero's clumsy puppy gait—like sneakers tumbling in a clothes dryer.

A couple of blocks from our house, we came to a dead-end street with a guardrail separating it from a quiet neighborhood of older Tudor-style homes. The houses were rich with architectural character; the generous front lawns were lush with landscaping. I enjoyed walking in that neighborhood because the homes were set back from the road, making lengthy conversations with the residents difficult, unlike our community of tightly spaced bungalows with short front yards that made chatting with the neighbors unavoidable.

The neighborhood on the other side of the guardrail was Hero's favorite place to walk too, but for an entirely different reason. He had befriended many people who lived there, a few special ones he'd taken to his heart. I leaned into him and ran my hand down the length of his back. "Feel like going through this morning?"

The route we usually took circled to yet another guard-railed dead-end street that led back to Kismet Avenue, the road on which we lived. It was a long jaunt, and I wasn't sure if Hero was up to it. But again, he surprised me by wagging his tail and leading the way, squeezing through a gap between some bushes at one end while I climbed over.

Immediately on the other side, to the right, lived the first of Hero's special friends, Smokey. That wasn't his real name, but because he was a chain-smoker, and I didn't know his real name, it was the one I'd assigned to him. Every morning that Hero and I had passed by Smokey's house, no matter what the weather was like, there he'd be in his garage, sitting in a tattered, 70's-avocado recliner. I knew nothing about Smokey, aside from what I'd seen, which left me to fill in the blanks of his life. I'd decided his wife, whom I'd caught a glimpse of once, didn't allow smoking in the house, and he, being a prisoner to his habit, had no choice but to spend most of his days outside.

As we got closer to Smokey's house, I could smell his cigarette smoke, and knew that meant he was in his usual place. "Who's walking who this morning?" he called out when he spotted us.

He said the same thing every time we passed by. It had been clever and apropos back when Hero was an eager puppy, pulling me along by the leash, but after a while, I became annoyed with him for not coming up with something different to say. I looked down at Hero plodding beside me. "I believe I have control this morning."

Smokey chuckled. It never got old to him. "Long time no see, huh?" he said, his words swirling through puffs of smoke.

"Yeah, we took a break." I felt the leash grow tense in my hand—Hero's way of telling me he wanted to see his friend—so I unhooked him, and he trotted up for a visit while I waited on the street. Smokey and Hero wallowed in each other's affection for a few minutes, and then Hero returned to be leashed up again. I threw up my hand and waved at Smokey as we walked away.

"Have a good one!" he hollered.

Next, we came to the house where Water Lady lived. I gave her that name because she used to leave a bowl full of water at the end of her driveway for Hero, who somehow knew it was for him and stopped to gratefully lap it up. Water Lady must have watched for us because every morning, as we passed her house, she opened her front door and waved.

Hero paused at her driveway, like always, and looked for the water bowl that wasn't there, then at Water Lady's door, expecting to see her. We waited a few minutes, but she didn't come out. She was not a young woman, and it occurred to me that she could've possibly passed away. "Come on, boy, let's go," I said, tugging at the leash. But Hero, determined to see his friend, staunchly stood at the edge of Water Lady's front yard and continued to stare at the house.

Finally, she appeared at the door, dressed in a floral house robe. Hero greeted her with a jubilant bark. "I thought that was you," she said, her feeble voice barely audible. "If I'd known you were coming, I would have put some water out."

"Oh, that's okay. We're not taking a long walk today."

"Well, it's good to see you both." She raised her hand to us as she went back into her house.

Satisfied that Water Lady was all right, Hero started walking again. We still had one more stop to make. At the far end of the street, on the top of a hill, lived Margaret Meow—her name I knew because she'd introduced herself; I added the Meow part because she had so many cats—Hero's favorite of all the people who lived on the other side of the guardrail.

Hero loved cats. Whenever he came upon one, he never tried to chase after it aggressively, like most dogs do, but instead walked up to it humbly, his tail anxiously flailing as if he wanted to play. The cats didn't return his affection, though, and usually ran away as soon as they spotted him. Except for one morning when we happened upon a big gray tabby, basking in a shaft of sun, that was too lazy to move from her comfy spot. She allowed us to slowly approach her, but as soon as we came too close, she hissed and swiped a fat paw across Hero's nose. He retreated with a whimper; his feelings hurt more than anything else. After that, he was cautious around cats but he never gave up on seeking them out and trying to befriend them.

The day we met Margaret Meow, she was sitting on her front porch in a white wicker settee. Cats were in her lap and curled at her feet, hopping through a swinging pet door and perched in every window. Trying his best to get to them, Hero pulled me into Margaret's yard. "Sorry," I said, reining him back. "My dog has a thing for cats."

"Does he now?" Margaret said. "How sweet; why

don't you let me take him to the back yard where most of them are?"

"Most of them?"

"Yeah, I know. *I* have a thing for cats too. I can't seem to stop rescuing."

"I'm not sure if that's a good idea," I said. "Cats don't like Hero."

"Some of them won't like him, but some will. The more there are, the better his odds."

As expected, as soon as Hero walked into Margaret's back yard, most of the cats scattered in every direction, but a few—five or six—stayed behind. At first, they circled him suspiciously; then, one brave kitten walked up to Hero and weaved her slender body in and out of his hind legs. Another sleek black cat craned her neck toward his muzzle; he lowered his head in response, and she pushed her tiny face into his. Slowly, more of them showed up to join the party, and the next thing I knew, Hero was on the ground, cats all around him, cats all over him. He was in heaven.

We had a long way to go before we got to Margaret's. As we continued up the hill, Hero hesitated at the house where an old but hyper terrier had once diligently guarded his territory. When Hero and I first started walking, the terrier bristled and barked at us until we were out of his sight. Over the years, we watched him go down, becoming less and less aggressive, barking once, maybe twice when we passed, until finally, toward the end of his life, when he tried to bark, no sound came out. The old terrier had been dead for several years, but Hero still stopped and looked up at the porch for a few minutes as if to pay his respect.

As the street began to incline more and more beneath us, Hero slowed his pace to a crawl, then suddenly pulled over and collapsed on the curb. It was heartbreaking to watch him look longingly up the hill toward Margaret's house, unable to go any farther.

I sat beside Hero, put my arm around his neck and cried. *How did I allow this to happen? Why did I let this creature burrow deeply into my heart, knowing he would have a short lifespan?* I was asking for the pain when I loved him so much that I could not bear to live without him. Hero put his head on my lap to comfort me. "We should go home now, boy. We'll visit Margaret Meow another day."

## CHAPTER 7
# ZANE

After Addison turned down Zane's coffee invitation, at first, he was at a loss for what he could do to get to know her. He thought about it on and off for two days straight until finally, while in his office between patients, an idea came to him.

During his lunch hour, he drove downtown to Harvey's, a men's clothing store, and bought some dress pants with a raw hem. One of Zane's favorite things about Driftwood was that there was only one men's store, one coffee shop, and one hardware store. Some folks around town grumbled that the limited selection was inconvenient, but Zane liked that he didn't have to ponder where to go for what he needed. He believed in simplicity, narrowing your choices.

Zane, now a man on a mission, entered the dry cleaners—the only one in Driftwood—his unhemmed pants in hand. Lily greeted him with a warm smile, like she was genuinely pleased he was there. He took the gesture as a good sign. He figured if Addison hated him, Lily would most likely have hated him too, or at least felt uncomfortable facing him.

"Hi Lily, nice to see you again," he said.

"You too, Zane." She glanced down at the bag he was holding. "What can I do for you today?"

"I need to have a pair of pants hemmed."

"Sure." She reached under the counter and brought up a small metal box. "I think I still have your inseam measurement on file." She fingered through the index cards. "Here it is, thirty-six, right?"

"Right."

"So, when do you need them?"

Zane put the bag on the counter. "No hurry."

"Good, because I'm swamped right now." Lily opened the bag and looked inside. "I see these are new, so I assume you don't want them cleaned."

"No, just hemmed."

"And pressed?"

"Sure."

She jotted down the information and then put away the file box. "Okay, I think I have everything I need. I'll give you a call when they're ready."

"Thanks." Zane suddenly realized Lily had been so efficient he hadn't had a chance to do what he'd come in to do. He lingered at the counter, searching his mind for a reason to stay longer.

"Is there anything else I can help you with?" she asked, giving him a you-can-go-now smile.

"No, that'll do it." He took one step toward the exit, then stopped. "Oh yeah, I meant to ask, how's Hero doing?"

"When I last talked with Addy, she said he was

feeling much better."

"Good. Hero's in decent shape for a dog his age."

"Uh-huh."

Circling a subject was not one of Zane's strong points. He was all about direct approaches. "Strange how Addison ran out of the exam room like she did. What was wrong with her?"

Lily broke eye contact with him and started shuffling through a drawer behind the counter. He had obviously touched on a subject that made her uneasy. "Nothing, really; Addy overreacts sometimes."

"Was it something I did?"

"No, you didn't do anything wrong. Addy's attached to Dr. Jacobs; he's been Hero's vet for a long time, and she's not good with change."

"I figured it was something like that. I called her a few days ago and asked her to have coffee with me. I thought it might be a good idea for us to get to know each other better since I may be the one treating Hero for a while."

"Yeah, I heard."

"She told you? What did she say?" Zane was aware of the eagerness in his voice. He was acting like a horny junior high kid, giddy at the slightest hope his phone call had meant enough to Addison that she'd told her best friend. But at this point, what Lily thought of him was of no concern. He'd come too far to worry about pride now.

"Basically, you asked her to have coffee, and she turned you down."

"Yep, that pretty much sums up the whole conversation."

"Addy tends to be reserved around people when she first meets them."

"Tell me then, how does someone go about getting to know her?"

"Most people don't. Her inner circle is Gama—that's her grandmother—Hero and me."

"Well, I don't want to be most people. I'm going to level with you, Lily. I want to get to know Addison."

Lily smiled. "I understand that, and I'm not surprised. Guys love Addy. The mysterious, aloof thing she's got going on, it's like a man magnet."

Zane became the junior high kid again. "Do you think I have a chance with her?"

"To be honest, I don't know. So many guys have been right where you are, and most ended up getting nowhere with her."

"Is she seeing anyone now?"

"No, not anymore; she still has a bitter taste in her mouth from the last guy she was with."

"Bad break up, huh?"

"No, not really—she didn't give a crap about him —it's just that he was a real jerk. But Addy's tough; she's had to be. She hasn't had an easy life, you know. I'm sure you've heard about what happened to her parents."

"Yes, Reenie told me…so horrible."

"What Addy's had to endure is something you never get over, and she's a guarded person because of it. She's been that way since I've known her, and we met in grade school."

"How do I get in the circle?"

"You don't. Not unless she decides to let you in."

"How did you get in?"

"It wasn't easy. Addy wouldn't even talk to me when we first met. Literally would not say a word."

"Then how'd the two of you become so close?"

"I didn't push her, but I didn't give up on her either."

"Sounds like there's a fine line to tread."

Lily laughed. "Practically invisible. The best advice I can offer—if she ever gives you a chance—is to try not to ask many questions about her past. Particularly avoid the subject of the wreck; she doesn't like to discuss the details with anybody she doesn't know well."

Zane certainly understood avoiding the rearview mirror. "I get it; I try not to look back too much myself."

"I'll warn you, though, Addy can be... challenging. She's complicated, moody, and at times down-right reclusive."

"Nothing worthwhile is ever easy."

Lily grinned. "That's the spirit."

"Something tells me she's worth the trouble."

"She is. Caring and loyal to the bone, and believe it or not, once you get to know her, she can even be fun."

"So maybe I should wait a while before I try again."

"But not too long...."

Zane glanced at the clock on the wall behind the counter. "I'd better head back to the clinic before Reenie sends out a search party. Thanks for the advice, Lily." He turned to leave.

"Zane, wait a minute." She picked up the bag with the pants inside and extended it to him. "You may as well take these back to Harvey's for a refund."

"Why's that?"

"You can't use them. The waist is size thirty-six, and you're a thirty-four."

He had not been able to find his exact size in the limited selection of unhemmed dress pants at the store. "Looks like I'm busted." He laughed and took the bag. "Thanks again, Lily, for everything."

"Sure. And good luck."

When Zane got to the door, he turned around. "Maybe put in a good word for me?"

Lily winked. "I'll do my best, but I can't make any promises."

*

Driving back to the clinic, Zane was slightly more hopeful than before he talked to Lily. While she'd tried to be encouraging, she'd offered little in the way of viable help. Still, the visit to the dry cleaners had not been a total loss. At least now, with Addison's best friend on his side, he had a chance.

When Zane came to the Snake Shadow Crossing, instead of thinking of the wreck, he consciously tried to replace the bad memory with a good one. He pictured Zach and him riding their bikes on the crossing like they'd done hundreds of times when they took the river trail. The trail forked off about halfway through, and there were two paths you could take: one led through a wooded area and the other, over the crossing. He and Zach always chose the Snake Shadow path because there was a steep hill right before the crossing, and if they gained enough speed, they could coast their bikes down it.

He longed for those days of innocence. And seeing Zach at their ma's funeral made him realize how much he missed his brother. As they often do, the dire circumstances made him appreciate the importance of the family he had left. Knowing he always had a friend to turn to, someone who understood him and shared his history was what Zane liked best about having a twin brother. As kids, the two of them had been close, but not creepy close. They never dressed alike or sent each other telepathic messages. In fact, to keep from falling into the twin stereotype, they'd tried to be different from one another. Despite their efforts, every now and then, they would slip up and accidentally say the same thing at once. Whenever this happened, they became embarrassed, and both scrambled to cover it up, again at the same time, which made things even worse.

Zach, for the most part, had been a good brother. Growing up without a father, he, being the oldest by a minute and a half, had tried in his own way to fill the role of a strong male lead. When the family was short on cash, Zach took on odd jobs around the neighborhood, mowing lawns or raking leaves. Sometimes he picked up soft drink cans on the side of the road and took them to the recycling center for a few dollars, then gave the money to their ma to buy groceries.

If Zane had to choose one thing about his brother that he hated, it would've been the practical jokes. There was one, in particular, that came to mind. One afternoon, they were walking home from school when Zach turned to him. "Want to see something cool?" He then handed Zane a good-sized yellow envelope with RATTLESNAKE EGGS printed on the outside.

"What's this?" Zane asked.

"What it says."

"Where'd you get them?"

"Ricky Truman gave them to me."

"Where'd Ricky Truman get them?"

"From his cousin who lives in Georgia; open it."

The envelope was light in weight but puffy. Zane had never seen rattlesnake eggs and had no idea how big they were. For all he knew, they could've fit into an envelope.

"Go ahead; they won't bite," Zach said. "They haven't hatched yet."

Zane slowly opened the envelope, careful not to damage the eggs. Just as he pulled back the flap to peer inside, something that sounded an awful lot like a rattlesnake shot up his arm. He jumped back. "Crap! What was that?"

Zach laughed for at least two minutes before

catching enough breath to talk. "Guess one of them did hatch after all."

When Zane settled down, he discovered the "rattlesnake" was a large paperclip with a rubber band attached. Zach explained that the rubber band had been wound tightly around the paper clip, then placed inside the envelope so that as soon as it was opened, the tension would be released, and the paper clip would pop out and spin around, mimicking the sound of a rattlesnake. Even though Zane was sure the joke had robbed him of a couple of months of his life, it was a good one, and whenever the two of them got together, they still laughed about it.

One year, Zach got some fake blood for a Halloween costume and was so impressed with how realistic it was he went back to the K-Mart where he got it and bought up all they had left. For a good two weeks, there were blood pranks regularly: Zach running up to Ma with a bloody t-shirt acting like he'd been shot, blood in the toilet after he'd complained his kidneys were hurting, a mysterious blood trail leading from the front door to his bed.

After a while, Ma stopped falling for the injury jokes, so Zach resorted to putting the fake blood in her shampoo. She was a good sport, as she was about most everything, but she still made him pay for another bottle of shampoo with his allowance.

Ms. Pimpernel, their eighth-grade history teacher, was not so kind when Zach put some fake blood in the hand lotion she kept on her desk. Everyone in the class started laughing as she smeared it over her knuckles and up her forearms. When she looked down and saw her bloody hands, she let out a scream that echoed through the halls of the school. Zach got a week's detention and was grounded to the house for the duration.

Revisiting cherished childhood moments had made it easier for Zane to pass under the crossing, and he decided he would try the same thing again the following morning. There were plenty more fond memories to choose from as there had been many pleasant days before, and even after, the big nasty one. The problem was there weren't enough of them to make him forget.

*

The incident at the clinic with Addison was on Zane's mind all night, to the point where he became frustrated with himself for being unable to move past it. He couldn't erase the image of her terrified face before she ran out of the exam room. He turned on the TV and flipped through the channels, hoping to find something to occupy his thoughts. During his ma's final months, they'd watched many old movies together, but he was no longer interested in TV now that she was gone.

He put down the remote and went into his ma's room, once again intending to go through her things. It was something he would have to do sooner or later if he was going to sell the house. He decided the task might be easier if taken on in increments.

He opened her dresser drawer, pulled out a box, and sat on the bed with it. When he lifted the lid, he discovered it was full of photographs. *Figures,* he thought. His ma had always been obsessed with capturing every moment.

On top was a picture of Zach and him—they were around eight—a black cat they called Licorice at their feet. Licorice wandered up to the door one afternoon, starving and matted; Zane let the cat inside, fed it a bowl of milk and a can of tuna, and had named it before his ma got in from work. Even though Licorice was just a tomcat that only came around when he was hungry, Zane loved him like all animals. He knew the first time he went with his ma to the clinic and watched in fascination as Dr. Jacobs examined the animals, administered shots, and wrote prescriptions that he wanted to be a vet someday.

Licorice was the first of many strays Zane had insisted on taking in through the years. There was the malnourished beagle he'd found down by the river that he didn't have the heart to walk away from. His ma looked at the scraggly, stiff-legged old thing, with patches of hair missing, stinking of fish, and demanded Zane take him back to the river. She said a tomcat that came around once in a while was one thing, but an old dog would be a real commitment.

"But Ma, I'll take care of him," Zane pleaded. "You won't even know he's here."

"No, Zane, absolutely not," she said. "The dog

cannot stay."

"But Ma, he'll die out there."

"No, he won't. Somebody else will take him in."

Zane fought hard to change her mind about the old beagle, but every argument he came up with was met with a resounding *no*. Defeated, he and Zach headed out the door to take the dog back to the river. As they were leaving, their ma stopped them. "Wait a minute," she said. "Let me give the poor starving thing something to eat first." Zane could see in her eyes that she felt guilty for putting an old dog out on the streets to fend for himself. As she was heating up some leftover beef stew, she tried to justify her decision. "I can't support a dog. I can barely feed the two of you."

The stray inhaled the beef stew and licked the plate clean, then, with a full-belly grunt, plopped down in the corner of the kitchen and immediately fell asleep. Ma agreed to let him rest for a while but insisted he had to go when he awoke. The old dog slept for about an hour, then got up from the kitchen floor, waddled into the den where Ma was seated on the couch and curled up at her feet. "May as well let him stay the night, now," she said. "It's too late for you boys to be down by the river."

By the following day, Ma had started calling the dog Bones. She said the name fit because his hips and shoulder blades protruded, and he was so skinny you could count his ribs. That's when Zane knew for sure that Bones was in. Everybody knows once you name a dog, he's yours.

Turned out Bones wasn't as old as he looked and ended up living another three years, all of which he spent glued to Ma. He followed her from room to room in the house, always underfoot while she washed the dishes or did the laundry. She cursed him daily because she kept tripping over him, but she was the one who cried the most when Bones passed on.

After Bones, there were a couple more cats and another dog named Sunny that Zane had picked from the accidental litter of a neighbor's hunting dog. "Some mutt dug under the fence and got to her," said the neighbor, who'd planned on breeding the dog. They had Sunny only a few months before he ran off.

Zane was heartbroken that his puppy was gone. His ma felt sorry for him and agreed to let him pick another one from the litter. Thankfully, the neighbor still had a few pups left. "Better get two this time," Ma joked, "in case we lose another one." Zane picked out a brown, fluffy male with a speckled face and decided to call him Dandy. Zach chose the second puppy, a tawny female he named Daisy.

Zane learned his lesson after he lost Sunny and was careful to keep Dandy on a leash whenever they were outside, in case the pup had some wanderlust in him like his brother. Zane became more attached to Dandy than any pet he'd ever had, so much so that when he went off to school in Florida, he took the dog with him. Dandy died less than a month after Zane's ma passed away.

He missed his old friend almost as much as he missed his ma. He shuffled through the box of pictures, trying to find one of Dandy. There was a snapshot of every phase of their family's lives; surely, there was one of a dog who'd stayed by Zane's side since he was thirteen. Finally, after practically emptying the box, he found a photo of Zach holding Daisy and him holding Dandy. It had been taken around Christmas—he could tell because they were standing in the living room in front of the decorated tree—not too long after the Snake Shadow accident. Even though Zane had smiled for the photo, he could see traces of stress on his face.

He returned the pictures to the box, put the lid on, and placed it back in the dresser drawer. Once again, he had failed to make it through his ma's belongings. Zane was forced to accept that he could not do the job alone, that when it came time for him to move, he'd have to throw everything into one big box and take it to North Carolina, where he and Zach could go through it together.

Standing in his ma's room, Zane was suddenly flooded with memories. Whenever he thought of her, he always thought of secrets. Take to your grave secrets. "Sometimes it's necessary to stay quiet to protect the ones you love," he remembered her saying.

"But how do I know what secrets to keep and what to tell?" he asked her.

"It's easy," she explained. "Just ask yourself if anyone would be hurt if you told. If so, it's best to let life play out as it may."

Secrets. Zane's ma kept them better than anyone. One of those secrets was his father.

## CHAPTER 8
# CORINNE

*1999*

C orinne was at work when she got the phone call. On the other end of the line was a man with a stern voice. "This is Officer Daniels with the Braxton Police Department. Can I please speak with Corinne Isaac?"

She had the impulse to hang up right then. She knew the officer would tell her something about the boys, and the news was bad; she could feel it. *Were they hurt? Had the police found out about what happened at Snake Shadow?* Either way, she had to face it; her boys needed her. "This is Corinne Isaac," she answered.

"Miss Isaac, sorry to bother you at work, but we just got a call from a lady who said she picked your twins up hitchhiking on the highway north of Driftwood. Do you know anything about this?"

"Hitchhiking? No, I don't."

"They asked the lady for a ride to the bus station in Braxton. Told her they were headed to Indianapolis. Luckily, the lady is from Driftwood and recognized the boys. She took them to the bus station, but after dropping them off, she called the police."

"Thank God they're okay."

"We were getting ready to send someone to the bus station to talk to the boys, but we thought you should know first."

"Thank you for calling, but there's no need to send someone. I'll go get them right now. Could you please call and ask the station attendant to keep them until I get there?"

"Don't worry, they're not going anywhere; they didn't have enough money to buy the tickets."

\*

Driving to the bus station, Corinne struggled to see the road through her tears. She knew Zach and Zane were bound to want to see their father sooner or later, but she thought she had more time to prepare. What a stupid assumption. They were thirteen years old. How long did she expect them to wait? It had been a tough year for them. They needed a father now more than ever.

Maybe this would've never happened if she had been more open from the start. But in all fairness, she knew hardly anything about Danny herself. The twins were seven when they first asked her about him. They'd looked up at her with expectant eyes waiting for her to tell them the story of the father they'd never met.

"Your dad lives in another country far away from

here," she'd explained. "He lives in Canada. Do you know where that is?"

They both shook their heads.

"Let me show you." She went to her bedroom, brought out her big world map, and spread it on the kitchen table. "We're here," she said, pointing to the state of Indiana. Then she slowly slid her finger north to Canada. "And your dad is all the way up here."

"Wow, that's a long way from us," Zane said. "How did you meet him if he lives so far away?"

"His grandparents live in Indianapolis, where I used to live. We met while he was there visiting them one summer."

Zach looked at her suspiciously. "Why does our dad live so far from us now?"

"Well...Canada is where he was born, and his parents live there, so I guess it's where he wants to be."

"But how come he doesn't live with us like other kids' dads," he asked.

"Honey, some people just can't live together."

"Is that why he never comes to visit us, because it's too far away?" Zane asked.

"That's part of the reason."

Zach stood up from the table. "We want to see our dad," he announced, speaking, as he always did, for both Zane and himself. "We want to go to Canada and look for him."

"Oh honey, we can't do that. Canada is not like Driftwood; it's a big place. He could be anywhere. I wouldn't even know where to begin looking."

"We'll find his name in the phonebook," Zane said, trying to help. "Do they have phonebooks in Canada?"

"Yes, I'm sure they do, but it's not that easy. Besides, we don't have the kind of money to take a trip like that right now."

"You can have all my allowance," Zach said.

"And mine too," Zane added.

"That's generous of you both, but we would need a lot more money to travel to another country."

"When we save up enough, then can we go?" Zane asked. "Please, Ma."

"We'll see."

Corinne's vague answers and vague promises had pacified her boys then, but she'd detected an urgency in their voices that told her it would not be long before they demanded more. She had no idea what she would do when that day came because, for all she knew, Danny might not even want to see his sons.

Just under six months later, her doubts were put to rest when, out of nowhere, Danny contacted her. He had moved to Indianapolis, was staying with his grandparents, and working for a small construction company, but planned to get his own place soon. Danny told her he'd had nothing to do with his parents' actions—the money, the pressure for her to put the boys up for adoption—none of it. He was eager to know all about Zach and Zane and asked if he could see them. He wanted a chance to compensate for his absence from their lives and offered to help with their support.

Corinne believed Danny when he said his parents had acted behind his back, and although she thought he was being sincere at the moment, she was unsure of his long-term intentions. She didn't see the harm in him assisting them financially—she certainly needed the money—but she wasn't ready to let him meet the boys yet. Corinne was afraid Danny might dart in and out of their lives, which, in her mind, would've been worse than not having a father at all. Even so, she was willing to work with him. If he proved his consistency through financial support and correspondence with her, they could possibly discuss visitation.

After Corinne hung up from talking with Danny, she was hopeful. She wanted Zach and Zane to know their father, and Danny to be a part of their lives. In the coming days, she found herself daydreaming about the boys having a real family; she saw the three of them camping, going on fishing trips, to ball games, and doing everything fathers and sons do together. Still, she didn't want to get her hopes up too high, and she didn't want to get her boys' hopes up either, so she decided not to tell them until things were more concrete.

As he'd promised, Danny sent a monthly check, no set amount, just whatever he could afford. Now and then, he called to see how the boys were doing. In return, Corinne mailed him school pictures and copies of report cards. This went on for almost a year. Then, right when she was about to give in and let Danny see his sons, the money and phone calls suddenly stopped.

She tried to reach him at the number he'd given her, and a woman answered the phone. Corinne panicked and hung up. She was hurt and disappointed, but more than anything else, she was angry. Not because Danny had moved on, but because he'd moved on without his sons. He could've had a girlfriend, a wife, or whatever and still been a father to them. And she was angry at herself for getting caught up in the fantasy, for breaking over and mentioning to the boys that she'd contacted Danny and that he lived in Indianapolis. Big mistake. She should've gone with her initial gut feeling and acted on what she knew would happen instead of what she wanted to happen.

Naturally, knowing their father was only a few hours away, Zach and Zane began asking to see him more and more. Corinne was running out of excuses; she had to do something. One night after a few glasses of wine, she got the nerve to try Danny's number again. She could've lived on without an explanation, but the boys deserved answers. She didn't care if Danny had a wife or even another kid; she was determined, as she dialed his number, to demand to speak to him, regardless of who picked up.

But she never had the chance because no one answered the phone; the line had been disconnected. She hung up and dropped her face into her hands. She couldn't bring herself to tell her boys their father no longer wanted to see them, that he probably had a whole new family. They would have never understood, and the news would've broken their hearts. She didn't know what to do, so she did what she had a bad habit of doing in such situations: froze and did nothing at all.

Until they asked.

Zane's desperation brought tears to Corinne's eyes. "Ma, will you please call our dad and ask him to come here so we can meet him?"

"I would if I could, sweetheart, but I don't know how to get in touch with him anymore. His phone's been disconnected. I think he may have moved."

"Back to Canada?"

"Possibly; I don't know."

"So, does that mean we're never going to meet him now?" Zach asked.

"No, I'm not saying that. Maybe your dad will call us soon to let us know where he is."

"But what if he doesn't call? What if he never calls?" Zane said.

"Let's give him a chance to. If he does, we'll work something out, I promise."

She'd meant what she said. If Danny had called, she would've given him another chance; she would've done it for her boys.

If only he had called.

Almost five years had gone by; they'd grown tired of waiting for her to do something and decided to take matters into their own hands. No, she couldn't blame her boys for this. It was her fault; she'd driven them to take drastic measures. She should've let Danny see them when he wanted to. *What if it's too late now? What if he no longer wants to see them?*

Zach and Zane were standing in front of the bus station when Corinne pulled up. As soon as she stepped out of the car, Zane ran up to her. "Ma, don't be mad."

She threw one arm around him and extended the other to Zach. "I'm not mad; I'm thankful you're both okay."

"We wanted to go see our dad," Zach said.

"I know you did, and I understand." She held them both tight for a few minutes until her trembling stopped. "Let's go home, shall we?"

"We didn't mean to scare you, Ma," Zane said in the car. "We thought if we told you where we were going, you would try to stop us."

"How were you expecting to find your dad in a big city like Indianapolis?" Corinne asked. "You don't even know his last name."

"Yes, we do," Zach said.

"But how?"

"We found the letters he sent you in your room."

They had been snooping through her things, and they knew better, but it was the least of Corinne's concerns. She would deal with it later, if at all. "But he could be anywhere. He could've moved back to Canada."

"Well, at least it would've been a place to start," Zach said. "It's better than doing nothing."

He was right. She could've done more, tried harder. There was a way to find Danny, and she knew exactly what it was. "If you want to see your dad, you should be able to," she said. "And I'm going to make it happen if it's the last thing I do."

*

Later that evening, while the boys were watching TV, Corinne slipped into the kitchen and did what she should've done years ago—called information and got Danny's grandparents' number.

Maxine, Danny's grandmother, answered the phone. Corinne told her she was a friend of Danny and that she'd heard he had moved to Indianapolis.

"After a long pause on the other end of the line, Maxine said, "Is this some sort of sick joke?"

"No, I'm trying to locate Danny."

"Who is this again?"

"It's Corinne Isaac. Don't you remember me? I used to live next door."

Maxine's voice softened. "Oh yes, now I remember. You're the nice girl who showed Danny around town that summer he spent with us."

It was evident from Maxine's response that she didn't know Danny had two sons, but Corinne decided it wasn't her place to say anything. "I haven't seen him in a while and was wondering how he's doing."

"How he's doing?" Maxine said.

A silence so heavy fell between them that Corinne thought they'd been disconnected.

"Maxine? Hello?"

"You really don't know, do you?"

"Know what?"

"Honey, Danny is dead. He's been gone for almost four years now."

Corinne put her hand over her mouth so the boys wouldn't hear her gasp. Her knees buckled, and she had to lean on the refrigerator to keep from falling. "How did it happen?"

"It was an accident," Maxine's voice cracked. "A tragic accident."

Corinne heard Maxine put the phone down and muffled voices on the other end, followed by more dead air. Finally, someone picked up. "Miss Isaac, this is Arnold, Danny's grandfather. I apologize for Maxine...what happened to Danny is still difficult for her, for both of us, to talk about."

"I'm so sorry, Arnold, I didn't know...."

"That's okay. If you give me your address, I'll send you a copy of the obituary and the newspaper clipping about the accident. That should explain everything."

"Of course."

Long after Arnold had hung up, Corinne, oblivious to the droning dial tone, stood with her back pressed against the refrigerator glaring at the phone in her hand as if it were responsible for what she'd just heard. Finally, she put the phone receiver back on the hook and covered her mouth to stifle the painful sobs rising from her chest. She allowed herself a few minutes of mourning, then straightened up and wiped away the tears with her shirt sleeve. Corinne was never going to see Danny again; death was absolute, permanent. She knew she could get through this; she was a survivor. But how would she tell the boys their father had died before they'd even had the chance to meet him?

## CHAPTER 9
# ADDISON

Hero and I, returning from a morning walk, were making our way up to the house when I noticed Lily's car parked in the drive. It was out of the ordinary for her to drop by so early without sending a text first. I pulled my phone from the rear pocket of my jeans and checked my messages; there was nothing from her. When I got to the back door, I could hear Gama and Lily having a spirited conversation in the kitchen, but the minute Hero and I stepped inside, the room grew quiet.

Lily was sitting at the table with a cup of tea. Lily didn't even like tea. "Hey Addy, how's it going?" she said.

"Okay...I guess. What are you doing here so early?"

"Having tea with Gama."

"Since when do you drink tea?"

"Since I tried this cinnamon spice stuff; it's delicious." She took a sip from her cup.

"You came by for tea?"

"No. I came to talk to you, and Gama offered me the tea."

I unhooked Hero's leash from his collar, and he headed toward his water bowl. "So, what did you want to talk about?"

"I wanted to see if you might like to go out tonight."

Lily and I had not been out since we returned from college. "Where?"

There weren't many places to go in Driftwood. No movie cinema, no mall. One drive-in theater, and Justine's Pub—a windowless, depressing place with colored Christmas lights strung year-round—was the only bar and grill in town. You could go there day or night, and there'd be the same two people seated at the bar. Betty Sharp, a chain-smoking retired beautician, and Serge, a Vietnam vet who told embellished war stories to anyone who would listen. Justine's served flat draft beer, and cheap whiskey poured into Crown Royal bottles. She didn't think anyone was wise to her whiskey trick or that the wine was boxed that had also been funneled into bottles, but someone caught her doing it once, and now everyone in Driftwood knew. Only out-of-towners drank wine or hard liquor there. Your best bet at Justine's Pub was to order canned beer and watch her open it.

"I thought we could drive to Nashville, do some Christmas shopping at a mall, and then maybe stop by Mom's house. She'd love to see you. She asked about you on Thanksgiving."

"But it's almost Christmas. The traffic is awful this time of the year."

"That'll make it even more fun."

"The malls will be packed."

"Like I said, it'll be an adventure. Tonight we can go to a club. Get a hotel room so we can stay out for as long as we want."

Gama touched Lily's arm. "Now, if you girls have a drink, you'll take a cab, won't you?"

Lily put her hand on top of Gama's. "Of course, we will."

I had no desire to visit a city the size of Nashville during the busiest month of the year; too people-y for me. I searched my mental file for stored excuses not to go. There weren't many; I had no social life. "But I recently started a new stained-glass project."

"Oh sweetie, it seems like that's all you do lately," Gama said. "You've been spending way too much time in the basement."

"What's wrong with the basement?"

"Nothing, it's just that you're so young. You need to be out having fun," Gama said. "Your project will be here tomorrow when you get back."

"But Hero…."

Lily shot that one down before I could even get the words out. "Hero's feeling much better. He'll be fine here with Gama."

"I don't know…."

"C'mon, Addy, do it for me. There's supposed to be a great Reggae band at this bar that I've wanted to go to forever."

"I don't really know that much about Reggae."

Lily stood up from the table. "Well, I do, and if

you won't go with me, I'm going by myself. You don't want me to go to a bar in a big city all by myself, do you?"

"What kind of friend would you be if you let her go alone?" Gama asked.

They were tag-teaming against me; I couldn't win. "How can I say no?"

"You can't." Lily took me by the arm. "Come on, I'll help you pack an overnight bag." She pulled me into my bedroom, opened my closet, and began flipping through my clothes.

"What are you searching for?" I asked.

"Something for you to wear tonight." She turned around and looked at me. "Don't you own anything that says *party?*"

"No, Lil, my clothes don't talk much."

"Doesn't matter; we'll get you something at the mall." She snatched my duffel bag from the closet floor with one hand and, with the other, dug through my chest of drawers until she found some panties, a pair of jeans, and a t-shirt. "This will be okay for the ride back home tomorrow." She picked up a mascara tube and lip gloss from my dresser. "Where's your make-up bag?"

"I don't have enough make-up to justify buying one."

"Guess we'll have to shop around for that too. We'll grab your toothbrush from the bathroom on the way out." She took my arm again. "Get your coat, and let's go."

"Don't we have to stop at your place and pack

your things first?"

"My stuff's already in the car."

"Talk about a set-up."

Gama shoved a brown paper sack into my hand as we walked through the kitchen.

"What's this?" I asked

"In case you get hungry on the way." She shooed us toward the door. "Now go have some fun!"

Hero tried to follow us out. "No, buddy, you can't go this time." I took his face into my hands and kissed the top of his head. "You stay here with Gama."

"Don't worry about Hero," Gama said. "I'll take good care of him."

"Good Lord, Addy," said Lily. "It's only one night! Get in the car already."

*

About half an hour into our trip to Nashville, Lily turned down the volume on the radio. "Hey, guess what? I heard that old Tudor on Collins Street—you know my dream house—is going to be available to rent again soon."

"Oh yeah, are you thinking of moving?" Lily lived in a cramped apartment above the dry cleaners where she worked because it was convenient, but I knew she wasn't content there.

"I think that house would be the perfect place to start a business."

"Are you ready to open your clothing boutique?"

For as long as I'd known Lily, she'd designed

and made her own clothes: blouses from old floral sheets, floor-sweeping skirts from damask drapes, vests from patchwork quilts. In school, the kids called her Bag Lady Lily and teased her viciously because of how she dressed. It didn't help that she was the only one in Driftwood with dreadlocks, wore ragged, fingerless gloves, and carried a huge, bulging hobo bag.

As it turned out, Lily had been ahead of her time with her bohemian style, which had now become a hot new trend. When we were in college, people offered to pay her to make them clothes using her unique designs. She had dozens of sketches and could've made some money if she'd wanted to, but she was holding out for bigger, better things. Unlike me, she had a plan for her degree and knew exactly what she wanted to do with her life. She'd been saving the money she made from her job doing alterations for the dry cleaners to open a boutique.

"Maybe, but I'm talking about a business for both of us."

"Both of us?"

"That's right. Last night I came up with an amazing idea. A partnership where I can sell my designs, and you can sell all the wind chimes hanging in Gama's basement, and those other things with the feathers and beads. What are they called again?"

"Sun catchers."

"Well, they're not catching anything but dust in the basement."

"But my stained glass is only a hobby. It's not good enough to sell."

"How do you know that? You've never let anyone see what you've made. I mean, it's worth a shot, right?"

"I don't know...."

"Okay, then think of it as a clothing boutique where we'll hang some of your pieces in the front window to see if anyone's interested."

"I guess there would be no harm in that."

"And I thought eventually you could branch out and make window panels, maybe even actual windows for houses."

"Wow. You've really thought this through."

"Sure, I have. I'm serious about it. Oh, and here's the most exciting part. I've already come up with the cutest name for the business."

"What's that?"

"Kaleidoscope."

"Kaleidoscope? I love the name and can see how it could relate to stained glass, but what about your clothing?"

"You know I like to use lots of color in my designs."

"True."

"So what do you say, you in?"

"Well, you certainly could make a living, but I don't know about me."

"What? Do you think you're the only person on earth who likes stained glass?"

"How much is the rent?"

"It's not bad, but I need to save some more so I'll have a cushion until things get up and running." She cut her eyes at me. "Not everyone's rich like you." Money was the one thing I never had to worry about. My parents had been insured with double indemnity policies, the proceeds of which had been in the bank drawing interest for thirteen years. "But if I had a partner to help with the finances…."

"Do you really think my stuff would sell?"

"Absolutely." She extended her palm to me. "What do you say, partner?"

I slapped her hand. "Okay, let me think about it."

*

When we got to Nashville, we checked in at a Marriot Hotel, had lunch at a deli, and then headed for Lily's mom's place.

"Maybe I can get her to do a lip reading for you," Lily said during the drive there. Her mom read Tarot cards and palms, but her specialty was lip readings.

"So, how does one go about reading lips anyway?" I asked.

"Your lips are like your palms; every line has a meaning. There are initials, dates, and symbols only Mom knows how to read. When someone calls to make an appointment, she tells them, even the men, to bring red lipstick when they come. When they arrive, she has them put on the lipstick and then gives them a piece of notebook paper to make a print of their lips."

"It sounds intriguing."

"Trust me; you'll love it."

Ava's house was almost exactly as I'd pictured, complete with beaded curtains, crystals, and burning incense. After we chatted for a while, she agreed to do a reading for me. I didn't have lipstick, so she provided one, and I kissed the paper, as instructed. We sat at a round table with a pink tasseled cloth as Ava studied the impression of my lips for a good five minutes before she finally spoke.

"Well, to begin with, I found Lily. There she is, right there, the *L*. See it?" Ava circled a tiny area of my lip print with a pen, then drew a line from the circle and wrote *Lily* on it.

I squinted and tried, but I could not find the *L* she was talking about. What she circled looked like ordinary cracks to me. "Yeah, I see."

Ava began making more tiny circles, explaining each crack's meaning as she went along. "It looks like you will have two children, both girls."

"Gama will be happy to hear that."

"You are creative and love animals."

These were things she already knew about me. "Uh-huh."

"Your future husband and soul mate is an N...his name starts with N. Nick, Nate or Norman. Know anyone by those names?"

"No, not that I can think of."

"It could be either first or last name."

"No one comes to mind."

"Well, maybe you haven't met him yet, but you will soon."

Ava closed her eyes, apparently shifting to clairvoyance. "I can see him, a handsome man, tall. There's fire behind him. Maybe his job has something to do with fire." She opened her eyes. "He's a fireman; I'm sure of it."

"A fireman?" I went through the names of the men who worked for the Driftwood fire department. Whitey Nicholson was the only *N* name of the bunch. Whitey was married with three grown kids and probably pushing fifty-five.

"You've had a lot of sadness in your past," Ava continued—again, common knowledge. "But this man will make you happy beyond belief." She began moving quickly, circling and explaining, and soon she lost me. When she'd finished, the notebook paper was filled with initials, dates, and notations about what my future would bring. She tore the sheet from the legal pad. "Here, this is for you to take home."

Although Ava and Winnie, to avoid paying taxes on the money they made, never asked anyone for payment after a reading, everybody knew, through word of mouth, that they were supposed to put at least five dollars, cash only, in a vase by the door before they left. As Lily and I walked out, I slipped a folded ten-dollar bill into the vase.

"Hey, I just thought of something," Lily said as we got into the car. "Wouldn't it be funny if that *N* Mom saw in your lip reading was actually a *Z* turned sideways?"

"Huh?"

"Z as in *Zane?*"

"Forget it. He's not a fireman."

Our next stop was the mall to buy something for me to wear that night. Lily picked out a form-fitting black mini dress at Macy's and asked me to try it on. The dress was not at all my style. It fit, but I didn't feel comfortable wearing it, so I passed. We compromised on a royal blue wrap blouse that Lily claimed made my eyes pop, and she talked me into some gold stilettos to wear with my jeans. She ended up buying the dress for herself.

We went to the hotel room to get ready for our night out. I showered and dressed, except for the stilettoes, and then stretched out on one of the double beds to wait for Lily to finish. When she finally came out of the bathroom, she was wearing the black dress from the mall, which looked much better on her because she had the curves to fill it out. She was stunning in plum-colored lipstick against her deep skin, her dreadlocks gathered into a high ponytail. Lily's thick, black hair had always been my favorite part of her looks. When she didn't have it in dreads, it hung in luscious ringlets. She said she got her dad's Puerto Rican hair. "That's about the only good thing I got from him," she once joked.

She stood before the full-length mirror putting on gold dangle earrings. "Are we ready to go?"

"I've been ready for half an hour."

*

"This is supposed to be an awesome local band," Lily

said as we entered the club.

"How'd you find out about this place?"

"Mom. She's always looking for reasons to get me to come to Nashville."

The club was packed. As we headed to the bar to order drinks, every guy in the room turned and looked at Lily. She was radiant that night as if she had a spotlight on her. We couldn't find a table, so we stood near the stage with our drinks in hand. Even though I didn't know any of the songs playing, the rhythm was infectious, and I found it impossible to keep from bobbing my head to the beat.

When the band took a break, Lily whispered, "Did you see that hunk of caramel on the drums?" She squeezed my arm. "Look, there he is, over by the bar. Oh my god, I think he's walking this way! Is he Addy? Tell me; I can't look. Is he?"

"I think he's coming this way."

The hunk of caramel walked past me and straight up to Lily. "Hi, my name is Andre. I'm in the band."

"You are? I didn't notice," she said, adjusting her dress. "I'm Lily, and this is my friend, Addy."

"Good to meet both of you," Andre said, his eyes fixed on Lily. "I only have a few minutes before I get back on stage, but can I buy you ladies a drink?"

"Sure, I could use another one," Lily said. "What about you, Addy?"

I held up my glass, half full of Chardonnay. "No, I'm good."

"Lily, would you like to walk with me to the bar to make the order?" Andre asked.

She looked at me. "Do you mind?"

"Of course not."

"We won't be long," she said.

Lily was a tall, voluptuous girl but looked petite beside Andre's broad, towering frame. I watched them interact at the bar, leaning in close as they talked, touching each other's arms. They made a striking pair.

When Lily got her drink, Andre joined the rest of the band on stage, and she came back and stood beside me, seemingly at a loss for words.

"Well?" I said.

"Addy, I saw my future in that man's eyes. Andre is the one I'm going to marry, the father of my future kids. It's kismet."

"Or wishful thinking."

"Did you catch his Jamaican accent?"

"Yes, it went well with the dreads."

"See, we're meant for each other; we even have the same hair. So, tell me, what do you think of him?"

"He seems nice."

"You hesitated. Why'd you hesitate?"

"I was swallowing my wine. But honestly, Lily, I can't make a sound judgment based on the thirty seconds I was around him."

"Why not? That's how long it took to decide you didn't like Zane."

"It's not the same; I didn't have a red warning when I met Andre."

"Good. Because you're my best friend, and it'd be

a deal-breaker if you didn't like him." She put her hand on my shoulder. "And I would really miss you."

"At least I know where I stand," I said. "So, does Andre get another break, so you two can talk some more?"

"I don't know, maybe. But it doesn't matter anyway; I came here to hang out with you and I intend to do just that. There'll be plenty of time for Andre and me. I gave him my number. He'll call." She tugged at the tie of my new wrap blouse. "Come on, I feel like dancing!"

## CHAPTER 10
# ADDISON

The next morning, Lily and I slept in until checkout at 10:00. Lily was hungry, so we stopped at a McDonald's drive-through and picked up a couple of breakfast sandwiches. By 12:30, we were back in Driftwood.

As soon as I stepped into the house, I noticed Hero wasn't there to greet me, nor did he come when I called his name. I glanced over at his leash hanging on the hook by the door to confirm that Gama had not taken him for a walk.

"Hello, I'm home," I called out as I headed toward the living room. When I got there and found Gama asleep on the couch, I instantly knew something was not right. She always took her morning nap at 10:00, and rarely slept more than an hour. I looked up at the clock on the living room wall. It was 12:37.

"Gama? Are you okay?" I bent down and touched her on the shoulder.

She jumped, and her eyes popped open. "My Lord Addison, you scared the living daylights out of me."

"Sorry. Where's Hero?"

"He's not in the kitchen?"

"No, he isn't."

"He was a few minutes ago."

I rushed through the house from room to room, searching but didn't see Hero anywhere. I went back into the living room. "Gama, I can't find Hero. When did you last see him?"

"Let's see…it was a few minutes ago when I let him out to do his business."

"Do you recall what time it was?"

"Right before my nap, I remember *The Price is Right* was coming on."

"That was over two hours ago! Did you forget to let Hero back in before you fell asleep?"

"Of course not."

"Well, where is he then?"

Gama wrung her hands. "Oh, Lord."

"What is it, Gama?"

"My knee was acting up, so I took one of those pills the doctor gave me. I must have overslept."

I ran outside and searched all around the house. Hero was nowhere in sight. I walked up and down the street, knocking on the neighbors' doors, but no one had seen him. I went through the guardrail; there was no sign of him there.

When I got home, Gama was calling everyone she knew on the landline. I grabbed my cell phone and dialed Lily's number. "You've got to come over right away," I blurted out as soon as she answered. "Hero's gone!"

"What do you mean he's *gone?*"

"He's missing…lost!"

"How in the hell did he get lost? He can barely

walk."

"Gama forgot to let him back in after he went out. That was over two hours ago."

"Okay, okay, calm down. Hero can't be too far away. I'll be right over. We'll find him."

*

When Lily arrived, we went into the neighborhood again and asked everyone to search their back yards. After we'd hit the last house within walking distance, she turned to me. "What do we do now?"

"We keep looking until we find him."

"Maybe we should check outside the neighborhood," Lily suggested. "You said he's been feeling much better since he's been on medication."

"It doesn't make sense that he would wander that far. He's never strayed from the house, even as a puppy."

"But it wouldn't hurt to look."

As we were getting into Lily's car, suddenly, the unthinkable occurred to me. "What if Hero went off somewhere to die?" I asked. "I've heard animals do that. They somehow know when it's their time and go into the woods to be alone."

"Get that out of your head. Hero would never do that to you. He'd fight to stay alive until he saw you first."

We drove around the surrounding neighborhoods knocking on doors and giving out my phone number. No one had seen Hero, but everyone promised to contact me if they did. Gama called every thirty minutes to see if we'd found him. Whenever her number popped up on my caller ID, I thought she'd phoned to tell me Hero was back home; and each time I answered, I was disappointed.

After we'd combed every inch within a five-mile radius of the house, we drove to the Humane Society to see if Hero was there. He wasn't. When we got into the car to continue the search, Lily looked over at me from the driver's seat. "Addy, don't you think we should get something to eat?"

It was around five o'clock, and we hadn't eaten anything since before noon. I wasn't hungry, but I couldn't expect Lily to continue without food. "You go ahead," I said. "I'm going to look a while longer. I'll walk back home later."

"I'm not dropping you off this far from your house."

"Give me twenty more minutes, and then we'll take a break."

*

Gama was on the front porch when we drove up. "No one has seen him?" she asked.

"No," Lily said as we took the steps up to the porch. "It's like he's vanished."

"But that doesn't make sense," Gama said. "Hero would never leave."

"What did you expect him to do, Gama? He was outside by himself for over two hours!"

"Do you think I did this on purpose? I love Hero as much as you do."

155

"Couldn't you have taken your nap after I got home, just this once?"

"But I could've sworn I let him back in the house."

"Wait a minute," Lily said. "Addy, I know you're upset, but that's no reason to take it out on Gama. She isn't used to looking after Hero on her own."

Lily was right; Gama had done the best she could. "I'm sorry," I said. "I guess I'm just worried."

Gama took me into her arms, and I let go of the tears I'd been holding back. "Hero's okay, honey, and we will find him," she said.

I felt Lily's hand touch my back. "Let's all go inside and get something to eat, then we'll try again."

Gama heated up some left-over vegetable soup, and we sat at the table in the kitchen to eat. I picked at my food for a few minutes to make Lily happy, then got up and grabbed a flashlight from the garage. "I'm going back out."

Lily and Gama joined me, and we searched the neighborhood again on foot. A few people came out of their houses to help, and then a few more until the whole street was filled with the good-hearted folks of Driftwood, their flashlights flitting through the dark, tracing the lawns.

Ten o'clock came and went and Gama never even mentioned going to bed. It was a first. As the night went on with no sign of Hero, the neighbors eventually gave up. Around midnight Gama suggested we go back home to check the answering machine to see if anyone had called.

Exhausted, we huddled on the front porch wrapped in blankets. When it got too cold, we migrated inside to the living room. Gama fell asleep in a chair, Lily, beside me on the couch. Every hour or so, I walked around the house to see if Hero had somehow found his way back home.

When you lose someone you love, the regret—what you should or shouldn't have done—drags you to dark places. My thoughts wandered back to the days after the wreck when Hero first entered my life. In my confused and shattered state, it felt like he was trying to take the place of Mom and Dad. I wanted him to go away, but he wouldn't. The more I rejected him, the more he tried to bond with me. In the mornings, I woke up to his head resting on my stomach, his soft puppy eyes looking up at me. Whenever I went to the bathroom, he got tangled in my legs.

Once he nearly made me trip and fall, and I shoved him aside with my foot. "Why won't you leave me alone?" I shouted. He lowered his head, tucked his tail, and scuttled to a corner of the room. Even though he was hurt by my rejection, I remember seeing something more in his eyes. He looked at me as if to say, "I get it; you're not ready yet. I'll wait."

After that, Hero kept his distance. He still followed me wherever I went but left plenty of space between us. At night, he slept on the floor at the foot of my bed, waiting for me to come around.

Then, one morning, I woke up, and he was gone.

I walked through the house, searching for him and calling his name.

"He's in here," Gama said. I followed her voice to the living room where I found her sitting in the rocking chair, Hero in her lap. "I guess he finally got tired of being pushed away," she said.

When Hero saw me, he sat up and eyed me with interest, but remained with Gama. I was surprised by my excitement when I saw him, and how relieved I was that he was okay. Without thinking, I opened my arms to him, and he jumped down from Gama's lap and ran to me, wagging his whole body. I got on the floor to greet him, and he smothered me with puppy kisses. It was at that moment that our bond began.

Somehow Hero wiggled his way into my heart, dug and dug until he found a soft spot. And he didn't stop there; next, he went for my soul. During those first miserable months without my parents, just as Gama distracted herself from the reality of her loss by looking after me, I clung to Hero with the same desperate need for a reason to live. He'd been beside me at my lowest point and had remained with me ever since. He'd been abandoned; I'd been abandoned. Only Hero came close to knowing the depth of my pain.

*

It felt like I'd just dozed off when I was startled by the sound of my phone ringing. I looked at the time; it was almost 6:30 in the morning. My mind raced as I unwrapped myself from the blanket: *Could it be someone calling about Hero? Is it good news or bad?* I took a deep breath and answered the phone.

"Good morning, Addison. This is Zane Isaac."

"Listen, Dr. Isaac, I don't mean to be rude, but we're in the middle of a family crisis here, and I can't tie up the phone for long. I'll have to call you back later."

"Hold on, don't hang up. I know all about your crisis because I have the family member who caused it here with me."

I sprung to my feet. "Did you find Hero?"

"That's right; looking at him now."

By then, Lily was wide awake, sitting on the edge of her seat, still cocooned in her blanket. Gama, who naturally had been up since five, came out of the kitchen. They were both staring at me, their eyes round with suspense.

"He's been found," I whispered to them.

Gama threw her hands up in the air. "Praise the Lord!"

"Is he okay?" I asked.

"He seems to be fine, aside from a little dehydration," Dr. Isaac said. "I gave him all the water I had with me."

"I'll come and get him right away. Where is he?"

"Well, now that information might cost you."

"*Cost* me? Cost me what?"

"Not much. Just that cup of coffee I was asking about the other day."

*What's with this man and coffee?* "Are you bribing

me?"

"Yes, I am. I tried asking nicely, and that didn't get me anywhere."

"Okay, okay, coffee it is. Now, where's Hero?"

"He's on River Bend Road, near the Snake Shadow Crossing."

"Snake Shadow? Wonder how he got all the way over there?"

"I was thinking the same thing. It's a long way from home for an old, arthritic dog to roam."

"Doesn't matter; I'm glad you found him. Do you mind staying with him for a few minutes longer until I get there?"

"Oh, I wouldn't leave him for anything. But I don't think you need to worry about him going anywhere. He won't move from this one spot on the side of the road."

"Okay, I'm on my way." I started to hang up and then stopped. "Dr. Isaac, thank you."

"Zane," he said. "Please call me Zane."

"Thank you, Zane. Thank you so, so much."

Lily snickered. "Zane Isaac found Hero? Now that's rich."

"You're enjoying this, aren't you?" I began searching around on the floor for my shoes.

"Loving it."

"Did I hear you right?" Gama asked. "Hero's at the Snake Shadow Crossing?"

"Yes, I guess he wandered off, and that's where he ended up."

Lily stood, folded her blanket, and threw it across

the back of the couch. "Do you actually believe it's a coincidence that Hero ended up where he first found you?"

"What, do you think he went there looking for me?"

"Yeah, I do. What surprises me is that he had the stamina to make it."

"I'm telling you, Addy," Gama said. "That dog's your guardian angel."

"That he is." I gave her a hug. "Do you want to go with Lily and me to get him?"

"No, I'll stay here and make breakfast. I'm going to fry up some bacon for Hero. I'm so happy to hear he's safe!"

"Well, we have Zane Isaac to thank for that," Lily said.

"I already thanked him." I found my shoes under the couch and stepped into them. "What are we waiting for? Let's go get my boy."

Lily got her purse and car keys, and we headed for the door. When we passed my room, I ducked in, snatched a brush from my dresser, and ran it through my hair as we walked to the car.

"Getting all pretty to see Zane?"

I whacked Lily with the brush. "No, I just haven't touched my hair since yesterday morning."

"Did I hear you say something about coffee when you were on the phone?"

"Yes, we're having coffee. Are you satisfied?"

"So, will you give this guy a chance now?" Lily asked as she was backing the car out of the driveway.

"What do you mean?"

"Now that you know why you got the red warning when you saw his tattoo, there's no reason for you to be afraid of him anymore."

"What are you saying?"

"Think about it. Hero was there when you got the warning that day at the clinic, and nothing else besides him getting lost has happened since, right?"

"Right?"

"Well, isn't that how it works?"

"Sometimes."

"There you have it. The warning was to let you know Hero was going to be lost. Zane's not a horrible person after all."

"I will admit it was nice of him to stay with Hero."

"You know they say everything happens for a reason."

"I suppose. At least now I won't have a problem taking Hero back to the clinic next month to get more medicine."

"I was thinking the reason was your date with Zane."

"It's not really a date. More like a truce. With coffee."

"I'll bet he doesn't think of it as a truce."

"And why do you say that?"

"Just a hunch." She grinned. "So, after the coffee date, do you think you'll go out with him again?"

"What makes you so sure he'll ask me?"

"He kind of...told me."

"What do you mean he told you?"

"He came by the cleaners. Had some more suit pants that needed hemming."

"And when did this happen?"

"A few days after we were at the clinic."

"What? And you didn't tell me?"

"Since you'd already turned down his coffee invitation, I didn't see any reason to bring it up." She flipped down the overhead mirror and wiped the sleep from her eyes.

"Well, are you going to tell me what he said?"

"Oh, so now you're interested?"

"Curious, that's all."

"Like I said, he brought his pants by the cleaners to get hemmed. The funny thing is they were brand new—still had the tags on them—and the waist was the wrong size. He'd obviously bought them on the way over, so he'd have an excuse to come in and talk to me."

"So, what did he want to talk to you about?"

"He wanted to know the reason you didn't like him and why you ran out of his exam room that day at the clinic."

"And what'd you tell him?"

"Don't worry; I didn't say anything about your warnings, only that you were partial to Dr. Jacobs."

"What did he say?"

"He said he wanted to get to know you. He really likes you, Addy. You should give him a chance. There's no excuse not to now."

"I don't know...it might be too soon after Cole."

"Oh, bull crap! He doesn't even count. You were

with Cole only because you knew you'd never fall for him."

"Okay, I'll give you that."

"Any more lame excuses you want to offer up?"

"Has it ever occurred to you that there might be someone else I'm interested in?"

"Oh yeah, who's that, the cable guy?"

"Kevin Winslow."

She looked at me, shocked. "From school, Kevin Winslow?"

"He's the pharmacist over at the drugstore."

"Yeah, I know. When did this all start?"

"Not too long ago."

"So, you're seeing Kevin Winslow?"

"Right now, we're only talking, but I think we may be moving in that direction."

It wasn't entirely a lie. Kevin Winslow and I had talked once. To pacify Gama, I'd started a conversation with him one Sunday after church service. He wasn't a big talker either, so the whole situation was awkward, to say the least.

Lily busted out laughing. "You've got to be kidding me."

"What's so funny?"

"You with Kevin Winslow."

"Why? What's wrong with him?"

"Look, if you want to go out with Kevin Winslow, that's okay by me, but somebody should tell Melissa Courtney."

"Who's Melissa Courtney?"

"Kevin's fiancée."

"He has a fiancée?"

"As of September; the wedding's in May."

"Is there anything that happens in this town that you don't know about?"

"Addy, I work at the only dry cleaners in Driftwood."

"Well, maybe I won't be dating Kevin Winslow, but I still don't want to go out with Zane."

"Why not? Are you afraid you might like him?"

"No, that's not it at all."

"Okay, I'm going to say some things, and you'll probably be pissed at me when I'm done, but I don't care. I love you too much to keep my mouth shut any longer."

"Wow, sounds serious."

"Addy, it's terrible what happened to you, probably one of the worst things that can happen to someone, but you don't get to opt out of life because of it."

"What are you talking about? I live as much as anybody."

"No, you go through the motions. You get up, shower, eat, and do whatever else is expected of you. That's not living."

I felt my throat constrict. It reminded me of fourth grade when she called me out for pretending I couldn't speak.

"I know you're afraid—hell, we're all afraid—to get too close, care too much, because there's always the chance the people you love might be taken away like your mom and dad were. When you love someone, you give them the power to hurt you, and that's scary, but the other side of that coin is the most fulfilling part of the human experience. And I want that for you."

Lily knew me better than anyone. That's why I loved her. That's why I hated her. I had no rebuttal for anything she'd said. I turned my face toward the window so she couldn't see my eyes water.

When we got to River Bend Road, near where I'd landed when I was thrown from the car, I noticed a parked SUV and then saw Hero's familiar form stand up in the ditch.

"Pull over, there he is!"

As soon as I got out, Hero ran to me, and I threw my arms around him. "Hey Buddy, I missed you!" The tears Lily had started in the car were now pouring down my face.

"How'd you find him anyway?" Lily asked Zane, who was standing nearby.

"I was on my way to work and caught sight of him in that ditch, the same place he was when you got here, sitting as still as a statue. He remembered me—he wagged his tail—but when I called his name, he wouldn't come. So I grabbed a bottle of water from my car, poured some into my cupped hand, and he drank every bit. I thought maybe the water bought me some trust, so I tugged at his collar, hoping I could get him to go with me to the clinic, but he wouldn't move."

I turned to Zane. "I'm so grateful to you for calling and staying with Hero until I got here."

"No problem."

"I guess we should be going now," I said, looking at Lily. "Gama's making breakfast."

"I was hoping you would bring Hero into the clinic before you take him home," Zane said. "When I found him, I did a quick check for injuries but I'd like to do a more thorough exam. It won't take long."

"Of course," I said. "I want to make sure he's okay."

"Good. And we can make the final plans for our coffee date while you're there."

Lily gave me an encouraging wink.

"Yeah, we can do that," I said.

## CHAPTER 11
# ZANE

The following Wednesday, at 10:38 a.m., Zane entered the Ugly Mug Café in Driftwood. He'd taken an early lunch, and had Reenie schedule his appointments to give him an extra hour. He found a seat at a table near the entrance, an intentional choice, so Addison would be sure to find him. He sat with his back turned to the door because he didn't want to appear too anxious, even though he had been since Monday morning when they made their date.

Zane suggested they meet at The Ugly Mug because it was the best place in Driftwood to get a good cup of coffee. Reenie and her husband Rex owned the café, which was like a Starbucks, only with much more character. Besides coffee, they served Danish, donuts, and scones, and their lunch menu included Paninis and gourmet grilled cheese sandwiches.

The theme of the café was in celebration of the ugly coffee mug—the gifts and vacation souvenirs that get pushed to the back on the highest shelves of our kitchen cabinets. Customers were encouraged to bring in their own coffee mugs to be considered for display. If Rex decided it was worthy of a place on the wall, the customer received one free item of their choice from the menu. It was a fun place with the whimsical feel of a nonstop ugly Christmas sweater party.

Across the restaurant, Rex, a jolly, mountain of a man who made Zane happy whenever he saw him, was moving from table to table, warming the customers' coffees. Rex spotted Zane and smiled broadly, revealing a gap in his teeth where he was missing a canine. Reenie said he was too stubborn to go to the dentist to get a bridge, and now he'd had the gap so long it had become his signature.

"Look who it is!" Rex bellowed as he walked across the room, still holding the coffeepot. "Been a while since I've seen you in here." He thrust his big, meaty hand into Zane's. "Hell, it's been a while since I've seen you anywhere."

"Easy, now, you're beginning to sound like your wife." Zane stood to shake Rex's hand. "How've you been?"

"Oh, fair to middling," he said. "Thanks for coming in! And thanks for bringing another ugly mug to add to our collection!"

"Huh?"

Rex chuckled, causing his round belly to bob under his apron.

It took Zane a few seconds, but he finally got the joke. "That's a good one."

"I've always wanted to say that to a customer, and I figured a good-looking guy like you, and being a doctor too, your ego could handle it."

"I don't know whether to thank you or be offended."

"Neither. Have a seat. What can I get for you today?"

"I think I'll have an espresso."

"The hard stuff, huh? Anything to go with it?"

"Not yet; I'm waiting on someone."

"What time is she supposed to be here?"

Zane looked at him, puzzled.

"Reenie told me."

Zane wasn't surprised or angry. That was just Reenie. "Around eleven."

They both glanced at the clock behind the counter. "So, any minute then. I'll be right back with your espresso."

Zane sipped his espresso, watching the clock, which seemed to have stopped, and waited for Addison to arrive. Naturally, he was nervous but mostly excited, akin to how he'd felt as a kid in those long few hours before Christmas. At 11:02, the bell above the café door rattled. Zane jumped in his seat and turned to see who was coming in. It wasn't her.

He decided to try to occupy his mind by challenging himself to select which mug displayed on the walls he thought was the ugliest. He scanned the rows upon rows of cups. Some had faces with bucked teeth and crossed eyes; others were character mugs like the Grinch and Darth Vader. There were mugs shaped like toilets and handguns, mermaids and butt cheeks. After much consideration, he finally chose one that looked like a lopsided pile of poop.

By 11:16, Zane had finished his espresso and felt jittery, so he switched to coffee. At 11:22, he heard the doorbell again. An older couple walked in; he watched them make their way across the room and sit down. *What if she doesn't come? What if she's forgotten?*

Rex came to Zane's table with the coffee pot at 11:26. "Need a warm-up?"

"Sure."

"Don't worry; women are always running late," Rex said, looking at the clock. "I've been married over twenty-three years, and I'm pretty sure I've spent half of it waiting for Reenie to get ready." He patted Zane on the shoulder and then moved to another table.

Zane went back to his ugliest mug contest to choose a runner-up. The thought crossed his mind that he was being stood up, and wondered what the protocol was on this type of thing, how long he should wait before giving up and returning to the clinic.

He thought of Addison's frightened face when they met and couldn't help but wonder if there was something she wasn't telling him. Then he remembered how she'd openly smiled and thanked him when she came to the Snake Shadow Crossing to get Hero, an entirely different girl from the one who'd run out of the clinic. He had been deeply touched by her that day, watching her reunited with her beloved friend, her emotions gushing forward, Hero licking the tears from her face. "How will this girl ever make it when her old dog dies?" he'd asked himself.

At 11:31, the bell above the café door rattled once again. Zane couldn't bring himself to turn around and confront the disappointment. He glanced at Rex, standing behind the counter, who winked and nodded. She had arrived.

"Hey there, Addison," Rex called out and pointed to Zane by the door. "Somebody's waiting for you."

She slid into the booth across from him, her cheeks flushed, her hair windblown. She had obviously walked to the coffee shop. "Sorry I'm late, Zane."

*She called me Zane without me correcting her. That's a good sign, right?* "You're late?" Zane checked the clock like he hadn't been counting the minutes. "Wow, didn't even realize what time it was."

Addison smiled as she removed the fuzzy gold scarf that Zane noticed made her eyes disarmingly bright.

Rex came over to the table, rescuing them both from those first awkward moments. "How you been, Miss Addison?"

She slipped off her Sherpa-lined denim jacket and put it on the seat beside her. "Just fine."

"Sure am glad you found that dog of yours," Rex said. "A lot of folks were worried."

"I meant to thank you, Rex; I really appreciate your help with that." Gama had called Reenie the night Hero went missing, and she and Rex had shown up with their flashlights to join the search.

"You're welcome. That's what we do around here; we look out for each other. Now, what can I get you?"

"Umm, I think I'll have a cappuccino, French vanilla, please."

"Gotcha."

When Rex turned to walk back to the counter, Addison stopped him. "Hey, Rex? Have any chocolate chip scones left?"

"Sure do. I heard you were coming and saved some for you."

"I'll have one of those," she said.

Zane's stomach had finally unclenched enough to allow him to eat. "Make that two."

Addison looked at Zane. "And I can't thank you enough for your part in finding Hero."

"I really didn't do all that much."

"Yes, you did. You didn't have to stay with him. Let's be honest, I wasn't exactly nice to you when we met."

Recalling his conversation with Lily, Zane decided not to address Addison's comment about what happened at the clinic. "I'm a vet; I love animals, and it's my job to do what's best for them," he said. "But I must admit I'm glad I was the one who found him. It opened up the opportunity for me to show you that I'm not such a bad guy after all."

"Lily told me you came by the cleaners."

"She did?" Her remark caught him off-guard, but he was all about efficiency and liked people who got to the point. "There really are no secrets in this town."

"I'm afraid not. If you've got secrets, you should probably move."

"You're not mad that I talked to Lily, are you?"

"No, not mad; surprised, maybe."

"Really? I thought I clarified my intentions when I called and asked you to have coffee."

"I figured you were only being nice."

Rex brought over Addison's cappuccino and the scones. "Can I get you kids anything else?" he asked, refilling Zane's coffee cup.

"No, this will be fine," Zane said.

Addison broke her scone in half. "I love these things."

"First time for me."

"You're joking."

"I've always been a blueberry muffin guy. Never tried scones at all."

"Better watch yourself; they're addictive."

Zane didn't want to get sidetracked with small talk about scones. He needed to steer the conversation back to them, but he couldn't think of a smooth way to do it, so he followed Addison's lead and jumped right to the point.

"I'd like to see you again to get to know you better," he said.

She broke off a chunk of her scone, popped it into her mouth, and washed it down with a gulp of cappuccino. "That's sweet of you, and I'm flattered, but I'm not in a place right now to start seeing anyone."

"Well, I can certainly understand that." Zane took a bite of his scone, trying to think of something to say that might change her mind. Then he remembered Lily's advice about not pushing. "Truthfully, it's Hero I want to get to know."

Addison studied Zane for a second and then grinned. "Hero, huh?"

"The thing is, I lost my dog not long ago, and Hero reminds me so much of him."

"I'm sorry. What was your dog's name?"

"Dandy."

"Love that. How did Dandy die?"

"Old age." Zane saw an opportunity to slip in a subliminal message. "I knew it was coming, but it was still rough."

"Hero's going to break the record for the longest living dog."

Zane's attempt to prepare Addison for Hero's death had done nothing to quash her denial, and he didn't want to take a chance on upsetting her by going any further. "As his vet, I'm certainly going to do everything I can to keep him around as long as possible."

What breed was Dandy?"

"Mutt."

"That's the best kind."

"You'll get no argument from me." Zane realized they were getting sidetracked again. "So, I was thinking, you know, to help me better deal with my loss, how would you feel about me taking Hero for a walk every now and then."

"Sure. I guess I can do that. But you do realize Hero and I are a package deal."

"Well, if you *have* to come, I suppose it would be okay. Why don't we start tomorrow afternoon?"

"Tomorrow?"

"What? Is Hero busy?"

"It's just that I didn't expect it to be so soon."

He dropped his head and peered down into his coffee cup ruefully. "I really miss Dandy." She smiled at him, and he took that as a yes. "Six-thirty okay?"

*

Zane's coffee date with Addison was over before he was ready for it to end. As soon as they'd parted ways, he began looking forward to when he would next see her. Back at the clinic, Reenie hit him up for the details the minute he walked in. "I hear there was a lot of smiling at the cafe, so it must have gone well."

"How'd you know that?"

"Rex called."

"Of course, he did."

"He calls me every day at lunch. Today he just happened to mention seeing you and Addison." She struggled to keep a straight face when Zane raised an eyebrow at her response. "Okay, okay, I told him to call when you left to let me know how he thought things went. It did go well, didn't it?"

"It did, after a shaky start. Addison was late, and I began to think she wouldn't show up at all. She walked there. Can you believe that? I mean, it's not that far from where she lives, but nobody walks much anymore. Does she not drive at all?"

"Come to think of it, I haven't seen her drive, always Lily. She never goes anywhere without Lily."

"I like Lily, but I was sure thankful to see Addison didn't bring her to the coffee shop."

Reenie laughed. "No kidding."

"Wonder why she doesn't drive?"

"Maybe she's afraid to get behind the wheel because of how her parents died."

"Could be; I didn't think of that."

"Anyway, are you seeing each other again?"

"Yeah, sort of; we're taking Hero for a walk down by the river tomorrow afternoon."

"Well, that's a good start. Lord knows if there's any way to get to that girl's heart, it's through her dog."

"We'll see how it goes." He picked up the files for his afternoon appointments and headed to his office. "At least this time, she didn't run away as soon as she saw me."

## CHAPTER 12
# ADDISON

When I told Gama that Hero and I were going for a walk by the river with Zane Isaac, you'd have thought I'd just announced that I was pregnant with her first great-grandbaby. "I'm so happy for you, honey!" she said, wrapping her arms around me.

"Gama, we're only taking a walk."

"I know, I know. So, when are you going?"

"He's picking me up this afternoon."

"Why didn't you say something before? I would've straightened the house."

I glanced around the kitchen. "What do you mean? The house is fine."

"Look at the dishes." We'd just finished dinner, and our plates were still on the table. She gathered and took them to the sink. "What time is he coming?" she asked as she began rolling her blouse sleeves up.

"Relax; he won't be here until 6:30."

"Oh, Addy, I'm so proud of you. It's good to get out and meet new people. And Zane Isaac is such a nice young man."

"Do you know him?"

"No, not personally, but Reenie from the animal clinic thinks the world of him; says he's got a heart of gold."

"What else does she say about him?"

"Well, she told me he recently moved back to Driftwood from Florida when he found out his mom had cancer. Dropped everything to come home and look after her. Now that's a good son."

"His mom has cancer?"

"Had; she died a few months back of breast cancer, the aggressive kind. She was only like, forty-five."

"Oh wow, so young."

"She was a beautiful woman too. We never met, not formally, anyway, but I saw her around town now and then. Years ago, she worked at the clinic as a receptionist."

"Reenie's job?"

"Before Reenie, I think I remember seeing her when we first took Hero."

"Why did she stop working there?"

"I believe that's when she moved away."

"Wait a minute; I'm confused. I thought you said Zane returned here to take care of his mom."

"He did. Corinne—that was her name—moved back to Driftwood later, after the twins were both grown, same house and everything."

"Twins?"

"You didn't know Zane has a twin brother?"

"No, I hardly know anything about him."

"I don't know much, but I've always heard good things about Corinne. You'd think there would've been talk since she was a single mom—you know how people are—but I've never heard a bad word about her. All she ever did was take care of those boys. Over the years, I remember seeing her at the grocery store and whatnot, and she always had them with her."

"If she worked at the clinic, I must have seen her there, but I don't remember."

"Oh, sweetheart, that was a challenging time for you. You weren't paying too much attention to your surroundings."

"So, how long has Zane been back in Driftwood?"

"Less than a year, according to Reenie."

"I can't believe I haven't run into him somewhere around town."

"I can. Unless he goes to the hobby shop a lot or hangs out in the basement, you wouldn't have."

"Not you too, Gama; I got an ear full the other day from Lily about how I need to be more engaged in life."

"Well, I've got to side with her on this one."

"What do you mean *this one?* You always side with Lily."

"That's not true."

A knock at the front door ended what was sure to have been a heated debate. "There's Zane now," Gama said, drying her hands. "You get the door; I need to go put my lips on." On her way to the half-bath, she stepped into the living room to fluff the pillows on the couch. "Go!" she hollered back over her shoulder. "Invite him in."

Hero, who'd been napping in the corner of the kitchen, suddenly appeared beside me flailing his tail with excitement. As soon as I opened the door, he pushed past me to get to Zane.

"Hey, old boy," Zane said, kneeling to scratch behind Hero's ears.

"Before we go, would you mind coming inside for a minute?" I asked. "Gama wants to meet you."

"Sure, I'd love to meet her too."

Gama popped into the room with carnation pink lips. Without hesitation, she walked up to Zane and embraced him. She passed hugs around like warm rolls, even when she met someone for the first time. "It's so good to meet you, Zane!" She pulled back from him, still holding onto his arms. "I was so sorry to hear about your mom."

"I appreciate that," he said.

There was a lapse in conversation, an invitation to jump in, but I couldn't. It's not that I didn't feel bad for people when they lost a loved one; I did—gut-kick bad—and I naturally understood the intensity of their pain, but I was the worst at expressing sympathy. After my parents died, I had to listen to everyone chant the same things over and over: *Sorry for your loss. My condolences. They're in a better place.* None of it sounded sincere. "Yes, me too," I finally added.

"I never had the pleasure of knowing her, but people have told me she was a wonderful woman,"

Gama said.

"Yeah, she was." He turned to me. "I know it happened long ago, but I'd like to offer my sympathy to both of you for your terrible loss."

Gama reached over and took my hand. "Thank you, Zane," she said, speaking for us both.

Then came the silence that's inevitable after people talk about the dead. We were at a place where things could've gone dark fast if someone didn't change the subject. "We'd better get going on our walk while Hero's still got the energy," I said.

As I prepared to help Hero into the SUV, Zane pulled out a portable dog ramp. "It was Dandy's," he said, unfolding the ramp. "Toward the end, he had trouble too."

"Don't take this the wrong way," I said as we were getting in the car. "But I can't get over how quickly Hero befriended you. I wasn't kidding when I told you he doesn't like men. He backed the pizza delivery guy off the front porch a few days ago. I'm surprised he's letting you anywhere near me."

"Why does he only go after men, if you don't mind my asking?"

"It's a stupid, uninteresting story involving an ex-boyfriend."

"Oh, I see."

"I won't go there right now. Let's just say it ended ugly with Hero chasing him out the door."

"Ouch!" Zane reached behind him and tousled Hero's head. "Way to go, buddy!"

"What about you?" I asked. "Got any scary-ex

stories?"

"Nope, no drama; things merely didn't work out."

"Did you break up recently?"

"It's been several months."

"How long were you together?"

"A few years; she was a nice girl, but not the one for me." He began fiddling with the the stereo dial. "What kind of music do you listen to?"

"Most everything; but recently, I've acquired an affinity for Reggae."

"Not sure what station to tune into for that."

"Anything's fine." He flipped the dial and landed on a country station. I was thankful the music filled the gaps in conversation.

After a few minutes, he turned the volume down. "So, where do you work?"

As soon as his question landed in my mind, I realized I was embarrassed that I didn't have a job. My unemployment hadn't bothered me before, but then no one, aside from Gama, had ever mentioned it. "I'm, umm, between jobs right now."

"Oh, that's right; of course, you aren't working yet. Reenie told me you haven't been home from school for very long."

Suddenly I remembered my conversation with Lily about the business partnership. "I have something in the works, though," I said.

"You do? I'd love to hear about it."

"It's in the planning stages now."

"Well, give me the gist then."

"Lily and I are going to open a shop downtown."

"Your own business? What will you sell?"

"It's mostly for Lily. She designs clothing."

"So, you'll help sell her clothing line?"

"Yes, and we're also thinking about selling some of my stained glass pieces."

"You make stained glass art? I love that stuff. You'll have to show me your work sometime."

"Sure, I could do that if you're interested."

"I am. I envy artistic people. I don't have a creative bone in my body."

"We're going to call it Kaleidoscope."

"Awesome name."

"It's Lily's brainchild."

Zane pulled into the driveway of a small cottage-style house not far from the river trail. "Why are we stopping here?" I asked.

"I thought this would be a good place to park the car while we walk."

"That's fine with me, but the people who own this house might not appreciate it."

"Don't worry, he doesn't mind."

"You know the owner?"

"I guess you could say that. It's me."

"You live here?"

"It was Ma's."

I looked at the white clapboard-sided house with a red, arched door and ivy climbing up the sides of the front porch. "Wow, what a neat place."

"I'll have to give you a tour."

*

We'd walked only ten minutes when Hero needed to stop for a rest. Zane and I sat on one of the benches facing the river and looked out onto the murky water, Hero on the ground between us. Once we reached down to pet Hero's head simultaneously, bumping our hands, and then looked at each other and broke out laughing.

Right away, I picked up that Zane didn't speak unless he had something noteworthy to say, and since I wasn't much of a talker either, our conversations were in fits and starts, mostly when something interesting or unique passed in front of us. During these brief interactions, I began to appreciate Zane's good looks. He was a rather boring, textbook sort of handsome in that he checked all the boxes: clear skin, full lips, strong jawline, and a defined nose proportioned to his face. Cole had symmetric features, too, only in a creepy android way; whenever I looked at him, I had to tilt my head to make him appear human. Unlike Cole, Zane had slight imperfections that intrigued me. Like the smattering of gold specks in one of his eyes, and the sprigs of wheat-colored hair that spilled into his face. But what made him truly attractive was a simmering Adrien Brodyesque intensity that oozed sex appeal. After thirty minutes or so of his sparse conversation and pensive silence, you're drawn in and begin to wonder things, imagine things, and before you know it, you're picturing yourself in bed with him.

We picked up where we left off when Hero was

ready to go again. It had been so long since I'd walked the river trail, I'd forgotten, until I spotted the fork up ahead, that there were two paths, one of which led over the Snake Shadow Crossing. I knew Zane would most likely want to take that one; everyone did because it was more interesting than walking through the woods. Or so people said; I, of course, had never walked the Snake Shadow path.

As we got closer to the fork in the trail, dread began to rise from my chest because I knew I would either have to walk over the crossing or talk to Zane about something that made me uncomfortable. When we were almost there, I decided to gut up and push through. I'd passed under the Snake Shadow Crossing countless times, and I figured walking on it couldn't be much worse. But at the last minute, something unexpected happened. Zane cut in front of me and, and without missing a step, continued to the route through the woods. Neither of us said anything, but I knew he'd done it because of the wreck. That thoughtful move alone earned him extra points with me.

Near the trail's end, a chilly wind blew up from the water and made me shiver. I tightened my scarf. "It's getting too cold to be out," I said. "Maybe we should head back."

"Yeah, you're probably right. I know of a nice little house with a fireplace not far from here. Warm you right up."

"Sounds tempting, but…"

"I hear the guy who lives there makes a mean cup

of hot cocoa. Not that instant stuff either."

"Maybe another time; it's getting late. We should go home."

"Late? It's seven forty-five. C'mon, I want to give you that tour of the house. You'll love it; lots of character."

"Well, I would like to see the house…."

"Hero wants to go. Don't you, buddy?"

Hero somehow found his second wind and got waggly-tailed like he knew what Zane had said. He looked at me, begging with his eyes.

"Have any marshmallows to go with that cocoa?" I asked.

"Marshmallow cream."

"Good enough."

\*

The inside of Zane's house was as inviting as the exterior. The walls were ship-lapped in bleached wood and adorned with pastel waterfront art, and jute area rugs were tossed about the oak hardwood floors. As we were walking in, I noticed some cardboard boxes in one corner of the room, and right inside the front door, propped against the wall, was a For Sale sign.

"Are you selling the house?"

"I'm thinking about it."

I read the sign: *Call the Brady Bunch for all your Real Estate needs.* "Looks like you're pretty serious; you already have a realtor."

"That's my Uncle Brady's real estate company. He

dropped the sign by the other day."

"Are you moving someplace else in Driftwood or leaving town?"

"I never planned on staying in Driftwood. I only came to help Ma after she got sick."

"What about your job at the clinic?"

"That was never meant to be permanent either. But I won't be going anywhere until Dean feels better."

"So, where would you move?"

"I'm considering North Carolina. I have a brother who lives there."

"Your twin?"

"How did you know I had a twin?"

"Remember, there are no secrets here."

Even though I wanted to know more about Zane's family and his life, I decided to let the subject dead end there. I was afraid my prying questions would lead to his prying questions.

Hero, who had sauntered through the door like he owned the place, plopped down on a plush area rug in the living room. Zane grabbed a handful of twigs from a wicker basket by the hearth, piled them in the center of the fireplace, and lit them with a long match.

"You look like you've done this before," I said.

"Once or twice." When the twigs were burning, he arranged three logs—tee-pee fashion—on top of them. "If you'll keep an eye on this for me, I'll get started on the cocoa."

"Sure, I can do that."

"Come on, boy." Zane motioned for Hero to follow him. "I've got something for you in the kitchen." Seconds later, Hero returned carrying a dog treat and settled in front of the fireplace to eat it.

When the fire was steady, I stepped into the kitchen, which was right off the living room and peeked in. The room was small but functional; you could almost stand in the center and reach everything you needed. The walls were deep gold, and the cabinets were painted white with wrought iron hardware. The proud focal point was an old pine butcher block island with vintage metal stools around it.

Zane was busy at the stove; when he saw me, he looked up and smiled "Almost done."

"I do love this house," I said. "How long did your mother live here?"

"The first time, thirteen years; the second, around seven, so, about twenty years."

"You must have grown up here then."

"I did until I was around thirteen."

"So, except for the months you took care of your mother you've been away from Driftwood for a long while."

"Not that long. How old do you think I am anyway?"

"I don't know...late twenties? You'd have to be at least that old if you graduated from veterinary school."

"I'm twenty-six, an old man compared to you. What are you, about 21?"

"Nice job at shooting low. I'm twenty-two."

"Get ready to experience the best hot cocoa you've ever tasted," Zane said, pouring the chocolate into two brown earthenware mugs. He pulled a jar of marshmallow cream from a cabinet, spooned a big dollop into each cup, and then gave one to me. "Let's drink this in front of the fire," he said. "That is if there still is one."

"Oops, I forgot." I rushed back into the living room and found only embers in the fireplace.

Zane came in behind me. "Let's see if I can breathe some life back into this thing."

"Sorry."

"No big deal. Have a seat, get comfortable."

As he fussed with the fire, I stood before the tight furniture grouping, trying to decide where to sit. My choices were an overstuffed blue and green striped couch, a coral-colored club chair with a matching ottoman, and two mint green slipcovered side chairs flanking the fireplace. Hero, now finished with his treat, was waiting to see where I landed so he could curl up somewhere near me. Usually, without even thinking, I would've gone for one of the chairs; it was my way, not wanting anyone too close. But surprising myself, I decided on the couch, risking the chance that Zane might sit beside me.

I watched him wedge a poker between the logs, his balloon-tattooed forearm on full display. This time when I saw it, I felt nothing but curiosity. "That's an unusual tattoo. What's the story behind it?"

He picked up a bellow from the hearth and pumped quick sprays of air into the embers. With a hiss, the flames came alive. "Does there have to be a story?"

"There's always a story. Unless you woke up one morning after a night out drinking and can't remember how you got it."

"Oh, I remember, all right."

"Why did you choose a balloon? I've seen all kinds of tattoos—roses, reptiles, women—but never a balloon."

"I guess you could say it's symbolic."

"Of?"

"It's there to remind me to let go of something difficult that happened long ago."

"This *something* sounds like a girl to me."

"No, nothing like that; it's just a piece of my past I needed to put behind me."

"So, you got a permanent mark on your arm to remind you of something you want to forget?"

"I never thought of it that way." Satisfied with the fire, he turned and, without hesitation, sat in one of the side chairs. "How's your cocoa?"

*Why did he choose a chair instead of the couch? Maybe he wants to be near the fire in case he needs to tend to it again. Or perhaps he simply doesn't want to sit beside me.*

"It's that bad, huh?" he said.

"No, the cocoa's good. I was thinking what a cozy place this is."

"Yeah, I know. Maybe that's why I always want to

stay inside. Reenie says it's a character flaw, being a homebody. She's always saying I need to get out more."

"You too? Seems like that's all I've heard from Gama and Lily lately."

"I don't know about you, but I stay home because there's no place else I really want to go. Don't care for bars or any crowded, noisy places."

"Same here."

"It doesn't take much to entertain me," Zane said.

"Guess some people would consider us boring."

We exchanged smiles behind our cups of cocoa.

"I see you've already started packing," I said, noticing the bare tabletops.

"Oh no, not yet; I've just been boxing up a few of Ma's things."

Looking around the room, a photograph on the mantle caught my eye. It was of a young woman, her hands on the shoulders of the two boys standing in front of her. She was leggy-tall and wide-eyed, with thick brown hair rippling down her shoulders. I got up from the couch and took the picture off the mantel to look closer. "Is this your mother?"

"When she was younger."

"Gama was right; she was beautiful."

"Yes, she was."

"She looks like somebody on TV...."

"Brooke Shields?"

"Yes, that's exactly who she looks like!"

"When I was a kid, we couldn't even walk down the street without somebody stopping us to tell her."

"Must've been interesting growing up with a mom who looked like a movie star."

"Let's just say my friends wanted to sleep over a lot when I was a teenager."

"I'll bet. So, who does your dad look like, Johnny Depp?"

"Don't know. I never saw my dad."

"Oh, Zane, I'm so sorry. I wouldn't have made a joke of it if…."

"That's okay; you had no way of knowing."

"You've never even seen a picture?"

"Nope, from what I understand, Ma didn't have much of a relationship with him beyond the obvious. It was a summer fling. They were both young."

"You said you never *saw* him, so I'm assuming he's passed away too."

"He died when I was around nine, but I didn't find out about it until four years later."

"Do you mind if I ask how it happened?"

"Car accident."

"That's something else we have in common."

"Only your situation was much worse. But I have to say that even though I never knew my dad, somehow, when Ma told me he was gone I still felt the loss."

From the ache in his voice, I got the feeling he was talking about more than his father's death. I got the feeling he was also talking about a balloon tattoo.

"Of course, you did." Suddenly I felt ashamed for

having wrongly judged him.

"But Ma more than made up for his absence."

"Gama said she was a good mother."

"The best."

I pointed to the boys in the picture. "And this must be you and your twin brother."

"His name's Zach."

"Zach and Zane; I like it. Are the two of you close, you know, like twins usually are?"

"We used to be before I went away to school. What about you? Have any brothers or sisters?"

"No. It's just Gama and me." I put the photo back on the mantel and returned to the couch.

As soon as I sat down, Hero got up from his place at my feet and walked over to Zane, who welcomed him with an outstretched arm. "He reminds me of my Dandy."

"You obviously love dogs. Why don't you get another one?"

"I plan to as soon as I settle somewhere."

Zane put his hand on Hero's head. "But who knows? Since I've made such good friends here, I might stick around a while." He looked over at me and grinned.

"Tell me about Dandy."

"The best friend I ever had. I got him right after I found out about my dad's death. It was a difficult year for me but having him around helped."

"Dogs really are therapeutic. I don't know what I would've done without Hero."

Being with Zane was surprisingly easy, bonding

over shared experiences, sipping chocolate in front of a crackling fire, with Hero sleeping at my feet. There were stretches of silence when we gazed at the flames, but it wasn't uncomfortable. I didn't feel any pressure to talk, no pressure to do anything but be. Ironically, I felt safe with this guy I'd once been so afraid of.

Around 9:30, when I was down to the last lukewarm swallow of my second cup of cocoa, I took my mug into the kitchen, put it in the sink, and then went back into the living room. "Guess we need to be getting home."

Zane stood up. "Let me throw another log on the fire, and I'll drive you."

A wave of disappointment washed over me. I expected him to try to get me to stay longer. "Okay," I said, pulling my coat from the hall tree by the door. "Come on, boy, let's go," I said to Hero. He rolled over, ignoring me as if he didn't want to leave either.

When we got to my house, Zane walked with us to the door. "Thank you for letting me hang out with Hero." He smiled. "And you're not bad company yourself."

"Thanks for the cocoa; it actually was the best I've ever had."

"My pleasure," he said. "You know, some moderate daily exercise would be good for Hero's arthritis."

"I try to take him for a short walk every morning if he feels like it."

"Tomorrow, if you don't mind waiting until the

afternoon, I'd like to tag along again, if that's okay. After the walk, I can make us dinner at my place."

"Tomorrow?"

"If you'd rather I not go...."

"No, it's not that...but Christmas is only a few days away."

"It is, isn't it? Guess it kind of snuck up on me this year."

"I'm sure you have last-minute shopping to do and plans with your family for the holidays."

"Yes, and you probably do as well."

I thought of Gama and me staring at the blinking lights on the Christmas tree. "Of course, family stuff."

"I'd still like to make you dinner, maybe sometime after Christmas?"

"Well, then there's New Year's Day."

"Okay, after New Year's."

"You don't have to go through the trouble of cooking."

"But I want to. Nothing fancy; my culinary skills are limited. Hope you like spaghetti."

"Who doesn't? Is there something you'd like me to bring when we come?"

"No, but you can make the salad. I'll have everything you need at the house."

"I can do that."

"Don't think you're getting off easy, though. I like big salads, so be prepared to do some serious vegetable chopping."

"Sounds good."

"Okay, bye." Zane turned and started walking in the direction of his car. About halfway there, he stopped. "After the first of the year, right? I'll call you."

As soon as we got inside, Hero headed straight for his bed, and I went into the living room where I found Gama on the couch, sleepy-eyed and bundled up in an afghan, watching TV. She perked up when she saw me. "Hey, you're home! How was your walk with Zane?"

I sat beside her. "You know, Gama, it went really well."

"You sound surprised."

"Actually, I am. To be honest, I didn't care for Zane when I first met him."

"Why? He seems so nice."

"Just a feeling, but I guess my instincts were wrong."

"Tell me all about your evening."

"We walked the river trail until it got cold, then Zane invited us back to his place for hot cocoa. He lives right by the river in the cutest house."

"But what do you think about Zane?"

"He's nice and really good with Hero."

"Are you going to see him again?"

"After New Year's Day; we're having dinner at his place."

"You know, Addy, I have a good feeling about that boy." Gama had a good feeling about everybody. She got up from the couch. "I think I'm going to turn in."

I glanced at the clock on the wall. She was right

on cue. "Good night, Gama."

"Night, sweetie; remember to shut everything off before you go to bed," she said, making her way down the hallway to her room.

I was flipping through the TV channels when I got a text from Lily: *Are you home yet?*

I started to text her back but then decided to call instead.

She answered immediately. "I was going to call you earlier, but I was afraid I might interrupt something…if you know what I mean."

"There was nothing to interrupt."

"Well, how was it? Did you have a nice time?"

"I made it home alive, so I guess Zane's not an ax murderer."

"Good to hear. Did you get around to asking him about the tattoo?"

"Sort of."

"I'm dying to know. What does it mean?"

"He didn't come out and say exactly, only that the balloon symbolizes something he wants to forget, something that made him unhappy."

"See, I told you."

"I think it might have to do with his father, who died in a car accident before Zane had a chance to meet him. He didn't give the details, just skimmed over the subject."

"It sounds like he's a private person. Hmm, who does that remind you of?"

"That's why I didn't press him. He's entitled to his privacy."

"So, did you guys do anything besides walk Hero?"

"We went back to his place."

"Okay, now we're getting somewhere." I could hear a smile in her voice. "So, what happened then?"

"He started a fire."

"What kind of fire?"

"The kind with logs and matches."

"And?"

"We drank the cocoa."

"And?"

"We talked. That's it."

"No spooning on the couch?"

"Nope."

"What about a kiss?"

"Sorry to disappoint you."

"So, do you like him now?"

"Sure, he's okay."

"Are you going to see him again?"

"We plan to get together after the holidays. He's making us dinner at his place."

"Now *that's* a date. Not a truce coffee or a dog walk, but a real date."

"You think so? I get the feeling he only wants to be friends."

"He's not gay, Addy."

"But I'm not picking up signals that he's interested in me, you know…physically."

"You're terrible with signals. Let me remind you that Zane came to the cleaners to ask me if I thought you would go out with him. Bought a pair of pants he couldn't even wear so he would have an excuse to come. A guy doesn't get any clearer."

"You're right; he must like me. Why else would he have gone to all that trouble?"

"He more than likes you. He's got the hots for you."

"No, he doesn't...you think?"

"Positive. Give him some more time to make his move."

"Okay, if you say so."

"Speaking of hot chocolate, guess who called me tonight?"

"The father of your future kids."

"Yep, and we're going out this weekend."

"Wow, that was fast."

"No sense waiting when you've found the man you're going to marry."

"Guess not."

"He offered to drive up here—he lives right outside of Nashville—but there's no place decent to go in Driftwood, so I'm going down there this Saturday. I was planning to visit Mom on Christmas Eve anyway."

My heart sank. Lily and I usually exchanged gifts on Christmas Eve. "When are we having *our* Christmas?"

"Christmas eve with Mom, Christmas with you and Gama, if that's all right with the two of you."

"That'll work."

"Listen, I need to hang up now and get to bed. I have to be at work early in the morning."

"Okay, but before you go, I want to tell you one more thing. It's about the business partnership we were discussing the other day."

"Yes?"

"Let's do it."

"Are you serious?"

"We can start making plans after the first of the year."

"Oh, Addy, that's the best news ever!" she squealed. "Can you hold on a minute? I'm going to have to put the phone down."

"Why?"

"I need both my arms to do my happy dance." A few seconds later, she picked the phone back up. "You won't regret it; we'll make a good team."

"I know," I said. "We always have."

## CHAPTER 13
# ZANE

Zane sat on the edge of his couch, staring at the phone in his hand. He'd selected Addison's name from his contacts and had his thumb hovering above the call button. She had made it clear to him that she wanted to wait until after the holidays before they got together again, but she didn't say anything about talking on the phone.

Just as his thumb was about to land, he thought of Lily's warning not to move too fast. He considered himself lucky to have gotten this far with Addison and didn't want to risk messing things up now. He tossed the phone on the couch and walked away from it so he wouldn't be tempted to try again.

He went into the kitchen to get a beer from the fridge. While there, he checked the time on the microwave clock; it was 5:30. He had about an hour to shower and get dressed for dinner with Reenie and Rex at their house. He was looking forward to the evening. Since his ma's death, his home-cooked meals had been few and far between. And he was thankful for something to occupy him, making the days he had to wait before seeing Addison again seem to go by faster.

He dressed and headed out the door early to give himself plenty of time to stop on the way and pick up a bottle of wine to take with him. As he drove to Reenie's, his mind wandered back to when he had last been with Addison. While they were walking the river trail, there'd been a few instances when he had wanted to reach for her hand, but he'd resisted, remembering Lily's advice. Later, at his house, she'd looked so sweet cozied up on the couch with her cup of cocoa, he'd wanted to sit beside her, but he knew he couldn't be close to her and not take her into his arms.

When he pulled up to Reenie's house, he noticed a car in the driveway that wasn't hers or Rex's. Reenie hadn't mentioned anyone else was coming. Did he have the wrong night? No, he was sure they'd agreed on Christmas Eve, seven o'clock. Maybe a friend popped in for a short visit. It was the holidays, and everyone knew Rex and Reenie's doors were always open.

He glanced at his watch; he was a few minutes early. He grabbed the bottle of wine and made his way to the house. When he rang the doorbell, Reenie appeared wearing a red sweater with a Christmas tree applique and snowman earrings. "Merry Christmas!" she chirped.

Rex popped in behind her in a Santa hat. "Come on in," he said.

"Merry Christmas!" Zane gave Reenie the wine he'd brought, then stepped inside, peering around the front door, curious to see whose car was parked in the driveway and bumped into Kim Webber.

"Kim...hello," he said, cutting his eyes at Reenie to let her know he was displeased that she'd gone behind his back.

"Did I not mention we invited Kim too?" Reenie asked.

"No, I'm pretty sure you didn't...." Zane caught himself before he said something that might hurt Kim's feelings. "But what a pleasant surprise."

"You don't mind, do you, Zane?" Kim asked.

"No, of course not; it's just that I wasn't expecting to see you."

"Must've slipped my mind," Reenie said. "I'm always scattered this time of the year...so much to do." She started walking toward the dining room and motioned for everyone to follow. "Dinner is ready. Rex, would you open this lovely bottle of wine Zane brought?"

When they all got to the table, making matters worse, Reenie insisted Zane and Kim sit side by side. Zane was uncomfortable with the situation, to say the least, but he was hungry—he hadn't eaten much that day in preparation for what was sure to be an abundance of food—so he was willing to let things ride.

Rex and Reenie began marching from the kitchen to the dining room, carrying bowls and platters filled with holiday food. Just as Zane thought they were finished, Reenie brought out a green bean casserole—a dish without which no festive meal in the Midwest was complete—and placed it on the table in front of him. The instant the rich aroma filled the air, he was taken back to that night.

He remembered easing open his bedroom window, trying not to wake anyone, and being startled by his brother's voice. "What are you doing?"

Zane looked across the room at Zach sitting upright on the top bunk. "I'm going to the crossing to look for Sunny."

"Ma already did yesterday, and she couldn't find him."

"Well, I'm looking again. Are you going with me or not?"

Zach hopped out of bed. "We'll need a flashlight. I'll get one from the kitchen drawer."

"Hurry, and don't wake Ma."

They climbed through the window, got their bikes from the garage, and walked them to the front of the house. They tried to be especially quiet when they passed their ma's bedroom because they knew the wrath that would descend upon them if they got caught. Sneaking out in the middle of the night was bad enough, but sneaking out when they were grounded—seriously grounded—would bring punishment they didn't even want to think about.

When they reached the crossing, they began searching for their lost puppy where they'd last seen him. After half an hour of no luck, Zach was ready to give up. "See, I told you he wasn't here. Let's go back home."

"But he has to be somewhere; he couldn't have disappeared."

"Ma said the pound may have picked him up. Maybe we can get her to take us there tomorrow to see." Zach said, putting the flashlight on the ground so he could zip up his jacket.

"What are you doing?" Zane asked. "I can't see."

"It's cold out here."

"Let's look one more place before we go home."

Zane led the way as they ventured closer to an area they'd been trying to avoid, the burnt ground in the ditch where the car had caught fire. A smoky, fetid odor lingering in the air made Zane's stomach churn.

"What's that, over there?" Zach asked, pointing to a small light-colored object on the ground a few feet ahead.

"Maybe it's Sunny curled up into a ball trying to stay warm."

The boys hurried to the object but realized it wasn't their puppy when they got a closer look.

"What is it?" Zach asked.

"Looks like a bowl of some sort."

"Well, see what it is."

"You see what it is."

"I'm holding the flashlight."

"Oh, all right." Zane picked up the bowl—white glass with a plastic lid, heavier than he thought it would be—and stood there a few seconds glaring at it in his hands. He wasn't sure why but he was afraid to open it.

Zach nudged him with the flashlight. "Don't just stand there; see what it is."

Zane slowly pulled back one end of the lid and peeked inside. "Looks like green beans." Then he recognized the unmistakable oniony smell. "I think it's a green bean casserole."

"Why would a green bean casserole be here?"

Zane replaced the lid. "I don't know." As he was putting the dish back on the ground where he found it, a car pulled up behind them, parked on the side of the road, and a man stepped out and started toward them.

"Who's there?" the man asked.

Shielding his eyes from the blinding headlights, Zane realized the man had gotten out of a police car. "It's Zane and Zach Isaac," he called out.

The officer squinted to see in the dark. "What are you boys doing out here so late at night?"

Zane opened his mouth to answer, but Zach's voice came out instead. "We lost our puppy, and we're here trying to find him."

"Your puppy?" the officer asked. "When did he run off?"

"Earlier tonight."

Zane looked at his brother, wondering why he'd lied.

The police officer studied the boys for a few minutes, then said, "I think I know what you're really doing here."

Zane's heart lurched; for a second, he thought about making a run for it.

The officer walked up and stood right in front of them. "You may have come here to look for your lost puppy but then remembered yesterday's car wreck, and curiosity got the best of you."

Zane was trembling so much that he couldn't even respond.

"We didn't mean any harm," Zach said.

"You boys have no business snooping around here. Get home and back into your beds before your ma wakes up and finds out you're gone."

"Sorry," the boys said, in unison, as they got on their bikes.

"I won't tell Corinne this time," the officer said as they rode off. "But don't let me catch the two of you nosing around here again."

Looking at the green bean casserole on Reenie's dining room table, Zane realized why he hated the dish so much. The casserole had turned two fatalities of a car wreck into two people who'd never made it to a Thanksgiving dinner.

Reenie noticed him staring. "Zane, do you want some of that casserole?"

"Oh...no thanks."

"That's right, I forgot. You don't like green beans."

During dinner, Reenie mentioned that Kim had been Driftwood River Queen twice as if that would seal the deal. There was nothing wrong with Kim. She was attractive, by anyone's definition, but in Zane's mind, few women could compete with Addison Quinn's natural, wholesome beauty.

When they'd finished eating, Rex suggested they

have their dessert in the living room, where it was more comfortable. Once they were there, Reenie excused herself to go make the coffee. "Rex, would you mind helping me in the kitchen?" she asked.

Rex looked at her curiously. "Since when does it take two people to operate the coffeemaker?"

She took Rex by the arm. "Since I said so."

Rex looked at Zane and shrugged apologetically as Reenie drug him with her to the kitchen.

After about five awkward minutes alone with Kim, Zane decided to address the obvious. "I'm sure you've figured out why we were invited here tonight."

"Sure, I have," she said. "But is that so bad?"

"No, it isn't. At least it wouldn't be under different circumstances."

"I'm not sure I understand what you mean."

"Kim, I'm going to be honest with you; I've recently become interested in someone."

"Oh? Anyone I know?"

"I don't want to say too much yet; we only recently started seeing each other."

"Well, at least tell me if she's from here."

"Actually, she's from Indianapolis."

"Well, whoever she is, she's one lucky girl."

"You know, I think *I* might be the lucky one."

"You care; I can see it in your eyes," said Kim. "Can I give you some friendly advice? If you find out she's the one, you need to hold on to her with everything you have. Don't make the same mistake I did."

Zane knew she was talking about her recent

divorce. "I'm sorry about you and Johnny."

"Hey, don't be. Besides, I may be getting a second chance. I didn't tell Reenie because I was afraid it might hurt her feelings—she went through so much trouble to set up this dinner—but Johnny and I are talking again."

"Kim, that's wonderful! If it's what you want."

"It is. Reconciliation is a strong possibility. Fingers crossed."

"I truly hope things work out."

Rex and Reenie finally made it back with the coffee and some fresh baklava. During dessert, Kim got a text that Zane guessed by the smile on her face was from Johnny. Shortly after, she thanked Rex and Reenie for a nice evening and told them something had come up and that she needed to go. Before she left, she warmly embraced Zane and whispered in his ear, "Good luck with that Indy girl."

As soon as Kim was out the door, Reenie beamed with pride. "That went well," she said.

"Yes, it did," Zane snapped back. "But not in the way you think."

"What was that hug and whisper all about then?"

Zane gave her a harsh look. "Reenie, you need to stop trying to fix me up."

Rex sighed and sat heavily in his recliner. "I told you he wouldn't like this. I saw the way he was looking at Addison at the cafe. I knew this was a bad idea from the get-go, but you wouldn't listen to me. Woman, I swear that head of yours is set with cement."

"Quit your ranting, you old fart, and let Zane talk for himself."

"Rex is right. You set me up with Kim even though you knew I was interested in Addison. Why would you do that?"

"Because I'm not so sure Addison Quinn is the right person for you."

"That's not for you to decide. But why would you think that?"

"I learned some things about her you probably should know before you become too involved."

"Whatever it is, I can tell you right now it's not going to make any difference in how I feel."

"Maybe not, but would you hear me out anyway?"

Zane took a seat on the couch, and Reenie sat beside him. "Okay, what have you got?" he asked.

"Remember I told you Addison's parents were killed in a car wreck?"

"So, something horrible happened to her; that doesn't make her a bad person."

"Let me finish. I also found out Addison was in the wreck, too...the only survivor. I was right; that's how she got the scars."

"Reenie, like I told you before, I don't give a damn about those scars."

"It's the scars on her inside that I'm worried about. I think you should be aware that Addison had some serious mental issues after the wreck. She even had to see a therapist."

"Who wouldn't after what she went through? Anyway, that was long ago. I'm sure she's fine now."

"I don't know; how she acted at the clinic the other day was awfully strange. What if she's still unstable?"

"If she is, it's my business; I'll deal with it." Then the thought occurred to Zane that the information Reenie was passing on might not even be true. "Where did you hear this?"

"Helen, the lady who does my hair, told me."

Zane laughed sarcastically. "Well, then it must be reliable."

"Apparently, it was a big deal around here," Reenie said. "One of the worst wrecks that ever happened in Driftwood."

"Driftwood? I thought you said the wreck took place in Indianapolis."

"I didn't say that. How could I have known? It was before we even moved to town. I *assumed* the wreck happened in Indianapolis because that's where Addison's from, but it happened in Driftwood, near the Snake Shadow Crossing, and on Thanksgiving, of all days. They were on their way to Kathleen's house for dinner."

Zane knew his face had lost all color; he'd felt it drain, but he tried to remain expressionless, so Reenie and Rex wouldn't know his mind had just exploded. "Reenie, I appreciate your concern but...."

"I don't want you to get hurt, that's all."

"I understand you mean well, but I'm a big boy. I can look after myself."

She got up and started gathering the dessert plates and coffee cups. "I sure hope you know what you're doing," she said as she disappeared into the kitchen.

Driving home, Zane's hands were shaking on the steering wheel, and his thoughts were racing. He had always known there'd been a survivor, a kid —his ma had told him that much—but he never thought he'd ever meet, let alone fall for her. When he asked his ma about the people in the wreck, she said there was no use telling him their names since they were from out of town, and he wouldn't have known them anyway. Then they moved to Braxton, and he got busy with school and sports, and after a while, it all became history.

Over the years, he'd thought about the survivor many times and wondered what her life was like. He could've easily done an Internet search and found out, but what good would it have done other than satisfy his morbid curiosity? Having witnessed the wreck was traumatizing enough. Did he really need to see their faces and learn their names? And there was a part of him that was afraid to know more. Afraid he might discover that the survivor, after years of being shuffled around from foster home to foster home, might have resorted to addiction or even committed suicide.

He now wished he'd done that Internet search. He wouldn't have been in such a predicament if he'd had the courage to find out. Or would he? He asked himself the hard question: *Would I still have pursued Addison if I'd known she was the survivor?*

*Absolutely.* He didn't even have to think about

it; he'd never been drawn to anyone like he was drawn to her. At first, the attraction had been mostly physical. Then he found her to be intriguing. After they got to know each other better, he discovered they were so much alike. They both hated crowds and bars and loved animals. They'd both suffered the pain from the loss of a parent. In his mind, this new development only strengthened their bond. Something else they had shared. But would Addison feel the same way if she knew?

Zane was not sure what to do with the revelation that had been thrust upon him. He wished he could return to the ignorance he'd enjoyed a few hours earlier. He went over his ma's checklist about secrets:

*Would anyone gain anything if the secret was out?*

No. Nothing would bring Addison's parents back.

*Would telling the secret do more harm than good?*

Maybe; dredging up the pain could possibly cast a dark shadow over their fledgling relationship.

Zane saw no good reason to tell Addison he had been on the Snake Shadow Crossing when the wreck happened. After all, his involvement was inconsequential; he'd simply been at the wrong place at the wrong time. It's not like the wreck was his fault.

## CHAPTER 14
# CORINNE

*1999*

I t was a severe knock on the door, rapid and firm. This was not a casual visit from a friend.

When Corinne looked through the peephole, the first thing she saw was the police uniform. Panic swiftly set in. Then she recognized the officer was Mack Sterling and felt a little better. Mack had always had a thing for her.

Corinne sometimes forgot she was anything other than a mother, but now she needed to resurrect the woman within her. She glanced into the mirror on the wall by the door. What happened yesterday had aged her ten years overnight on the inside, but the face looking back at her could still pull off youthful innocence. Her eyes were puffy from crying; however, it was early, so Mack would assume she hadn't been awake long. She straightened her bathrobe, removed the elastic band from her hair, and pulled her honey-colored waves forward, so they cascaded around her shoulders. She took a couple of deep breaths—in through the nose, out through the mouth—and opened the door.

"Hello, Mack," she said with her sweetest smile. "What brings you here so early?"

"Good morning, Corinne. Hope I didn't wake you."

"Oh, no, I've been up for a few minutes." She noted that Mack was looking her over.

"Did you have a good Thanksgiving?"

"Yes, we did. Just the three of us, but it was nice."

"I wasn't sure if you'd be home. It occurred to me, driving over, that you might've had to work today."

"The clinic is open, but Dr. Jacobs was kind enough to give me the day off so I could have a long weekend."

"Are the boys still in bed?"

"Yes, they're sleeping in; it must be all that turkey they ate."

"Sorry to bother you on your day off, but do you have a few minutes to talk? It's kind of important."

"Of course." She stepped aside so Mack could enter the house. He followed her into the living room, where they both sat. "Sounds serious. Is there something wrong?"

"Unfortunately, yes. There was a car wreck yesterday out on River Bend Road. It was a bad one; two people are dead."

"Oh, no!"

"There was one survivor, a young girl. It was her parents who were killed."

"That's awful! And that poor little girl. Who were they...do we know them?"

"No, I don't think so. They're from out of town, somewhere around Indianapolis."

"What a shame, and on Thanksgiving too."

"I stopped by to ask if your boys, by any chance, were riding their bikes around the Snake Shadow Crossing yesterday."

An image of Zach and Zane, clad in orange, surrounded by burly men with crude tattoos flashed through Corinne's head. Her precious babies bent over in the shower and gang raped by smelly thugs, forced to whittle shanks from toothbrushes to stay alive. They were only thirteen, but she knew their young age wouldn't be enough to save them. She'd heard stories on the news about juvenile offenders being tried as adults. The gavel would come crashing down, and their lives would be over just like that. She imagined them reaching for her as the guards take them away, pleading for help, but by then, it would be too late.

Corinne's stomach knotted, and her heartbeat pounded in her ears as Mack waited for her response. She was sure her boys were not responsible for the wreck that killed those two people, but would everyone else see things her way when the grieving family stood before the judge demanding justice? Of course, she felt terrible for the ones left behind, especially the girl, and she understood the human need to assign blame and seek retribution, but she had to protect her own. That's what a good mother does.

"No, they were with me all day," she said. "We

had our Thanksgiving dinner around one and then played Monopoly for the rest of the evening." She looked at the game board on the coffee table and was glad Zane had not done what she'd asked him to for once.

"I didn't think they would've been out riding bikes in the rain on Thanksgiving," Mack said.

"Why do you ask?"

"The lady who reported the accident said she thought she saw a couple of kids on the crossing. She didn't get a good look at them, but I know your boys like to ride down that way, and I thought if they were there, they might've seen what happened. We're talking with everyone in the area with kids."

"Sorry I couldn't be of more help."

"Oh, that's okay; it doesn't matter anyway." Mack stood up. "It's obvious the wreck was caused by the slick road, and my guess is the driver was traveling faster than the speed limit. That big curve off the highway into Driftwood is tricky if you're not from around here. Plus, you know how out-of-towners always look up trying to see the shadows."

"Shadows that aren't even there. It's a wonder there aren't more wrecks."

"There have been quite a few, mostly fender benders, though. This is the first one with fatalities we've had in a long while."

"They need to do something about that place before someone else gets killed."

"Like what?"

"I don't know...put a sign up telling people to stop

looking for the snakes because there are none."

Mack chuckled. "You'd never get the city council to agree to that. They claim the crossing brings in tourists."

"Well, we wouldn't want to lose a buck to save a life, would we?"

"Guess not." Mack started for the door. "Sorry to have taken up your time."

"Don't be. It's always good to see you."

"You too, Corinne, take care."

As soon as Mack had left, Corinne's knees buckled, and she had to steady herself against a wall to keep from collapsing. She watched from the front window as the police car pulled out of the drive and disappeared down the road.

Corinne had not planned on lying. She never planned on lying; the decision was always made in an instant. She was not a liar, in the true sense of the word. Her lies were always clean—necessary lies, she liked to call them—to protect the ones she loved. And she'd had no other choice, really. At least that's what she would tell herself days later when the guilt started creeping in.

After the lie, Corinne fleetingly thought of her mother. She almost, *almost* knew how her mother had felt when she'd asked Corinne to give the twins up for adoption. Despite her odds, she was determined to keep her babies, and still, even with the hellacious mess Zach and Zane had gotten her into, she had no regrets about her decision. She had thought her parents were being cruel and insensitive, but she now realized they were only trying to protect their children, the same thing she'd just done.

Corinne knew lying about something so important does not come without consequences. She braced for the stressful days to follow. Carefully choosing every word, listening intently, but not too intently, for any new developments. Yes, the road ahead was going to be rough for Corinne and her boys.

\*

One evening, a week or so later, Corinne and the twins were eating dinner when a knock came at the door. She tiptoed into the living room, peeked out the curtain, and saw a police car parked on the side of the road in front of the house. Her first impulse was to not answer the door. She hurried back to the kitchen, gathered her boys, and huddled behind the table, trying not to make a sound.

Holding Zach in one arm, Zane in the other, the strangest thing popped into her head: the tree limb. She'd first noticed it in late winter, dangling precariously from the fork of a much smaller branch of a tree in her back yard. She knew the loose limb was going to fall; it had girth and weight; the question was when. In the coming months, she kept telling herself she should probably tend to it, but that was a job for a man, and Corinne didn't have one of those or the money to pay for one.

Weeks passed, she got busy with life—the boys

were toddlers—and before she knew it, spring was upon her. When the trees were filled with leaves again, and she could no longer see the dangling limb, she forgot all about it. Then one Sunday morning, she was washing dishes and watching through the window as the boys played in the yard when suddenly the limb fell to the ground, and with a loud crunch, landed smack between Zach and Zane.

Someone calling her name snapped Corinne back to the present problem. "Corinne, are you home?"

She recognized the voice. "It's Mack," she whispered to the boys. She remembered her car parked out front. "He knows we're home."

Corinne didn't know what to do. *Should we run?* She began planning it all out in her mind: They would take enough food for a day or two, a change of clothes, some warm blankets, and go into the woods behind the house to hide for a while. When she felt it was safe, they'd sneak back home for the rest of their things, and then she and the boys would flee to another country.

"Corinne? Zane...Zach, are you in there?"

"What are we going to do?" Zach asked.

She told the boys to put on their coats, and sent them to the back yard. "Stay out until I come for you," she said.

Then she went and answered the door. "Mack... hello."

"I was beginning to get worried."

"Sorry, I didn't hear you knock. I was at the back

of the house." As soon as she'd said it, she realized how stupid she sounded. Her house was tiny. The boys could say something in their bedroom, and she could hear it from the kitchen. "I had the vacuum running," she quickly added. "What brings you here this evening?"

"Do you have a few minutes to talk?"

"Sure. Come inside."

"Where are the boys?"

"Out riding their bikes."

"Isn't it kind of cold for that?"

"They're bundled up. Why do you ask?"

"Because I wanted to talk to you alone."

"What about, has there been another wreck?"

"No, it's personal," he said. "I came here to ask if you would consider having dinner with me sometime."

Corinne was ashamed of the thought that slithered into her mind—but not enough to keep her from following through with what she felt she must do. She liked Mack, although not in the same way he liked her. Still, she would accept the invitation she knew would lead to another, to keep him close, stay in the loop in case there were any new developments in the Snake Shadow accident.

"Of course; I'd love to go out to dinner with you, Mack," she said.

After Mack had left, Corinne realized that she and her twins had managed to dodge another tree limb, but she was afraid if she didn't do something soon to ensure their safety, another one would fall dangerously close. Or, even worse, come crashing down upon them.

## CHAPTER 15

# ADDISON

I was glazing the ham, and Gama was making the ambrosia salad. She stopped in the middle of peeling an orange and put it on the counter. "If you don't call Zane, I will," she said.

"It's too late to invite him now. I'm sure he's made other plans."

She picked up the orange again, gave it a grudged stare, and then finished peeling it. "Well, you should've already invited him. The poor boy's probably spending Christmas alone."

It wasn't the first time that day Gama had pointed out that I should've asked Zane to have dinner with us. She'd started on me early that morning. As usual, she was right, but there was nothing I could do to correct the mistake. "Gama, we don't know he's alone. Maybe he went to North Carolina to visit his brother."

"North Carolina? That's a long way to travel, considering he probably has to be back at the clinic tomorrow to cover for Dr. Jacobs."

"He mentioned an uncle who lives in Braxton. He could be going there." *Or he could be all alone at his house with a TV dinner in front of him.* I put the ham in the oven and then picked up an orange from the large mound in front of Gama. "You're making way too much ambrosia."

"Not if you invite Zane to come."

"Gama, drop it. I'm not calling him."

We peeled in silence for a few minutes until my cell phone chimed to let me know I had a text message. I figured it was Lily offering to bring something, even though she knew we would tell her not to, but instead, it was a message from Zane: *Just wanted to wish you and your family a Merry Christmas.*

I texted him right back. *Merry Christmas to you, too! Hope you're enjoying the holiday with your family.*

*Not there yet, getting ready to leave for Uncle Brady's. He and his wife have three grown kids, and they all have kids of their own...I've lost track of how many...but there should be a houseful.*

"See," I said to Gama, holding the phone up for her to read the text. "I told you Zane's going to his uncle's house for dinner."

"Is that Zane?" Gama asked, in her company voice, as if he could hear her. She didn't fully understand the concept of text messaging. "Well, at least I know he's not spending the day by himself."

I messaged back: *Have fun! Gama said hi.*

As I was putting down the phone, I got another text: *Mind if I call in a few minutes? I have something I'd like to ask you.*

*Sure.*

I stepped into my bedroom, shut the door, and

waited for the phone to ring.

"Hope I'm not interrupting anything," Zane said when I picked up.

"No, not at all; I was just helping Gama in the kitchen. What did you want to ask me?"

"Addison, I know we agreed we were going to wait until after the holidays to see each other, but I was wondering if you don't already have plans, why don't we bump up our dinner date and bring in the new year together?"

A crowd of drunken people wearing silly hats and blowing party horns flashed through my head. "What did you have in mind?"

"No bars or parties, just dinner at my house like we talked about."

I imagined the three of us cozy in front of the fireplace. "Actually, that sounds good."

"You're sure you don't have anything else you'd rather do?"

"I'm positive. You'll be rescuing me from attending a church event with Gama or being the third wheel at a party with Lily and her boyfriend."

"And you'll bring Hero, of course."

"Of course."

"Is five o'clock okay?"

"Five is fantastic."

"I'll see you then."

When I got back to the kitchen, Gama eyed me curiously. "What are you all smiley about all of a sudden?"

"It's Christmas, Gama, a day to be cheerful."

The doorbell rang. Hardly anyone came to the front door, and no one ever rang the bell. Gama and I looked at each other, baffled.

"Who could that be?" she asked.

"Beats me." I glanced down at Hero, his head was cocked to one side, and he was looking in the direction of the living room, but he made no move to get up. "Some watchdog you are. Come on; let's go see who it is."

I opened the door to a gigantic basket wrapped in red cellophane and tied with a silver bow. "Merry Christmas!" said a husky voice from behind the basket. It sounded like Rex McCormick, which would've explained why Hero didn't bark.

"Rex? Is that you?" I asked.

"I know there's a strong resemblance," Rex said, craning his neck from behind the basket. "But it ain't Santa Clause."

Gama joined me at the door. "Hi, Rex, come on in out of the cold!"

"Thanks, Kathleen, but I'm not here for a visit. I've come to make a delivery."

"Since when did you start delivering?"

"I only deliver to special people, and in my book, you girls are as special as they come."

"But we didn't order anything." Gama looked at me. "Did we, Addy?"

"No, I don't think so."

Rex extended the basket. "This is for the two of you...and Hero."

"Who's it from?" I asked.

"Well, you'll have to read the card attached to find that out."

"You sure you don't want to come in for a while?" Gama asked. "I'd offer you coffee, but I know you get enough of that at work. What about a nice cup of hot tea?"

Rex chuckled. "Sounds tempting, but Reenie's expecting me home for dinner." He turned and headed for his van. "Have a merry Christmas, ladies!"

"Merry Christmas to you, Rex, and tell Reenie the same!" Gama said, and then closed the front door. "Wonder who sent this."

"I don't know; let's have a look." I sat the basket on the coffee table and read the card aloud: *Wishing the three of you the best Christmas ever! Love, Zane.*

"Zane sent this? How sweet of him!" Gama pulled back the cellophane and explored the contents of the basket. Inside were a dozen chocolate chip scones, half a dozen blueberry muffins, a mason jar of hot cocoa mix with mini marshmallows, and a box of gourmet peanut butter dog biscuits. "We have to call and thank him," she said.

"He's probably on the road by now, headed to his uncle's house. I hate to bother him while he's driving."

"At least send him one of those phone messages."

"I will," I said as we returned to the kitchen.

As we passed the back door, Lily popped in, followed by Andre, carrying a shopping bag loaded with presents.

Christmas had now arrived.

The day would not have been complete without Lily. She was the closest thing to a sister I'd ever had. Those first few years after the wreck, she'd brought light into the darkness that engulfed Gama and me around the holidays. She came by, either Christmas Eve or Christmas morning, prattling about all the people who'd been to see her mom for a psychic reading. She could never afford to buy presents for us, so she made them, turning thrift shop sheets into potholders and dish towels for Gama, hats and house slippers for me, and Hero got a snappy new bandana to wear for the holidays. The gifts I'd given Lily through the years never quite measured up to the thought and effort she put into mine. But this year was going to be different.

Having heard Lily's voice, Hero hurried into the kitchen to greet her, but as soon as he spotted Andre, he stopped in his tracks and launched into frantic barking. After a few minutes, I managed to calm him, but he insisted on sitting between Andre and me on the floor.

"Come in, come in," Gama said and put down the gift basket to free her arms to hug Lily.

"Gama, this is Andre," Lily said.

Gama embraced him like he was one of her own. "Welcome to our home."

"Thanks for having me," said Andre.

Lily raised a bottle of Cabernet she had in her hand. "I brought the Christmas cheer."

Gama took the wine and put it on the counter

beside Zane's gift basket. "That's my girl." She turned to Andre. "Follow me, and I'll show you where to put those presents."

"Where's Zane?" Lily asked.

"Sometimes, I think you and Gama call each other to plot against me."

"Well, where is he? Is he coming later?"

"No, he isn't coming later. He's spending Christmas with his family."

"What family?"

"His uncle in Braxton."

"Did you ask him to come?"

"That's what *I* said," Gama called out from the living room.

"See what I mean...always two against one."

"So, you didn't invite him."

"I already feel bad enough without your help." I pointed to the gift basket on the kitchen counter. "Especially since he sent that."

"Zane sent all this?" Lily asked, walking over to look at the basket. "You should feel bad."

"That's enough." I picked up my phone from the counter and started toward my room, punching Lily on the arm as I passed her.

"Ouch!" she said. "Where are you going?"

"To send Zane a text to thank him."

"All he gets is a text message?"

"That, and to spend New Year's Eve with me."

"Really?" She threw her arms around me. "Finally, there's going to be a real date...and a kiss."

"How do you know that?"

"On New Year's Eve? Oh, there'll be a kiss, all right." She opened one of the kitchen drawers and began rummaging.

"What're you looking for?"

"The wine opener. We need to celebrate."

Gama came back into the kitchen. "What are we celebrating?"

"Zane and Addy's first kiss."

"Lily, stop it!" I said, then retreated to my bedroom and shut the door to write my text in private.

*Thank you for the gift basket you sent. What a surprise! I'm looking forward to New Year's Eve.* I stared at the phone for a few seconds, thinking about what I'd written, and then decided to delete the last line. Too anxious.

\*

After dinner, we all went into the living room and sat around the Christmas tree to open presents. Hero was still uncomfortable having a strange man in the house and continued to eye Andre with suspicion, growling intermittently. Hero's aggressive reaction was inconvenient and embarrassing, but how could I blame him for his confusion? He knew that even a seemingly kind man could turn nasty. After all, Cole had been a friend before he was an enemy.

"Dogs usually like me," Andre said. "I'm not a mean guy."

"It's not you," I assured him. "Hero's like this with all men when he first meets them."

"Except for Zane," Lily said.

The way Hero had immediately taken to Zane was a mystery that continued to baffle me. Hero clearly knew something I didn't.

Gama began passing out the packages. Everyone had something to open, even Andre. When she found out he was coming, she wrapped a box of homemade Christmas cookies so he wouldn't feel left out. Once all the presents were distributed, I kept an eye on Lily because I didn't want to miss seeing her face when she saw what I'd gotten her.

As soon as Hero's present from Lily was in front of him—she always put it in a bag so he could open it himself—he began pulling out the tissue paper, then his new bandana to get to the treat he knew was waiting for him at the bottom.

Lily first opened her present from Gama, a fabric store gift certificate. "I figured it was something you could use," Gama said. "You'll understand when you see what Addy got you."

"Gama, hush!" I said. "You'll spoil the surprise!"

"Oops," Gama said. "Well, hurry and open it, Lily."

I could barely contain my excitement as Lily tore away the wrapping paper, took the lid off the tiny box, and examined the contents. "A key?" She looked at me, bemused. "Did you buy me a car?"

"No, it's something even better. A note in the bottom of the box under the cotton will explain everything."

"Read it to us," Andre said as Lily unfolded the note.

"This is the key to your dream," she read. "It's official. Kaleidoscope is now a reality! Love and Christmas wishes, Your BFA." She turned to me. "Addy, what have you done?"

"It's the key to the house on Collins Street."

"You bought it?"

"Sorry, I don't love you that much. But I did pay the first six month's rent. That should be enough time for us to get things up and running."

Tears started rolling down Lily's cheeks. "I don't know what to say...I feel bad...about my gift to you."

"What are you talking about?" I held up the skirt she'd made me. "It's lovely!"

"Addy, really, this is too much."

"No, it isn't. It's not nearly enough; your friendship is worth so much more. Besides, we're partners, remember? I would've paid half the rent anyway."

She sprung from her seat, letting everything in her lap—wrapping paper, Gama's gift—slide to the floor, and then stepped over it to give me a big tear-soaked hug. "Thank you so much!"

"Don't get too excited; there's a lot of work to do. The windows need to be cleaned, and every room could use a fresh coat of paint. We've got to find racks to hang your clothes on."

"And some way to display your stained glass."

Gama turned to Andre. "Something tells me we're not going to see much of our girls in the coming months."

## CHAPTER 16
# ZANE

Zane hadn't thought about the kiss. When he asked Addison to spend New Year's Eve with him, he never even considered the possibility of intimacy. He was willing to settle for being in the same room with her and would consider himself lucky if she'd graced him with a rare smile by the end of the night. Just hearing her laugh would be better than sex. Better than sex with anyone else but her.

He had the rest of the evening down to a science: he'd stopped by the bakery to pick up a cheesecake for dessert, rented some movies to watch after dinner, and bought a bottle of champagne to toast in the New Year. But the kiss had slipped his mind completely. How could he, a man who made a habit of planning everything, have forgotten something so important?

Now that Addison was seated at the island in his kitchen, effortlessly sexy in a simple white t-shirt, black leather jacket, and a pair of faded jeans, her lips aglow with pink gloss, the kiss was all he could think about. There was going to be a kiss, he knew that. It was New Year's Eve. What else was he going to do at midnight, shake her hand? But what kind of kiss, and how would he execute it? He glanced at the clock. He had only four and a half hours to figure it out. Right now, he needed to think about dinner.

"You said something about chopping vegetables?" she asked, flipping her hair back from her shoulders.

"Yes, the salad." He opened the refrigerator, pulled out a head of romaine lettuce, two tomatoes, and a cucumber, and put them on the countertop in front of her. "If you see anything you don't like, speak up now," he said, scrabbling through the vegetable crisper.

"If there's a carrot somewhere in there, you can leave it."

"Okay. What about green onions?"

"Green onions are good."

He tossed a bunch on the counter with the rest of the vegetables. "Bell pepper?"

"Bell pepper, I can take or leave."

"Tonight, you'll take," he said. "They're good for you."

"When you said you like a big salad, you weren't kidding."

He grabbed a butcher block cutting board propped up against the backsplash and put it on the counter, then slid a knife from a cutlery stand and offered it to her. "Ready to start chopping?"

"Guess I'd better be," she said, eyeing the pile of vegetables before her. "That is if we want to eat sometime this year."

Addison went to the sink and turned on the water to wash her hands. Zane pushed up the sleeves of his sweater and joined her. While lathering their hands with soap, their arms touched, and she looked up at him and smiled. *There it is,* he thought, and it took everything he had not to lean down and press his lips to hers. *Is that what she wants me to do?*

He'd never had so much trouble reading a woman before. He would've recognized the signals if it had been any other woman. He knew them all: the hair twisting, biting the bottom lip, the soft touch of his forearm during a conversation. When he grabbed a paper towel to dry his hands, she reached back for the lettuce so she could wash it and brushed up against him again. Usually, "accidental" touching was a surefire sign that a woman was interested in intimacy, but he wasn't sure about her. She was unlike anyone he had ever known.

"So, what are you going to do while I'm making the salad?" she asked.

"Prepare the main course."

"What, boil some pasta and pour a jar of sauce over it?"

"Hey, there's an art to cooking pasta, not too chewy, but not too mushy. Plus, I always add my own seasoning to the sauce."

Addison looked up from her chopping. "I noticed you haven't put the For Sale sign out front yet."

"Yeah, I decided to hold off on that for now." Zane took note of Addison's grin.

"What made you change your mind?"

"A couple of things." His face suddenly felt hot when he grinned back at her. He couldn't even remember when he'd last blushed. But then again, he wasn't usually the kind of guy who'd ask a woman's best friend for dating advice either. Addison Quinn was taking him into unchartered territory. Whenever he was near her, he felt as if any second, the ground could shift under his feet. He scrambled for a new subject. "Speaking of that, mind if I get your opinion on something?"

"Sure."

"Since I might be living here for a while, there are some things I'd like to change, starting with the paint color in this kitchen."

"What, you're not a fan of seventies harvest gold?"

"It could stand some toning down. I was thinking about painting it a cream color. What do you think?"

"Umm, cream's kind of...blah. I believe your mom had the right idea with the gold. The morning sun through that window probably makes this room glow, but the shade's outdated. What about something in the middle like a pale, buttery yellow?"

"Isn't that the same thing as cream?"

"Kind of, but maybe a shade deeper."

"Sounds good," he said. "How are you with a paintbrush?"

"Messy."

"Messy help is better than no help."

"Why not? What's one more room to paint when I already have five?"

"Where?"

"Remember I told you about the business Lily and I were thinking about starting?"

"Sure, I do...Kaleidoscope, coolest name ever."

"Well, we've rented the building. Actually, it's a house that's already been zoned for a business."

"That's exciting news! Where's it located?"

"Collins Street."

"There are some cool houses on that street. Which one is it?"

"It's beside the antique shop."

"The one with the stone around the front door?"

"Yep."

"That's a prime location for a business."

"Yeah, we were lucky to get it, but the inside needs work. Chipped plaster, beat-up hardwood floors, and the rooms need to be painted."

"I'll make you a deal. I'll help you with Kaleidoscope if you help me paint this kitchen."

"Sounds like a fair trade. Five rooms, including the ceilings, for one tiny kitchen."

"That's what you think. Painting empty rooms will be much easier than all the trim work that has to be done in here."

*

At dinner, Zane was impressed by Addison's hearty appetite. She got a bit of spaghetti sauce on her white t-shirt, and instead of freaking out like most women would've done, she dabbed at it with a napkin, then laughed it off. They cleaned up the dishes with the comfort of an old married couple —he washed, she dried—then took their glasses of wine in front of the fire. So far, the evening had been ideal, but they hadn't gotten to the kiss yet.

Addison looked around the living room. "Where's Hero?" She'd been so busy helping Zane with the dishes she had forgotten all about Hero; now, he was nowhere in sight.

A jolt of panic shot through Zane when it occurred to him that Hero might've followed him when he went out for firewood. "I'll check out back," he said. "You look in the bathroom."

Hero was in neither of the places they looked, so they started to search the rest of the house together. When they were halfway down the hall, Zane heard a sound coming from the bedroom that he and Zach had shared when they were kids. He turned to Addison, who was following behind him. "Did you hear that?" he asked.

"What?"

"It sounded like snoring."

"I don't hear anything."

Zane grinned. "We must've woken him." He switched on the hall light, and it shone on Hero sitting sleep-dazed in the bottom bunk where Zane had once slept.

It had been a while since Zane had been in his old bedroom. Since his ma's death, he slept in the living room on a feather mattress he kept rolled up and stashed in the linen closet. He couldn't bring himself to sleep in his Ma's bed, and the feather mattress was much more comfortable than the cramped bunk, which was the only other alternative.

Entering his childhood bedroom was like stepping back in time. His ma had brought everything he and Zach had left in Braxton—soccer trophies, lava lamps, rock band posters—and restored their old room to how it had been before they moved away from Driftwood. He wondered why she hadn't thrown out all their junk and put the space to better use. Then it occurred to him it was probably the same reason he had yet to discard her things.

Addison went up to Hero and ruffled the fur on his head. "Well, look at you, making yourself right at home."

"Wonder how he got up there without help," Zane asked.

"The bunk is pretty low to the ground, and I've learned Hero somehow finds a way to do the things he wants to do," she said. "He seems to like this room; I hope you don't mind."

"Oh, no, it's fine."

Hero stood, circled twice, and then curled up on the bed again. "He acts like he's ready to go back to sleep."

"Hey, I rented a couple of movies," Zane said. "You want to watch them while we finish that bottle of wine?"

"Yes, I'd love to."

They were almost to the living room when he felt Addison's hand touch his shoulder from behind.

When he turned to face her, she planted a kiss full on his lips. It wasn't an invitation to have sex, but it was soft and lingering, and he was aroused by the spontaneity, and from being so close to her.

"I thought we should go ahead and get that out of the way," she said. "So the first one wouldn't feel like an obligatory New Year's kiss."

*The first one.* Zane liked the sound of that.

\*

Zane woke to movie credits rolling on the TV and Addison sleeping on the couch beside him. He didn't want to take her home but knew her grandmother was probably worried. "Addison," he said, bending over her. "Do you think you should call Gama to let her know you're okay?"

Addison's eyelids fluttered open. "What time is it?"

"It's almost one."

She sat upright on the couch. "I'm sorry I missed midnight."

"That's okay…I fell asleep too." He smiled. "We're a couple of party animals, aren't we?"

"What about the champagne you bought?"

"It'll save for another evening."

She picked up her phone from the coffee table and sprang to her feet. "I need to get home."

"But it's late, cold too. And after all that wine, I probably shouldn't be driving. Why don't you sleep on the couch for a while longer? I'll take you home at daybreak."

"I can't; Gama would be worried sick."

"Call her and explain the situation; she'll understand."

"I *am* tired." She sank back into the plush couch. "And this thing's like a magnet."

He chuckled. "It's the down-filled cushions. I'll get a quilt and pillow while you make the call."

Zane took Hero out, and then picked up an all-night log from the porch on his way back inside. By the time he'd returned to the living room, Addison had fallen asleep again. He took her phone from her hand and checked her log to make sure she'd called Gama. As he was covering her with the quilt, Hero passed in front of the couch and did a quick sniff-check to make sure she was okay before he headed back to the bunk bed.

Zane sat in the club chair, propped his feet on the ottoman, and listened to Addison's gentle breathing. With her hair away from her face, her scars from the wreck were fully visible in the shimmering firelight. Now that he knew she was the Snake Shadow survivor, he did not want her any less. In fact, if anything, it made him want her more. He wondered if his reaction was normal or some twisted, subconscious form of vindication. And there was something else to consider. If he thought passing under the crossing every day was a constant reminder of the wreck, what about those scars?

He shook all the unsettling thoughts from his head because, at this point, none of them mattered anyway. Whatever the reason, he'd already fallen for

Addison. That unexpected kiss in the hallway had pushed him over the edge.

## CHAPTER 17
# ADDISON

It was Saturday morning, and Lily and I were at the house on Collins Street—which we now felt confident enough to call *the shop*—staining the wood floors. We were side by side, butts in the air, working our way back toward the front door.

"How are things going with you and Zane?" Lily asked. "You haven't said much about him lately."

"Fine...I guess."

"Uh-oh, you guess? That doesn't sound good. Let's hear it; what's going on?"

"It's nothing, really."

"Okay, if you say so. But when you're ready to talk, I'm always here."

What she said took me back to the day Lily and I came to be. We were on break at school, sitting in our usual spot away from everyone else. Lily was rambling about a rash on her arm, and I, still in my silent phase, was listening when I noticed a couple of the popular girls coming toward us. I knew something was up because none of the popular kids ever came toward us. I nudged Lily to let her know.

The bookend girls, with wavy blonde hair and

sparkly lip gloss, stopped in front of us. "Hey Lily, your grandmother called," the one named Tiffany said. "She wants her quilt back." The two girls looked at each other and laughed.

Lily stood up and twirled and fanned her skirt, matador style. "How did you know this was my grandmother's quilt?" She giggled. "Well, it *was* her quilt until it became my skirt." Then she curtseyed, proudly holding her quilt skirt out for display. "Don't you just love it?"

Tiffany smirked. "It's hideous. Get a clue, Bag Lady, and stop wearing quilts and curtains to school."

Without thinking, I popped up and stood beside Lily. "Her skirt is beautiful," I blurted. Startled by the sound of my own voice—I hadn't said a word to anyone in almost three months—I clamped my hand over my mouth.

Lily started jumping up and down, clapping her hands. "I knew it! I knew you could talk if you wanted to!"

"Oh my God!" Tiffany shrieked, pointing at me. "Crazy Addy said something! Hey everyone, Crazy Addy can talk!"

A small group of kids began to gather around us. My secret was out; there was no retracting it, so I decided I may as well let loose. "Yeah, I can talk, and I've got plenty to say too." I stood defiantly close to Tiffany. "For starters, don't you ever talk to my best friend like that again!"

"And what will you do about it, Crazy Addy,

attack me?" She looked around at the other kids watching. "Hey, can somebody go get a straitjacket?"

"Crazy?" I stomped the floor in front of me. "You bet I am!" I lunged at her, and then, for added effect, growled.

Both girls jumped at once and started backing off.

Lily locked her arm in mine and pulled me away. "Come on, Addy. The idiots are beginning to multiply."

As we walked off, I called out to Tiffany, "Oh, and one more thing, you might want to brush your teeth once in a while. Your breath smells like butt."

From then on, it was Crazy Addy and Bag Lady Lily against the world.

Once Lily and I had finished staining the shop floors, we got our coats from the foyer and went out onto the front porch.

"It's what's *not* going on between Zane and me that I'm worried about," I said, sitting on one of the steps.

Lily sat beside me. "What do you mean?"

"Over the past few weeks, we've been together a lot. After we walk Hero, we go back to his place, he starts a fire, we watch TV, and then he drives me home."

"What's wrong with that? Sounds like a perfect date for you."

"It's not that I mind staying in, but don't you think something is missing from our evenings together."

Lily pondered a minute. "Oh...*that*."

"It's like we're buddies or brother and sister."

"No making out at all?"

"Nothing, except maybe a quick peck at the end of the night."

"You kissed on New Year's Eve, didn't you?"

"Yes, but I had to initiate it."

"Was he into it?"

"He seemed to be; that's what's so confusing."

"Well, you've always said you don't like guys to pressure you into having sex too soon."

"I don't, but I'd at least like the opportunity to turn him down."

"That's just mean."

"I'm kidding. But I am beginning to get a complex."

Lily snickered. "Makes you want to sleep with him even more, doesn't it?"

"I'm about to go nuts. Maybe Zane's not attracted to me in that way."

"Now you're being stupid."

"You think it's the scars?"

I had not completely lost touch with the little girl who'd once combed her hair over the scarred side of her face, one icy eye peering through the dark strands. Sometimes I could still hear the whispers swirling around me, see the kids openly gawk, then look away when I catch them, like they'd done something wrong. Like their parents had told them to never stare at the poor, disfigured Quinn girl.

"Hell. No." Lily took my chin into her hand. "You think your scars are much worse than they are.

Trust me, girl, Zane wants to have sex with you."

"Well, then what's holding him back?"

Lily looked down at her feet and started scraping a bit of stain from her sneakers with her fingernail. "It could be my fault."

"Your fault?"

"Yeah, I might have mentioned to him that he probably shouldn't rush things with you."

I shoved her so hard that she almost fell off the step. "Lily! Why would you do that?"

"Um, I don't know…maybe because you don't like to be rushed?"

"Yeah, but you've told guys that before and it didn't stop them."

"Has it ever occurred to you that Zane may want more from you than sex?"

"Okay, since you're playing couples counselor, what should I do to let him know I'm ready?"

"I guess you need to find a way to give him the green light."

"I've been flashing green lights since New Year's Eve."

"Then you might need to take a more direct approach."

"You mean make the first move."

"I can guarantee you won't be rejected."

I stood and zipped up my coat. "So, we're finished here for the day, right?"

"I suppose. There's really nothing more we can do until the floor dries," Lily said. "Hey, you're not mad at me, are you?"

"How could I be? I know you're only trying to help."

"You want to get some lunch then?"

"I would, but Hero's at Zane's."

"I'm sure Zane wouldn't mind watching him another hour."

"He probably wouldn't, but I promised him we'd paint his kitchen this afternoon."

"Do you guys need help? I've got nothing to do for the rest of the day."

"Thanks, but I think this is a job for just the two of us."

Lily grinned. "You're not going to get much painting done, are you?"

"I don't plan on it."

*

When I got to Zane's house, I let myself in, and Hero met me at the door.

"In here," Zane called out from the kitchen. When I walked into the room, he was masking around the window frame. The walls were bare, there was blue tape around the baseboards, and the cabinets were covered with plastic.

"Wow. You've been busy."

He turned away from his work. "Hey there!"

I held up the bucket of paint I had in my hand. "I stopped at the hardware store on the way."

"What color did you decide on?"

"It's called Churned Butter."

"Sounds like cream to me."

"No, it's more yellow than plain cream. You said you already had rollers and trim brushes?"

"Yep, over by the back door." He tore off a length of tape and smoothed it out under the bottom of the window. "We should be good to go whenever you're ready."

"There's one more thing we need to do before we start." I put the paint on the floor beside me, walked over to him, took the roll of masking tape he was holding, and put it on the counter. Then I slid my hands behind his neck, thrust my body into his, and kissed him in a way that there would be no mistaking my intention.

As we kissed, he pulled me in with enough force to let me know how much he wanted me, then slowly slipped his fingers under my top and up my back. When he raised his arms to take off his t-shirt, I saw his tattoo and remembered the red warning it had triggered. Sensing the hesitancy in my body, he stopped, brushed a strand of hair away from my face, and looked into my eyes as if to give me one last chance to back out.

I'm not sure what possessed me to do what I did next. It was something I'd seen in a movie once: a girl swept away by passion jumped into a guy's arms and wrapped her legs around him. And the guy, holding her with one arm, cleared a space on the counter, or desk, or whatever, with one swoop, and then they had unbridled, slightly rough sex.

It all looked so effortless in the movie, but when Zane and I were in a tangled heap on the floor, laughing so hard we could barely breathe, I realized those actors must have rehearsed that scene a hundred times before they got it right.

"Are you okay," he asked.

"My pride's a little beat up, but other than that, I'm fine. What about you?"

"I wrenched my knee when I went down, but no worries, I have a spare."

"I probably shouldn't have had that second donut this morning."

"Or I need to hit the gym more."

We started laughing again, and Hero came over and licked our faces, concerned we were hurt. When he realized we were all right, he began circling us, trying to figure out the game we were playing so he could join in.

"Hey Buddy," Zane said, "I think I can handle it from here." But Hero wasn't going anywhere; what we were doing looked like too much fun. Zane got up, scooped me off the floor as if I were weightless, and carried me to the couch.

*

Later, when I was putting my panties back on, Zane snatched them from me and threw them across the room. "What do you think you're doing?" he asked.

"I'm getting dressed so we can start painting the kitchen."

He grabbed my wrist and pulled me back onto the couch. "I don't care if that room ever gets painted now."

Hours later, after round three, I got up again. "Seriously, Hero needs to go out. And I'm starving."

"Hey, you're the one who opened the door, so don't expect it to slam shut again anytime soon." He smiled. "But I guess I do have to let you refuel."

We ordered a large pizza and inhaled the entire thing. As Zane was starting a fire, I noticed a couple of shoe boxes and a stack of photo albums in one of the chairs. "Are those family photos I see?"

"Yeah, they were in Ma's room. I got the albums to organize the photos; I just haven't gotten around to doing it yet. I'm trying to clear her room out so I can start sleeping in there. I bought a new pillowtop mattress from the furniture store the other day, and they're delivering it next week."

"If you'd like, I can help."

"Would you? I sure could use a hand."

"I'll tell you what. I don't think I have the energy left for painting, but I can sit in front of the fire and go through boxes."

Zane picked up the boxes and albums from the chair. "You sure you don't mind?"

"Of course not; it'll be fun. I'd love to see some baby pictures of you."

He took the top box and gave me the other one. "There's really no way to organize photos, but we can at least get them in these albums so they'll be easier to see."

"Okay, I'll get started," I said, lifting the lid.

There were very few pictures of anyone other than Zane and his twin brother. Obviously, his mother had adored them and built her life around theirs.

"Do you think there could be a picture of your dad in here somewhere?"

"No, I don't. Ma spent only one summer with him. When it comes to my dad, I've got to think like he died before I was born."

"I guess that's one way to look at it."

"It's the only way I *can* look at it."

About a quarter of the way through the box, I ran across some things besides pictures. "Hey, Zane, I found a few Mother's Day cards and other personal items. What should I do with them?"

"Set them aside, and I'll go through them later."

"Okay." I tossed a few cards on the couch to start a pile. Then I found a folded newspaper clipping that I thought I should look at to see if it was something important. When I unfolded the clipping, I immediately recognized the photograph above the article: "That's Hero!"

"What are you talking about?" Zane asked.

I read the headline: "Heroic Puppy Helps Save Injured Girl." Then I looked up at Zane. "It's an article about Hero that was in the paper after the wreck."

"Let me see it." Zane studied the clipping seemingly as perplexed as I was.

"Why would your mother have kept it?"

"I'm not sure, but I know she had a habit of saving everything."

"But why would she have gone through the trouble of cutting out a story about a dog she didn't know, and why would it be in a box with family photos?"

"All I can think of is that the story touched her heart. She loved animals. She worked for Dr. Jacobs at the clinic, you know."

"Gama told me she used to have Reenie's job."

"This is dated November 24, 1999. We didn't move to Braxton until January. She might have even been there when you first brought Hero in."

"Yeah, Gama said that too."

"So, that's what Lily meant that day at the clinic when she said Hero had found you."

"He was there when I was thrown from the car. We think somebody must have dumped him."

As if he'd been cued to do so, Hero came out of Zane's old room and stood before me. I mindlessly stroked his back, staring at nothing.

"Are you all right," Zane asked.

"Seeing that article kind of freaked me out."

"You'd had to have known Ma to understand." He refolded the newspaper and placed it up on the fireplace mantel. "I think I'd like to keep it since it's about our boy."

As I finished filling the album, I couldn't stop thinking about Zane's mother and the newspaper clipping. Clearly, everything else in her belongings revolved around her sons. That box was filled with nothing but photos of them and Mother's Day cards they'd given her. Why would she have bothered to save a newspaper article about a dog she may or may not have seen once? Animal lover or not, that seemed strange to me.

## CHAPTER 18
# CORINNE

*1999*

C orinne recognized Sunny right away. His distinguishing feature was unmistakable: one ear was pricked, and the other was floppy.

She had discovered he was missing two weeks earlier, on Thanksgiving. With all that had happened that day, she didn't even realize he was gone until that evening when she put a plate of turkey scraps on the kitchen floor, and he didn't come running when she called out for him. After she'd searched the house, she went back into the kitchen and stood before the twins, who suddenly seemed a little too interested in their turkey melt sandwiches. "Where's Sunny?" she asked.

When Zane lowered his head in shame, she knew something was wrong. "He followed us to the crossing today."

"You're kidding me. You left him there?"

"We had to, Ma," Zach said. "He ran off."

An image of Sunny wandering the streets, hungry and cold, popped into Corinne's head. "He's probably scared to death. What if he gets hit by a car?"

Zach and Zane offered to go back to the crossing to look for the puppy, but Corinne thought the idea was risky. She'd heard somewhere that the guilty always return to a crime scene. Her boys were not guilty, but she feared the police might think they were.

As the night went on, she couldn't shake the thought of Sunny out in the dark alone, so she decided to go to the Snake Shadow Crossing to look for him herself. For two hours, she searched the crossing and surrounding area and combed the path between there and the house but found no trace of Sunny. Finally, shivering and tired, her spirit crushed, she gave up and went home. Later, in bed, feeling broken and helpless, she wept into her pillow so the boys wouldn't hear. *What else is going to happen?*

When Corinne spotted the lost puppy waddling around in the vet clinic waiting room, her first thought was of her boys and how elated they'd be to know she'd found him. She would take Sunny home with her that afternoon, and it would be the one positive thing to come out of the whole Snake Shadow mess. From sheer excitement, Corinne almost blurted out his name but caught herself when a young girl swooped him up from the floor. Something in the way the girl held onto Sunny, both arms wrapped almost desperately around his neck, made Corinne take pause and consider her actions.

Then a woman approached the counter. "Hello, may I help you?" Corinne asked.

"Yes, my name is Kathleen Baker, and our puppy, Hero has an appointment at one."

"Of course. This is Hero's first time here, right?"

"It is. We brought him in to get the necessary vaccination shots and a general checkup."

"Absolutely," Corinne said, jotting down the information for Dr. Jacobs. "And how old is Hero?"

"I'm not really sure," Kathleen said. "You see, we found him on the side of the road a few weeks ago. But I'd say around two months if I had to guess."

It didn't take Corinne long to put the rest together: the bandages on the girl's face, the profound despondency in her eyes. She was the lone survivor of the Snake Shadow car accident, and Kathleen Baker was her grandmother. She glanced over at the girl, who was still clinging to Sunny. "How kind of you to take in a stray puppy," she said.

"We ran an ad in the newspaper to see if he belonged to anyone first," said Kathleen.

Corinne had been avoiding the paper because she didn't want to read about the details of the wreck. "Looks to me like Hero's where he belongs," she said. "Ms. Baker, if you'll have a seat, I'll let you know when the doctor's ready to see him."

Corinne had known a new patient was coming into the clinic that day, a puppy named Hero that needed vaccinations; she'd created the file herself. But how could she have possibly made the connection? If she had known, she would've taken the day off, feigning illness, just to avoid her current situation.

She thought about going home—she certainly felt sick—but Dr. Jacobs had a full schedule of patients and needed her help. She hunched down at her desk and tried to keep her face hidden behind the computer, afraid that if Sunny saw her, he'd come running up, wagging his tail, and the new owners would wonder why he was so excited about a receptionist at a vet clinic.

An agonizing ten minutes later, Dr. Jacobs called the front desk and told Corinne he was ready to see his one o'clock patient. As she opened the door to the waiting room, she was trembling inside; there was no way to avoid what would happen next. "The doctor will see Hero now," she announced.

As Sunny passed by her, he made direct eye contact. Corinne loved that puppy as much as her boys did, and it took everything she had to keep from snatching him from the girl's arms and running. Sunny wagged his tail briefly to let Corinne know he recognized her but made no other move. At that moment, she realized the secret was not hers alone; it belonged to Sunny too. As much as he loved Zach and Zane, he somehow knew the Snake Shadow survivor needed him more. Corinne gleaned a tiny bit of comfort from knowing that at least the survivor had a loving grandmother and now Sunny to look after her.

She decided she would not tell the twins about the survivor or that she'd seen Sunny; it would only upset them, and they were struggling enough as it was. First, the incident at Snake Shadow, then learning the father they never knew was dead. Corinne had always believed that some things were best left untold. Still, lately, her necessary secrets were mounting inside her, and sometimes she felt like she might collapse from their weight.

Now that she had come face to face with the survivor, an even more pressing problem had emerged: she realized Driftwood was too small of a town for her secrets. Thankfully, there was a solution. Brady had been after her to move to Braxton and work at his real estate company. He said she could start in the office and maybe later look into getting her realtor's license. Not only would she make more money, but she'd also broaden her horizon. She enjoyed working for Dr. Jacobs, but it was the only job she'd ever had. This development was just what she needed to give her a push to try something different.

She told herself that, but her heart was saying something entirely different. She didn't want to leave Driftwood. But what else could she do? If it had only been a couple of weeks since the wreck and she'd already run into the survivor, she knew the boys eventually would too. Corinne had almost broken down looking at that poor girl, orphaned and injured, and wasn't sure how Zach and Zane would react if confronted with a similar situation. She could not afford to take the chance to find out.

She would call Brady later that night, accept the

position in his real estate office, and start planning to move to Braxton. Moving would be easy; making Zach and Zane understand why they had to move would be the hard part. Their roots had grown deep in their thirteen years living in Driftwood. Ripping them away from their friends and a town they adored would toss salt into their fresh wounds. But they had agreed to hide what happened at the Snake Shadow Crossing, and there was no turning back now.

Corinne thought of the sadness in Zane's eyes when he realized they'd lost Sunny, and how he'd pleaded with her to let him get another puppy. Because he and Zach had acted irresponsibly when they let Sunny follow them to the crossing, she had refused, but was now having a change of heart. She couldn't undo the Snake Shadow incident or bring back their father. She couldn't get Sunny back either, but she could try to replace him. She decided she would call the boys and give them the good news. Maybe new puppies would make the dreadful news to follow more palatable.

## CHAPTER 19
# ZANE

A ddison was sitting across from Zane at their favorite restaurant, a pitcher of beer and an appetizer tray of hot wings on the table between them. She was up to her elbows in buffalo sauce, a crumpled pile of sticky napkins beside her plate. He loved how she dug into the hot wings with gusto, the way she approached everything in her life, all in, unconcerned about what the people around her thought; this, and so much more, made Addison irresistible to him.

Like early in the mornings, when she first got up, all sleepy-eyed, her hair a matted mess, and walked heavy—zombie stomped—into the kitchen to start the coffee. Despite her healthy appetite, Addison was not a large girl; but, in the morning, she sounded like a 350-pound linebacker walking through his house. As the day wore on, her steps lightened up, and by noon, she was walking like a five-foot-seven, 130ish-pound girl again.

Zane found this adorable, but his favorite of all her idiosyncrasies was how she used her feet like hands. Her toes were the same length as her pinky fingers and freakishly flexible. If she dropped a dish towel or a sock on the floor, instead of bending to retrieve it, she grabbed it with one of her hand-feet, as he called them, and then transferred it to her actual hand. He thought this was hilarious to watch.

Addison picked up a wing and double-dunked it into some blue cheese dressing. "It's impossible to eat these things without getting them all over you." She pointed the wing at Zane. "Why aren't you eating?"

"I love you." Zane had thought those three words so many times that he wasn't sure if he'd said them out loud until he saw the shocked expression on Addison's face.

She put down the wing, wiped her mouth with a fresh napkin, then took a long gulp of her beer and swallowed hard. When she'd cleared her mouth, she opened it to speak, but Zane stopped her.

"I know this is where you think you should say something, but you don't have to. I didn't tell you to hear you echo the words back to me."

The waiter approached the table to refill their water glasses, saving Zane from what was sure to have been the most uncomfortable moment of his life. "Are we ready to order here?"

*

They'd planned on going to a movie after dinner, but after seeing the packed cinema, because neither of them liked crowds, they decided to find something on TV to watch instead. They both agreed that since it was Valentine's Day, there would surely be a romantic comedy marathon.

When they got to the house, Addison cut up the plain chicken breast she'd ordered from the restaurant, and she and Zane hand-fed it to Hero. Zane did not usually condone feeding a dog food from the table, but he made an exception in this case. Hero's appetite was waning, and at this late stage in his life, they pretty much let him have anything they could get him to eat.

After they'd given Hero plenty of attention and belly rubs, Addison and Zane exchanged Valentine's gifts. They had both chosen sensible items appropriate for their time together. Addison gave Zane a stained-glass sun catcher she'd made—a bunch of balloons in every color but red—to hang in his kitchen window. "I figured you already had a red one on your arm," she said jokingly. He gave her a pale blue cashmere scarf. Handing her the gift, he realized it did not match what he'd said at the restaurant earlier, but he hadn't planned on saying it, not then, anyway. If he'd known, he would've bought her an aquamarine necklace to bring out her eyes instead of the scarf.

They hung Zane's new sun catcher, so they could see the morning light sift through it the following day, then settled on the couch to watch a movie. During a commercial, while Addison lay with her head in Zane's lap, she looked up at him and said, "You know my mouth was full of chicken at the restaurant, don't you?"

"I know, but I really want you to think about it."

Zane got up and went into the kitchen to open a bottle of chardonnay and get the box of chocolate-covered strawberries he'd bought so they could eat them while they watched the rest of the movie. When he returned to the living room, Addison had rolled out the feather mattress, and she was on it wearing nothing but her Valentine's Day present. He tossed the strawberries on a table and put down the wine. *God, I love this woman.*

*

It was six a.m., and Zane had been awake for hours, staring at the faint light from the window. He looked over at Addison sleeping beside him. She had one leg kicked out from under the quilt, stretched over Hero's back.

She spent the night at his place when they'd been drinking, or it was too late to wake Gama or too cold to get out—any excuse he could think of to keep her there with him. They were still sleeping on the feather mattress, rolled onto the floor. Zane had finally cleared out his ma's old room, and there was now a new pillowtop mattress on the bed, but Addison insisted she liked the feather mattress better. Zane knew the real reason she wanted to sleep on the floor was so Hero could lay with them whenever he wanted to.

He wondered how she would wake up that morning, now that she knew how he felt. He did not detected any change in her behavior the night before, even when they made love. Zane felt relieved since he'd been honest with her, as if a burden was lifted from his heart. He couldn't unsay the words he'd said at the restaurant, and he didn't want to. Now they were out there for the universe to handle.

His cell phone rang, and he hurried to retrieve it from the pocket of his jeans he'd thrown over the back of the club chair the night before. He stepped into the kitchen to talk so he wouldn't disturb Addison. It was Zach; the excitement in his voice reverberated through the phone. Michelle had the baby earlier that morning, a girl, seven-pounds-six-ounces.

As Zane was hanging up, Addison came into the room, Hero dragging along behind her. "Who were you talking to so early?" she asked, opening the back door to let Hero out.

"My brother, I just found out I have a niece!"

"Well, that's good news to start the day. When was she born?"

"Around four o'clock this morning."

"She was almost a Valentine's Day baby. What did they name her?"

"They decided to go with Cori, after Ma."

"What a sweet way for Zach to honor your mother." Addison went up to Zane and put her hands on his chest. "If we have a girl, we can name her after Gama."

Zane's heart skipped a few beats. *Did she just say she wanted to have a baby with me? Is this her way of telling me she loves me?*

"How do you feel about the name Kathleen?" she asked.

"I love it; we can call her Katy."

Zane glanced at the clock on the microwave, hoping there was enough time to coax Addison back into bed with him.

She looked at the clock, too, sensing what he had in mind. "We've got to get going," she said. "You need to be at the clinic soon, and I have tons of work waiting for me at the shop."

He grinned. "I know; it's just that all the talk about making babies inspired me."

## CHAPTER 20

# ADDISON

A s soon as Zane dropped me off at my house, I sent Lily a text: *Zane told me he loved me last night.*

My phone rang almost immediately. "I want to hear everything," she said when I picked up.

"We were at Joe's eating wings, and he said it."

"Out of the blue?"

"Out of the blue."

"On Valentine's Day...that's so cheesy but romantic-cheesy. So, you told him you love him too, right?"

"Well...no."

"What the hell, Addy? You love the man; why didn't you tell him?"

"He caught me off guard. And I had a mouth full of food."

"Can you imagine how crappy he felt when you didn't say it back?"

"What about *my* feelings? This is a big deal for me, too. I've never told a guy that before."

"Poor Zane, he opened his heart, and you just went on eating chicken wings."

"You don't understand; he didn't want me to say anything. He told me to think about it a while."

"That might've been what he said, but I guarantee it's not what he truly wanted."

"He's right. I *should* think about it."

"What's to think about? You love the guy; anyone can see it." Lily sighed. "Poor Zane."

"Poor Zane? What about me?"

"Whatever. I need to get a shower. I'll see you at the shop. We'll talk then."

I slammed down the phone and stormed into the kitchen. Gama was sitting at the table; she looked up from her crossword puzzle.

"Sometimes, that girl makes me furious!" I said.

"Well, you must admit she has a point."

"What do you mean?"

"Why didn't you tell Zane you love him?"

"Gama, were you listening in on my phone conversation?"

"I wasn't trying to, but I couldn't help but overhear; you were practically shouting."

"How can you and Lily be so sure of how I feel?"

"I'll tell you exactly how." She put down the pencil she was holding. "It's simple, really. He makes your heart smile."

"What?"

"You know when you pass a friend on the street and think you should smile to be polite?"

"Yeah, I guess."

"When you look at someone you love, you don't have to think about smiling. It's spontaneous, from the heart. You couldn't stop it if you wanted to. You smile when you talk about Zane, and I'd be willing to wager you smile when you see him too."

"I do not. *Do I?*"

"You do; you're just not aware of it. That's how beyond your control it is. I didn't realize I was doing it either until my mother told me the same thing I'm telling you now."

"So, when did you finally know?"

"Come over here and sit for a minute. I want to tell you a story."

"Is this going to be one of your long stories?" I asked, walking toward her. "Because I'm meeting Lily at the shop; we've got a lot of work to do."

"I know you're busy, so I'll get right to the point." She pulled out the chair beside her, and I sat in it. "Back when Grampa and I were young, even younger than you are now—if you can imagine that—we were at the local fair one night, and he was shooting a basketball, trying to win this stupid stuffed alligator I had my eye on. Now, it's important to understand that Grampa was not athletic, and couldn't hit that little goal to save his life. But he wouldn't give up because he didn't want to let me down. He turned to me and said, 'Kitty, if you want that alligator, I'm not leaving here until I win it for you.'"

"Aww, that's so sweet."

"I know, that's how he was."

"Did he win the alligator for you?"

"He did—an hour and fifty dollars later."

"That's an adorable story, Gama, but I don't understand what it's got to do with Zane and me."

"I'm not finished. Long before that night, my mother told me she could tell I was in love because I lit up when I saw Grampa and got all giggly whenever I talked about him. Of course, I was stubborn like you and didn't believe her. Not until I left the fair with a giant pink alligator tucked under my arm."

"Did you tell Grampa?"

"Right then and there."

"I don't think that's how it works for everybody."

"Sure, it is. You'll see. You've got no say in the matter; your heart's in charge now." Gama grinned, and then returned to her crossword puzzle. "All you can do is sit back and wait for your own alligator to arrive."

*

Lily and I had made significant progress toward opening Kaleidoscope. The hardwood floors had been refinished, and with Zane and Andre's help, the interior had been painted a conservative Parchment White. But we still had a long way to go before the house would be ready for the early March grand opening we were shooting for. We needed to make some racks for Lily's clothing and figure out a way to display my stained glass pieces. We also had to clean the windows, a job we should've already done but were putting off because neither of us wanted to tackle it.

When I got to the shop that morning, I expected Lily to still be aggravated with me because of our conversation earlier, but instead, she was all smiles when she met me at the door. Andre was there. Whenever he drove up from Tennessee, as he had for Valentine's Day, he usually spent the night in a bed Lily had set up for him in one of the back rooms.

"So, what are we working on today?" I asked as I took off my jacket.

"I know we need to wash the windows," Lily said. "But I figured if we waited a week or so, the weather might warm up, making the job more pleasant."

"That makes sense. So, are we building racks then?" Lily had suggested we build the clothes racks out of metal plumbing pipe, a clever solution that would be easy on our budget and add character to the shop.

"We could start on the racks...but I've got an even better idea."

I narrowed my eyes at her. "What have you come up with now?"

"You know you were saying we needed more display space and that you wished there wasn't a wall between the living and dining rooms?"

"Yeah?"

"I say we take the wall out."

"That would be nice, but you're forgetting this is a rental, and we can't just go knocking out walls."

"Yes, we can. I talked to the landlord this past weekend. She loved the idea of opening up the space and agreed to let us remove the wall if we have it done by a professional."

"Hiring a contractor is probably not cheap."

"True. But I happen to know one who's offered to do it for free."

"Who's that?"

"Andre. It's literally what he does. He works for his dad, who buys houses, remodels, and then sells them."

I looked across the room at Andre, leaning against the wall, eating a donut. "I thought you were a musician."

"I am. Flipping houses pays the bills. What I make from the band is fun money."

"So, what do you say, Addy? Should we go for it?" Lily asked with a lilt in her voice.

"Sure." We really did need the space, and I was pleased that Lily had a new project to distract her from what we'd discussed on the phone. I turned to Andre. "As long as you know what you're doing."

"Well, it isn't a huge wall, or load-bearing, so that's a plus," he said. "But it may be slightly more difficult since it's plaster-and-wood-lath. And without a doubt, it will be messy. But in general, taking a wall down is easy."

I had no idea what he was talking about, so I figured that meant he did. "Okay then. What are we waiting for? Let's tear this thing down!"

At Lily's request, Andre had brought his tools with him. He said we would also need a broom and several large garbage bags, which we already had, and gave Lily and me each a pair of safety glasses and an N95 mask. Then, sledgehammer in hand, Andre began knocking away the wall. He wasn't kidding when he said it would be a messy job. Lily and I stayed busy nonstop, filling bag after bag with debris and hauling them out to the dumpster.

As we discussed where to order lunch, there was a knock on the front door, and Hero and I went to see who was there. Standing on the porch were two men I didn't recognize. Hero barked for a few minutes, then lost interest and retreated to a back room of the shop, away from all the dust.

"Is there an Addison Quinn or a Lily James here?" one of the men asked.

"I'm Addison, and Lily's inside the house."

"Good. We have the right place then. We're here to install your new storefront sign."

I glanced at their van in the driveway: *Sign Me Up* was printed on the side. "But we haven't ordered our sign yet."

Lily must have heard the conversation because she joined me at the door.

"Says here the order was made by Kathleen Baker," the man said, looking through some papers in his hand. "Kaleidoscope lighted sign, multi-colored letters."

Lily and I looked at each other. "Gama," we said at once.

I turned back to the men. "How much is it going to cost?"

"The balance has been paid in full," he said. "So, can we get started now?"

"Yes!" Lily said, clapping her hands. "Please... start!"

As I watched the men unload the van, chill bumps covered my arms. I reached for Lily's hand. "This is really happening."

We called Gama and put the phone on speaker. "You didn't have to pay for the shop sign," I said. "It must have cost a fortune!"

"What else am I going to do with my money?" she said. "It's my grand opening gift to you girls. I'm so proud of you both."

We thanked her repeatedly, tears streaming down our faces. Gama cried with us. Even Andre's eyes started to water.

Lily and I were so thrilled that we wanted to set up lawn chairs in the front yard and watch our store sign being erected. But we needed to finish taking out the wall before Andre left that evening, so we had to settle for running outside every few minutes to check on the progress.

Around four in the afternoon, as we were sweeping the last bits of plaster from the floor, Zane walked in. "I finished at the clinic early," he said, bending to greet Hero. "I thought you guys might need an extra set of hands." He looked up at me. "You didn't tell me you were getting your storefront sign today."

As soon as our eyes met, a smile with a mind of its own stretched across my face. I thought of Grampa shooting basketball at the fair, and Gama with the pink alligator, and my smile grew even more.

"I love you," I said at the top of my voice.

Andre wolf-whistled.

"Hell yeah, she does!" Lily shouted.

I dropped the broom I was holding, ran to Zane, and jumped into his arms.

This time, he caught me.

## CHAPTER 21
# ADDISON

We had the grand opening of Kaleidoscope on March 3, in honor of Lily's birthday. The turnout was excellent, almost more than the tiny shop could handle. Rex and Reenie donated muffins and coffee, and Gama and her church friends put up banners and decorations. The flyers we had distributed in nearby cities paid off, and of course, almost everyone in Driftwood dropped by to show their support.

Lily put out most of her clothing designs in three sizes, and I displayed thirty or more stained glass pieces. We took orders from our inventory, enough to keep us both busy for a while. After a full day at the clinic, Zane came to the shop and helped us clean up. With everybody pitching in, all in all, the birth of Kaleidoscope was a huge success.

That night, Zane and I were too tired to chew food, so we heated a can of tomato soup and drank it for dinner. All the socializing had even worn Hero out; the minute we walked through the door, he went to his favorite spot in Zane's old bedroom to rest. Hero could no longer get into the bottom bunk, but he liked being in that room for some reason, so we put a fluffy dog bed in there for him.

Zane built a fire to take the chill off the house, and then he and I cuddled up in front of it on the feather mattress. It was Friday, and we were both looking forward to sleeping late the following day.

I was about to drift off when Hero walked into the room, stiff-legged and hobbling, the way he always was when he first got up. "Hey buddy, you need to go outside?"

The slow wag of his tail said yes.

I started to get up, but Zane stopped me. "I've got him this time; I need to get another log for the fire anyway," he said. "Come on, old boy; let's go out so you can do your business."

When they returned, Zane tossed the log onto the fire and jumped under the quilt, shivering. Hero had been sleeping with us lately and was usually content to curl up at our feet, but on this night, he wedged in between Zane and me. I put my arm around Hero's neck, and he touched his cold nose to mine and then closed his eyes. Zane put his arm around Hero too, and we heard swoosh, swoosh, thump, thump, thump as Hero's tail lifted the covers. Zane and I looked at each other, and using the last of our energy, laughed but said nothing; the moment was too flawless to mar with words. I knew, as it was happening, that we were creating what would one day be a cherished memory.

*

The following morning, a slice of sunlight from the front window cut across my eyes, announcing the arrival of a shiny new day. Beside me, Zane and Hero were in deep sleep. I lay there for a few minutes, looking at my two boys and thinking how lucky I was to have them in my life. I got my cell phone and took a picture; it was a space in time I wanted to capture forever.

I gave Hero a nudge and whispered in his ear. "Come on, buddy, let's go out." I stood up and threw a quilt around my shoulders. As I walked toward the door, I glanced back at Hero, but he wasn't getting up. "Come on, boy, let's go," I said loud enough to wake Zane. But Hero didn't move. I bent down and nudged him again. "Wake up, Hero." When he still didn't stir, I began shaking him. "Wake up!"

Zane placed his hand over mine. "Addison, wait a minute; let me look at him." He gently pressed two fingers to Hero's neck.

"Why are you doing that?' I asked. "He's all right. He's still asleep." I took Hero's face into my hands and felt the heat from his body. "See," I said. "He's warm. Feel him. Sometimes he's stubborn this way. Wake up, boy!"

Zane put his ear to Hero's chest and then looked at me solemnly. "He's gone."

"No, no, you're wrong! Feel how warm he is. Try once more to find his pulse."

Zane tried again and then shook his head. "I'm so sorry, Addison."

"No! He can't be dead! He was fine last night. You

saw him wagging his tail."

"He went in his sleep. That's the best way it could've happened, with you and me beside him."

"Hero's just tired. I'll let him rest a while longer, and then he'll be ready to get up. Go and make the coffee; we'll join you in a minute."

Because of the magical way Hero had entered my life, there was a delusional part of me that had managed to convince an irrational part that he was invincible. After the wreck, I lost consciousness, so I didn't see how he came upon me; as far as I knew, he'd appeared out of nowhere.

The first time I saw him, he was a wet ball of fur swaddled in a towel. "Look who I have!" said the nurse holding him. "It's your puppy! He must have been thrown from the car too." As soon as she placed him on the hospital bed beside me, he pushed his wet nose against my hand and wiggled under it until my palm rested on his head. "Amazingly, he wasn't injured," the nurse said. "We cleaned him all up and got special permission for him to stay in here with you."

Gama gave me a bewildered look. "Honey, I didn't know you got a dog."

I was as confused as she was. "I've never seen this puppy before."

"Now that's odd," said the nurse. "When the paramedics found you, he was right by your side. In fact, they said his yelping helped lead them to where you were."

"Poor little fella," Gama said. "If he isn't yours, I

wonder who he belongs to."

"He might have wandered from his owner," the nurse offered. "Or somebody could've left him there on purpose. Unfortunately, that area has always been a popular dumping ground for unwanted pets."

Gama picked up the puppy and nuzzled him against her neck. "It doesn't matter how he got there; I'm grateful he stayed with you until help came. That makes him a hero in my eyes."

The next day, the nurse posted an ad in the local paper that a lost puppy had been found near the Snake Shadow Crossing. When a week passed, and no one stepped forward to claim him, we decided to take him in.

Now, looking at Hero's motionless body, it was hard to believe he was the same rambunctious pup of over thirteen years ago.

After I'd sat there for nearly half an hour with Hero's head on my lap, Zane touched my shoulder. "Addison, I called Gama. She's on her way over to pick you up."

"Why did you do that? I'm not leaving him!"

Zane sat on the floor beside me. "Hero may have been suffering toward the end. You wouldn't have wanted him to continue like that, would you?"

"He didn't act like he was suffering last night."

"That's true, but it's a dog's instinct to hide their distress." Zane took me firmly by the shoulders and turned me around, facing him. "I realize I can never replace Hero in your heart, but I'm here with you now, and I want you to believe I'm not going anywhere."

I folded into his chest. "I'm not sure if I'm strong enough to get through this."

"You are. You've already proven you can make it through anything." He held me in his arms for a few minutes and let me have a purging cry before he spoke again. "Addison, I know this is an ugly thing to face right now, but we need to deal with Hero's remains soon before his body starts to decompose."

I sat up and wiped the tears from my face with the backs of my hands. "What should we do?"

"I'll get someone to help me take him to the clinic where we have the means to properly store him."

"Store him? How?"

"We have a facility where his body will be kept cold to slow the decomposition."

"How long will you keep him there?"

"A couple of days until you decide what you want to do."

"What do you mean, what I want to do?"

"That's up to you. You'll have to make some decisions, but I'll help you."

"What are my options?"

"Well, there are a few pet crematory services in Braxton. The one that we recommend at the clinic does a fine job, classy and respectful. They let you select an urn to keep the ashes in, and they even make a plaster paw print for you to keep."

"No, I'm sure I don't want Hero to be cremated; I can't bear the thought of him burning."

"Then we'll have to bury him. There's a local

Amish guy who makes quality wooden pet caskets. He stocks various sizes, so there shouldn't be any waiting period."

"Yes, that's better. I want the best casket available. It doesn't matter what it costs."

"Okay, I'll pick it up for you, and I promise I'll get the best one. Do you have an idea where you want to bury Hero?"

"I guess at our house in the back yard. Can I do that?"

"If you mean, is it legal? Yes, it is. Is that what you want?"

"Yes, but I don't know where to put him. Our yard is small, and Gama has so many flowers."

"What about here? There's plenty of room behind the house."

"You would do that?"

"Absolutely, and you can come to his gravesite whenever you want." Zane lifted one corner of his mouth in an attempt to smile. "If I had it my way, you'd always be here."

"Hero did seem to love this place."

"Then it's settled. I'll make all the arrangements and get what we need to bury him properly. We can even have a service if you'd like."

"That would be nice. And I want to get a headstone."

"I can recommend a place for that too."

"Zane, are you sure you don't mind doing this?"

"Of course, I don't mind. I want to do this for you. I love you, and I loved Hero too."

"I don't think I can watch him being put into the ground."

"Then you won't have to. I'll see if I can have him buried tomorrow morning. When it's done, we'll have a private service for him here."

"Oh, Zane, that's asking too much of you."

"No, it's not. Besides, I'm Hero's vet. It's part of what I do."

"You're much more than his vet. Hero loved you."

"Gama will be here soon." He carefully removed Hero's head from my lap, put his arm around my waist, and eased me to my feet.

When I stood up, my empty stomach turned, and I got lightheaded. Panic surged through me, and I dropped back to the floor. "No, I'm not ready to go; not yet."

"Okay, take a few more minutes then."

Zane stayed with me until we heard Gama drive up. "Come on," he said, lifting me to my feet again. "I'll walk with you."

Gama got out of the car, her face wet with tears, and extended her arms to me. "Oh, Addy, sweetheart, I'm so sorry."

I fell into her hug and let the floodgates open again. "Hero's gone, Gama."

"Where is our boy now?" she asked, rubbing my back in a soothing, circular motion like she'd done when I was a little girl.

"He's inside." I pulled myself from her arms. "Do you want to see him?" I asked, turning back toward the house. "I'll go with you."

"No, no, I don't think so," she said. "I'd rather remember Hero the way I saw him last."

Zane steered me toward the car. "Addison, you need to go home. I'll take care of everything."

Gama touched Zane's arm. "Thank you so much."

"No need to thank me. Hero meant a lot to me too." He opened the car door. "If there's anything you'd like to have buried with him, a picture of the two of you, a favorite blanket he slept on when he was a puppy, get those items together, and I'll drop by this afternoon to pick them up."

I took his hand. "Zane, this means so much to me."

"What about Sunday for the service?" he asked.

"Sunday is fine." I stood there with the car door open and gazed at the house for a minute. I wanted to go back inside and see Hero again, but I was afraid I wouldn't be able to tear myself away from him if I did. I got in the car, and Zane shut the door behind me.

"We'll talk about it more when I come by later." He tapped the top of the car to let Gama know it was time to get me away from there.

*

It was Sunday afternoon, and Gama, Zane, and I were seated at the island in Zane's kitchen, waiting for Lily to arrive so we could begin Hero's funeral service. We kept our conversations light—the newly painted kitchen, the unseasonably cold weather—because we all three were on the brink of breaking down. When we had nothing more to say, we were slowly paralyzed by our grief. We stared into our cups of coffee, avoiding eye contact—crying tends to have a domino effect. Finally, we heard a knock on the front door. Thankful for something to do, we all started to get up at once.

"I'll get it," I said.

I opened the door expecting to see Lily but instead was greeted by Rex and Reenie.

Reenie handed me a huge tray of cookies. "We're not too late, are we?"

"Too late for what?"

"For Hero's service," Rex said. "Kathleen told us about it."

"No, of course not, come in."

While we were still in the doorway, Lily drove up. Two more vehicles pulled in behind her, filling up Zane's driveway. A lady rolled down her car window and asked if she could park in front of the house. Right away, I recognized her voice; it was Margaret Meow.

Soon cars were lined up on both sides of the street, and Zane's tiny kitchen was overflowing with people, food, and chatter. Among them were Dr. and Mrs. Jacobs, Water Lady, Smokey, and his wife, who was pushing him in a wheelchair.

Shame wrenched my heart when I realized Smokey—I found out his name was Earnest—was unable to walk due to a war injury, and that was why he'd always insisted Hero come to him whenever we passed by his house. Hero had known the truth all along, and I would have too if I'd taken the time to get to know Earnest.

Zane went out of his way to see that the guests were comfortable in his home. He got some folding chairs from the garage and set them up in the kitchen so everyone had a place to sit, and made several pots of coffee to go with the cookies Reenie brought.

After everyone had socialized for a while, Gama separated herself from the crowd. "Can I have your attention, please?" she said, trying to raise her naturally soft voice above the murmur.

Rex, realizing no one could hear her, stepped in to help. "Excuse me," he said, in a tone as commanding as his appearance. "Kathleen has something she'd like to say."

A hush fell over the room.

"I want to thank you all for coming here to celebrate the life of an extraordinary creature that made our days brighter in his short time on this earth," Gama said. "I've thought about it, and I believe the best way to pay tribute to Hero is for each of us to share a fond memory of him." Gama scanned the room for volunteers. When no one made a move, she said, "I would be honored to go first."

"My favorite memory happened on a summer day when Hero was around a year old. I was on the back patio, shucking sweetcorn when I noticed him dragging one of the ears of corn—almost as big as him—out into the yard. When he found a spot to his liking, he plopped down and began peeling away the husks with his teeth. He continued until the corn was clean and then snatched another ear and did the same thing. Before I knew it, Hero had shucked half that pile of sweetcorn for me, and as good as I could've done myself." Gama paused, a little misty-eyed. "Now, you might think he removed the shucks just because puppies like to shred things. But why did he stop when he got to the corn?"

Zane went next. He talked about our walks along the river trail and the many ways Hero had filled the hole Dandy's death had left in his heart. Then, one by one, everyone at the service shared their own special memory of Hero. As I listened to them tell their heartfelt stories—some funny, others touching —I realized Hero had not belonged only to me but to every person in the room. He had existed humbly in the background of our lives; sometimes, we hardly knew he was there, but the void he'd left behind was too vast to fill. We would somehow have to learn to live with the emptiness.

\*

After everyone had gone home, Zane opened a bottle of wine, handed me a glass, and sat on the couch beside me. He dropped his head. "I didn't expect it to hurt this much. I feel like I've lost Dandy all over again."

Zane and Hero had connected the instant they met, and the bond they formed in a mere three months was uncanny. I put my hand on his. "I can't even imagine going through this twice."

We silently stared at nothing and said nothing for five minutes. Then Zane asked, "How would you like to take a road trip?"

What he said didn't register. The furthest thing from my mind was a vacation. "Now?"

"I could use a change of scenery, and it might be good for us both to get away for a while."

"That's what people always say, but getting away doesn't make things go away."

"I know, I know. The truth is, I have a baby niece I haven't met yet, and now that Dr. Jacobs is well enough to handle the clinic again, I'd like to drive down to North Carolina for a visit."

"You do need to see your new niece."

"Oh, and I forgot to mention, I'm not going without you," he said. "Please say you'll go; Zach and Michelle are anxious to meet you."

"How long does it take to get there?" I wanted to meet Zane's family, especially his twin brother. And having something to occupy me could not make things any worse.

"Lake Lure is about an eight-hour drive from here. But we can break it up if you want, maybe stay the night somewhere in Tennessee."

Without Hero, I felt like a vital appendage had been lopped off. No prosthetic could help me; I would forever walk unbalanced. No matter where I went or who was with me, that's how it would be. Zane knew this; he was simply offering me something temporary to lean on. "When do you want to leave?"

"I was thinking early Wednesday morning."

"This Wednesday?"

"Sure, it's as good a day as any."

"How long would we stay?"

"Only a couple of nights; I talked to Zach, and he said they weren't expecting any guests at the bed and breakfast until the weekend."

"I'll have to see if it's okay with Lily first."

"I'm sure she can manage the shop without you for a few days."

"You've already talked to her, haven't you?"

"I might have."

"Sounds like you've got everything under control."

Suddenly I felt drained, so I stretched out on the couch and put my head on Zane's lap. As I was about to close my eyes, I thought I heard Hero stirring in the back of the house. I looked at the door leading to the hallway expecting to see him walk through it any minute like he had so many times before.

## CHAPTER 22
# ZANE

Addison's eyes widened as Zane pulled the car up to a sprawling log home with a tin roof and wrap-around porch. "Wow, this is not at all what I imagined," she said.

"What did you expect?" Zane asked.

"When I think of a bed and breakfast, I picture a Victorian-style house with a steep roof and lots of gingerbread. This has more of a lodge-y feel. But I love it."

"They really lucked up when they got this place. They bought it from Michelle's parents for cheap. Plus, it was already an established business."

"Still, it must be hard work to keep it going, especially with a baby to care for."

"They have someone who comes in and cleans the rooms and does some of the cooking. And I think Zach told me Michelle's parents have been helping out since Cori was born."

"How many guests can they accommodate?"

"Four, I think."

"It's so big...it almost looks like two houses hooked together."

"Actually, it is. A screened-in breezeway separates the guest quarters from where Zach and Michelle live. The largest area, to the right, is the bed and breakfast. Each of the four bedrooms has a bath, and then there's the kitchen and a lounge."

"So that little portion on the left is their house?"

"Yes. That's where we'll be staying."

"Do they have enough space for us?"

"Oh, yeah; it's bigger than it looks." Zane parked the car and shut off the motor. "You'll see. Let's go inside."

As they took some slate steps up a slight hill that led to the house, the front door opened, and Zach came out to meet them. "Glad to see you guys made it," he said. "How was the drive?"

"Long," Zane said.

At first glance, the identical twins couldn't have appeared more different. Zach had a buzz cut under his ragged ball cap, a full beard, and was wearing a Metallica t-shirt with a flannel jacket. Zane wore his hair in an unkept style that said, "I've got more important things to do than sit in a barber shop," was clean-shaven, and had on a gray crew neck sweater.

After the brothers embraced, Zane introduced Addison to Zach, and then the three of them went into the house and were immediately greeted by a large yellow dog.

Zach looked at Addison. "That's Daisy, Dandy's sister."

Addison bent over to stroke Daisy's head.

"I've only seen photos of Dandy, but there is a resemblance."

"Actually, Daisy looks more like Sunny," Zach said.

"Sunny?"

Zane wanted to strangle his brother before he could say another word. He shot Zach a dirty look, but it didn't work.

"We had Sunny before we got Daisy and Dandy. They all three were from the litter of a Lab that lived down the street from us in Driftwood."

"What happened to Sunny?" she asked.

"We lost him when he was still a pup."

"Oh, no; how'd he die?"

"No, we actually *lost* him; he ran off one day, and we never found him. We think somebody probably picked him up."

"Let's hope so," Addison said as she scratched behind Daisy's ears.

Zane hadn't seen Daisy in so long he'd forgotten how much she looked like Hero. If he'd remembered, he might have somehow been able to prepare Addison before they arrived. But now it was too late; there was nothing he could do except hope she didn't notice, and that was unlikely because the resemblance was startling.

Addison looked back over her shoulder at Zane. "Who does she remind you of?"

There was no denying the obvious. "Hero," he mumbled.

"Who's Hero?" Zach asked.

"He was my dog; he just passed away over the weekend."

"Yeah, Zane told me. I'm so sorry." Zach reached over and ruffled the fur on Daisy's head. "I don't know what I'll do when this old girl is gone."

Michelle walked into the foyer with Cori, diverting Addison's attention away from Daisy. Zane could breathe again.

After introductions and a few minutes of swooning over the baby, Michelle invited everyone into the dining room, where dinner was waiting. "The two of you must be famished after that long drive," she said.

After dinner, while Addison was helping Michelle in the kitchen, Zach grabbed a couple of beers from the fridge and motioned for Zane to join him on the front porch.

Zane took a seat in an Adirondack chair. "Cori's amazing," he said.

"She's the best thing that's ever happened to me, next to meeting Michelle." Zach leaned back against the porch railing. "Addison's gorgeous," he said. "I can't figure out what she sees in you."

Zane took a sip of his beer, grinning. "Sometimes, I wonder myself."

"She seems to be having a hard time with her dog's death."

"It's still fresh. I thought bringing her here would distance her from reminders of Hero, but as it turns out, I might've made things worse."

"I guess every dog she sees makes her think of

him right now."

Zane sat his beer on the chair's armrest and then got up. "There's more to it than that." He pulled his wallet from his back pocket, took out a folded newspaper clipping, and handed it to Zach. "This was in Ma's things."

Zach unfolded the clipping and looked at the photograph. "Hey, this looks like Sunny." He glanced at the large block of text below the photo. He'd never been much for reading. "So, what's this about?"

"Hero."

"An article about Hero with a picture of Sunny?"

"That's Hero in the photo."

"Man, it sure looks like Sunny. He even has the one floppy ear."

"That's because it *is* Sunny."

"Huh?"

"Read."

As Zach read the article, his face slowly changed from confused to astonished. "Does this mean what I think it does?"

"Hero was Sunny, and Addison is the girl you just read about."

Zach turned up his beer and guzzled half the bottle. "Unbelievable. Of all the women in the world, you had to fall for the survivor of the Snake Shadow wreck. How did this even happen?"

"Addison brought Hero into the clinic for arthritis. You can figure out the rest of the story."

"You didn't have any idea who she was before you started seeing her?"

"Hell no! Why would you ask me that?" It was a sensitive subject with Zane.

"Because it's all a bit too...coincidental."

"We're talking about Driftwood."

"Okay, but it never came up after you started seeing her? Was the sex so good that you never spoke to each other?"

"Addison's private about her past. I knew her parents had been killed in a car accident, and while it occurred to me that she could've been in the wreck, too, I didn't know it was the Snake Shadow wreck. I figured it happened somewhere in Indianapolis, where they lived, and by the time I found out, I was too far gone."

They turned up their beers and stood quietly for a few minutes.

"So that's where Sunny ended up when he ran off," Zach said.

"And became Hero."

"But how did you not recognize him when you were with Addison?"

"As an old dog, Sunny didn't look anything like he did when he was a puppy. I remember him as being goldish brown with those funny, uneven ears. Hero was pale yellow, almost white, and both his ears were floppy."

"You just described Daisy."

"Now you understand why Addison got so emotional."

"Hell, I feel like crying, myself." Zach refolded the clipping and gave it back to Zane. "So, Ma obviously knew about all this. Why do you think she kept it from us? She saw how upset we were when we lost Sunny."

"Because if we'd known where Sunny was, we would've wanted to go get him. Ma couldn't risk the chance of someone putting two and two together and figuring out we were at the crossing the day of the wreck."

"She was protecting us like she always did."

Just as Zane returned the newspaper clipping to his wallet, Addison walked out onto the porch. Both men jumped when they saw her.

"What are you two talking about out here?" she asked. "I thought I heard someone say my name."

Zach, the better liar of the two, jumped to Zane's rescue. "I was trying to convince my brother he should move to Lake Lure."

Addison turned to Zane. "And what did you say?"

Zane could see himself living in Lake Lure, or somewhere like it, with Addison. He wondered how attached she was to Driftwood, how difficult it would be to talk her into picking up stakes and moving somewhere else with him. If she didn't want to go, didn't want to leave her grandmother, he would suck it up and stay because a future without her was unimaginable.

"Like I was telling Zach as you came out, that depends on Addison." Zane realized he had become almost as good at lying as his brother.

*

Friday afternoon, Zane and Addison were still in Lake Lure. They had planned to leave that morning —everything was packed in the car—but Michelle talked them into staying for lunch. Then time got away from them; now it was almost four o'clock, and they were all in the kitchen chatting over coffee while Cori napped.

Zane would've liked nothing more than to stay and watch another stunning sunset on the lake. He didn't have to be back at work for another week, and Addison seemed surprisingly at ease with Zach and Michelle. But the B&B guests were arriving later that night, so Zane decided it would be best to head home.

When there was a lag in the conversation, he got up from the table. "We need to get out of here so you can prepare for your guests."

Zach stood beside his brother. "As much as I hate to break up the party, I probably should get busy."

Zane and Addison began making their way toward the door, Zach and Daisy behind them. Just as they got there, Michelle came out of the kitchen. "Here are some cookies for the road." She handed Zane a red plastic box. "Hope you like Macadamia nuts. You can keep the container. It's one of those disposable ones left over from Christmas."

"Thank you, Michelle," Zane said. "It was so good to see you and to finally meet my niece. Give her a kiss for me when she wakes up."

Michelle hugged Zane. "Don't wait so long to visit next time."

He laughed. "We'll try to make it back before Cori starts first grade."

Michelle turned to Addison. "It was so nice getting to know you," she said, then leaned in for a hug.

Addison's body stiffened as she wrapped one arm around Michelle and patted her on the back. "You too," she said in a faint voice.

Zane noticed Addison was pale and had a peculiar, detached look, much like the one she had when they met. "Are you feeling okay, Addison?"

"Sure. Just a little sad to be leaving, I guess." She stroked Daisy's head.

"Well, stay longer then," Zach said. "We can work around you."

Zane turned for the door. "We'd like to, but you don't need to worry about us while tending to your guests."

Zach clutched the back of Zane's neck. "I wasn't asking you, clown head."

Zane elbowed his brother's ribs. "Come on, Addison, we'd better get going; it's a long drive back."

When they got into the car, Zane put the cookies in the back seat and then turned to Addison. "Are you sure you're feeling all right?"

"Yes, I'm positive."

"Did something happen that I don't know about? Sometimes Zach doesn't have a filter on that trap of his."

"No, no, nothing happened. Zach was great. Everything was great."

"Something's wrong; I can see it in your face."

"Can we just drop the subject?"

"Addison, talk to me."

She turned away and looked out the passenger side window. "Please don't make me tell you."

He reached over and took her hand. "I love you, and if there's a problem, I want to know about it."

"But if I tell you, you'll think I'm insane."

"No, I won't."

"Trust me; you will."

"Maybe I can help."

"Okay, but I'm warning you upfront; what I'm going to say is bizarre."

"What is it?"

"Would you mind parking the car somewhere first?"

"Sure." He pulled into the next place he saw, a convenience store, shut off the car motor, and turned to Addison, giving her full attention.

"A few minutes ago, as we left the bed and breakfast, I got this feeling…like a warning."

"A warning?"

"A red warning; that's what I call them."

"Them? So, you've had the feeling before?"

"Yes, but it's been a while."

"Why do you call them *red* warnings?"

"Because I have them only when I see something red."

"What did you see red?" He looked at his clothes, hers, and all around until he spotted the cookies Michelle had given them in the back. "The cookies;

they're in a red box."

"I told you it's bizarre, and I'm just getting started."

"Go on."

"After I've had a red warning, something bad always happens."

Zane felt he should be getting what she was trying to tell him, but he was not. "So, they're like premonitions?"

"Kind of, but not really; I never know what's going to happen or when, only that it will involve one or more of the people present at the time of the warning."

"So that means Zach, Michelle, you, or me."

"Or Daisy."

"How long have you been getting these warnings?"

"Ever since I was around eleven."

"And how often do they happen?"

"Not as much as they used to. This is the first one I've had since...." She looked away.

"Since when?"

"Since we met, I had a warning when I saw your tattoo."

"The balloon? Ah, it's red. That's why you ran out the way you did. So, what was the bad thing that happened after the warning then?"

"Hero got lost."

"Hmm, but that was a while after you were at the clinic."

"Sometimes that's how it goes."

"Tell me, what do you feel like when you're having one of these warnings?"

"Terrified, my heart starts pounding; sometimes, I even have trouble breathing. And the strangest part is everything in my sight loses color except the one red object that set off the warning."

"Could it be that you're afraid because you know something bad will happen?"

"No, because when I had the first few warnings, I didn't know they were connected to the bad stuff that happened afterward."

"Why red?"

"I don't know. But it's always a red object that causes a warning."

"Hmm."

"What is it?" Addison asked. "What are you thinking?"

"I'm not an authority on this kind of thing, but it sounds to me like your red warnings might be panic attacks."

"Panic attacks? But there's never been anything threatening going on before a warning."

"Panic attacks aren't always set off by obvious fear. It could be something deep within your subconscious mind. Since they're brought on by red, maybe you have chromophobia, a fear of color, in this case, red."

"There's such a thing as being afraid of a color?"

"Oh yeah, there's a list of phobias a mile long. People are afraid of everything from dust mites to donuts. As strange as it may seem, chromophobia is one of the more common ones. The question is, *why* are you afraid of red? Usually, a phobia results from trauma, most likely from early childhood."

"But it still doesn't explain why the bad things happen after a warning."

"This is just speculation, but could it be that the unfortunate events were coincidental, and you simply attached them to the warnings as an explanation?"

"What do you mean?"

"Think about it; bad things happen daily, so the chances of them happening around your panic attacks are very likely."

"That's the same thing Lily said." She looked down. "All these years, I thought I had a special power to predict danger when it was nothing but fear all along."

"Or, who knows? Maybe they really are premonitions."

Addison half-smiled. "On the other hand, if you're right, in a way, it's kind of liberating to finally have an explanation that actually makes sense."

"Yes, but even if your warnings turn out to be panic attacks, just because you put a label on them doesn't mean they'll go away."

"Maybe not, but I'd still feel better knowing what causes them. The way I see it, I've been dealing with—whatever's wrong with me—for a long time already; I've just been calling it something else."

"Can you remember anything from your past associated with red that could've caused your fear?"

Addison pondered a few minutes. "Yes, something that happened during the wreck."

It made sense to Zane that the trauma causing Addison's panic attacks was connected to her parents' deaths. As much as he didn't want to hear the details of the wreck, he knew it was a pivotal moment in their relationship. "Can you tell me about it?"

"The blood, there was so much of it, all over the windshield."

He knew all about the blood. He remembered how his stomach had turned when he saw it, realizing someone inside the car had been seriously injured. He could only imagine how Addison had felt. "And now when you see red, it reminds you of the blood that came from one of your parents, which causes you to experience the fear you felt all over again."

"But it wasn't my parents' blood; I know because it was there *before* Dad lost control of the car."

Suddenly Zane needed air. He cracked the car window. "Before, you say?"

"I realize it makes no sense for blood to have been on the windshield before we wrecked. But I know what I saw."

"Are you sure it was blood," he asked. "Could it have been something else?"

"Like what?"

"I don't know...maybe a wet piece of trash."

"Now you sound like Gama. Look, I've had over thirteen years to think about it. What I saw was blood or something that looks exactly like blood."

Her last three words flipped a switch inside Zane's head. He had an idea what caused the blood they both had seen on the windshield that day; however, only one person in the world could confirm his suspicion. He needed to make a phone call for the answer, but he couldn't do it in front of Addison.

He started the car engine. "I'll have to think about that one for a while."

Addison didn't want to talk about her red warnings anymore, so they discussed their visit with Zach and Michelle, and how adorable Cori was. Zane tried to present a calm exterior, even though inside, he was a tangled mess of confusion, anger, and possibly even regret.

They stopped in Nashville to eat. Over dinner, Zane convinced Addison to let him drive straight through, even though it would put them back in Driftwood after midnight. The sooner he was home, the sooner he'd be able to make the phone call. But how would he do it without Addison finding out?

When they were on the road again, she got out her cell phone to text Gama and Lily to let them know she was headed back to Driftwood.

"Do you want me to take you home tonight since you haven't seen Gama in a while?" Zane asked.

Addison looked at him inquisitively. "Why? She won't be up anyway."

"True, but it would be nice if she could see you first thing in the morning."

"Do you think I should?"

"I think it'd make her feel special."

"You're right; it probably would. I'll send Gama another text."

When Addison finished her text, she put her head on Zane's shoulder. "Are you okay?"

"Sure," he said. "Why do you ask?"

"I don't know...you seem...preoccupied."

"I'm just tired."

"We can still stop somewhere and get a hotel room."

"No, no, Gama is expecting you."

*

When the car became quiet, Zane realized Addison had fallen asleep. As he glared at the seemingly endless road before him, the day he'd spent years trying to push from his mind seized him and dragged him back to relive the nightmare.

He could see his ma in the kitchen stirring something in a pot, cracking the oven door every now and then to check the turkey. He pictured her, Zach, and him around the table with big smiles in lively conversation as they ate their Thanksgiving dinner, unaware of the tragedy ahead.

After they'd finished, he and Zach became restless. The rain that had pounded the roof for two days straight, forcing them to stay indoors, had finally stopped, and they were eager to get out of the house. Zach wanted to go bike riding on the river trail, and Zane was all for the idea.

Zach suggested they take some water balloons with them. When they were kids, they liked to have balloon wars or throw them against things and watch them explode. Zach kept a large bucket in their room, full of at least fifty water-filled balloons, ready for such an occasion. Since they planned to play war that day, they needed different colors. Zach always took blue and gave Zane the red ones. They stuffed their backpacks with as many water balloons as they would hold, then took off on their bikes, their new puppy, Sunny, tagging along behind them.

When they came to the Snake Shadow Crossing, Zach stopped and dismounted his bike. "Let's drop some balloons off here and watch them hit the pavement."

"But Ma told us to never drop anything off the crossing. Remember when Brody Hendricks dropped a fountain drink and it hit that lady's car?"

Zach walked over to the south side of the crossing, a balloon in each hand. "Yeah, but we're just dropping water balloons, and we'll make sure no cars are coming." He tossed one of his balloons into the air and then caught it. "There won't be much traffic today anyway. It's Thanksgiving; most people are eating right now."

"Okay, but we'd better not tell Ma." Zane slipped off his backpack, took a couple of balloons out, and joined his brother.

Zach dropped one of his blue balloons off the crossing, and they watched it splatter on the blacktop below. He looked at Zane. "What are you waiting for? Drop one of yours."

Zane rested his balloons on the stone wall and steadied them with his hands. "Wait a minute; I think I hear a car coming." He peered up the winding road behind him, through the branches of the oak trees, but couldn't see anything.

"Drop it before the car gets here," Zach said. "They'll wonder what the heck it is. It'll be funny! Go ahead!"

When Zane still didn't drop the balloon, Zach gave him a shove on the shoulder, causing one of the water balloons to slip out from under Zane's hand and wobble toward the road below.

The boys leaned over the wall expecting to see the balloon smash into the pavement, but instead, saw a car emerge from under the crossing. Suddenly, the car swerved off the road, flipped over, and with a loud crunch, landed in a ditch.

Stunned motionless, they stared in disbelief at the overturned car, its wheels spinning in the air. Right then, Sunny shot off the crossing. Zane started after him but was stopped in his tracks by a deafening boom and a vibration he would feel in his bones for years to come. When he turned around, he saw black smoke rolling up the side of the crossing and realized the car had burst into flames.

Zach tugged Zane's arm. "We'd better get out of here!"

"Why?"

"Why do you think, you moron? A car just wrecked underneath us, and we're standing here with our backpacks full of water balloons."

"But shouldn't we do something to help?"

"Like what? Look at that fire; there's nothing we can do."

"What about Sunny?"

"He'll find his way home; it's not that far." Zach ran to his bike and hopped on. "We need to go *now* before somebody comes."

Zane stood there for what couldn't have been more than a few seconds, hypnotized by the flames, acrid smoke burning his nostrils. He looked at Zach riding away and then back at the burning car. The choice was before him, and his decision would alter the rest of his life.

He picked up the other balloon from the wall of the crossing, got on his bike, and began pedaling for home as fast as he could.

When they got inside the house, their ma was in the front room reading. "You didn't stay gone very long for a couple of boys who were dying to get out."

"We changed our minds," Zach said. "We decided we want to play Monopoly instead."

"Good." She closed her book. "I'll set up the board." She took the lid off the game box and began issuing tokens, counting money. "Hey, did you boys hear that loud noise a few minutes ago? It sounded like a gunshot."

"No," Zach quickly replied.

She looked at Zane, who hadn't said anything since he'd been home. "Honey, your face is as white as a sheet. What's the matter?"

"It was an accident, Ma!" he blurted.

"What was an accident?"

"The wreck...it wasn't my fault!"

"You wrecked your bike?" She got up, went to Zane, and took him by the shoulders. "Are you okay?" she asked, checking him over.

"No, not me; there was a car wreck."

"What are you talking about?" She looked at Zach, who now had nothing to say. "Okay," she said, returning to the couch. "Start from the beginning and tell me what happened."

The boys began blathering at once—frantic, high-pitched, fragmented sentences.

Ma stopped them. "Zane, you go first." Of her two sons, she knew he was the one most likely to tell her the truth.

"We rode our bikes down the river trail like we said and stopped on the Snake Shadow Crossing."

"And we took some water balloons with us to drop off the side," Zach added.

"Off the side of the crossing?" She scowled. "What have I told you about that?"

"I know, Ma," Zach said. "But we were going to make sure no cars were coming before we dropped them."

"That's not the point. The point is you disobeyed me." She turned back to Zane. "So, then what happened?"

"I think I may have hit a car with one of the balloons," he muttered.

"No, you didn't," Zach argued. "The car wasn't

even there yet when you dropped it."

"Me? You pushed me and made it slip out of my hand!"

"Zach, hush," Ma said. She turned her attention back to Zane. "Okay, you accidentally dropped a balloon that may have hit the car, and then what?"

"The car ran off the road."

"Oh, no! But it got back on, right?"

"No, not exactly; it went into a ditch."

She gasped. "The ditches on that road are deep. Did you see anyone get out of the car when it was in the ditch?"

"No," the twins answered in unison.

She paused as if to gather her thoughts. "Well, I guess all we can do is hope whoever was inside the car is okay."

"But Ma, I don't see how they could be," Zane said.

"What do you mean?"

"The car exploded."

"Oh, my Lord!" She covered her mouth with her hand. "That must've been what I heard!"

"Whoever was in the car could've crawled out before it caught fire," Zach said. "It happens all the time in the movies."

"This isn't the movies." She got up, walked to the window, and gazed out into the overcast sky.

"Ma, if the balloon hit the car and somebody got killed, does that make us murderers?" Zane asked.

She turned to him; the horror that contorted her lovely features would haunt Zane for the rest of his life. She fell to her knees and began sobbing. Zane and Zach rushed to her side and put their arms around her.

"I'm sorry, Ma," Zane said. "Please don't cry." He wanted her to scream at them, exact the punishment he knew they deserved—at least then things would feel normal again—but all she did was hold them in her arms and cry.

They stayed on the floor for hours until the room became dark. Finally, without saying a word, Ma got up, wiped her face on the sleeves of her sweater, and went into the kitchen to make their supper.

The next morning, a knock on the front door startled Zane from sleep. He scrambled from his bed to the window and peeked out one side of the curtain. There was a police car parked in the driveway. He swallowed hard and tried to find his voice. "Zach...Zach, wake up; the cops are here!"

Zach jumped from the top bunk, ran to the window, and pushed up beside Zane. "Oh, no; they've come for us."

They heard their ma answer the door and voices coming from the living room, but they couldn't make out what they were saying. A few minutes later, the front door opened and shut again. The boys went to the window and watched the police car back out of the driveway and leave.

After a few more minutes, Ma called them to breakfast. They sat at the table while she made pancakes as if nothing had happened.

"Why was there a policeman here, Ma?" Zach asked. "Was it about the wreck at Snake Shadow?"

"Yes, of course, it was about the wreck. It was Mack Sterling. He wanted to know if the two of you were at the crossing yesterday. Does anybody want bacon with their pancakes?"

"What did you say?" Zach asked. "Did you tell him we were there?"

"I told him you were both here with me all day."

Zane looked at her, astonished. "You lied?"

She put down the spatula she was holding and turned to them. "You know I disapprove of lying, but there are good and bad lies. The lie I told Mack was a good lie to protect the ones I love." She walked over to the table and stood before them. "Neither of you is to blame for what happened at the crossing yesterday. It was an awful accident that the police are certain was caused by a combination of the slick, windy road and sudden change of speed limit coming off the highway."

"If the police are sure the wreck was an accident, why did they come here to ask if we were at the crossing?" Zach asked.

"Oh, he was only doing his job, honey. Some lady driving up the road after the wreck said she thought she'd seen a couple of kids there, so he was asking everyone in the neighborhood."

"If the wreck wasn't our fault, why did you say we weren't on the crossing?" Zane asked.

"Because there's no reason to raise unnecessary suspicion. I was afraid if anyone found out you were there, someone might try to blame you for what happened, even though you're innocent. You know how people around here like to gossip."

Zach looked at Zane. "See, I told you the balloon didn't hit that car."

"Of course, it didn't," Ma said. "And even if it did, a silly water balloon can't cause a wreck." She put her arms around them. "Boys, listen to me carefully. You need to understand that I could get into trouble if anyone found out I lied to the police. Now, it's your turn to protect me. We must keep this secret between the three of us forever. I want you both to promise me, right now, that you'll never, under any circumstances, tell anyone you were at the crossing yesterday. Can you do that for me?"

"We promise, ma," Zach said.

"We'll protect you forever," Zane added.

*

After Zane had taken Addison home, as soon as he pulled into his driveway, he shut off the car motor and got his cell phone out of the glove compartment. His hands shook as he searched his contacts for his brother's number. When Zach picked up the phone, Zane fired the question that had been on his mind for the last several hours. "Did you put fake blood in the water balloons we took to the Snake Shadow Crossing on the day of the wreck?"

"You called me in the middle of the night to ask me that?"

"Did you?"

"That was long ago, bro...."

"Just answer the damn question."

"It was supposed to be a joke."

"A joke? Why didn't you tell me about it afterward?"

"I didn't see the point...the joke was ruined. What difference does it make now anyway?"

"It makes a hell of a lot of difference. The fake blood you put in that balloon caused the wreck that killed Addison's parents."

"What? How do you know that?"

"She told me she saw a blood splatter on the car's windshield *before* the wreck."

"Holy shit."

"Holy shit's right."

Zane disconnected the phone and shoved the palms of his hands into his forehead. For years, he had believed the wreck wasn't his fault. His ma said it wasn't; even the police report concluded it was caused by the slick road. He thought the worse thing he'd done that day was run from the scene of an accident when he should have stayed and tried to help. Now he knew the truth: he was responsible for the deaths of two people and had possibly destroyed the life of a third.

## CHAPTER 23

# ADDISON

Tired from the trip, I slept in the following morning. When I finally woke up, around nine-thirty, my first thought was that Zane hadn't called yet. He called me every morning, if I wasn't with him, around eight, just to say hello. I checked my phone to see if I'd slept through the ring or if he'd texted instead. There was nothing from him.

Zane was dependable, and it was out of his character to stray from routine. But he had seemed exhausted on the drive back; it was after midnight when we got home. Thinking maybe he wasn't up yet, I went on with my day, spending time with Gama, telling her all about our trip, one eye on the clock.

Around lunch, when I still hadn't heard anything from Zane, I began to get concerned, so I decided to call him. His phone went straight to voicemail. I sent him a text. No reply. I waited half an hour, then tried him again. Nothing.

Something was wrong.

When two o'clock rolled around with no word from Zane, I began to worry. *Am I overreacting?* I got my phone; I needed to hear a voice of reason.

"Lily, I have a major problem," I said when she answered.

"What happened?"

"Zane hasn't called yet."

"Geez, I thought your house had burned down or something."

"No, you don't understand. I haven't heard from him since we returned from North Carolina."

"When did you get back?"

"Late last night."

"What? Give the guy a break!"

"But he calls every morning."

"So, he missed a day. Why don't you call him?"

"I already did, twice, but he didn't answer."

"He's probably beat from the trip."

"Yeah, I get that, but too tired to pick up the phone?"

"Maybe his phone went dead. Did you try him at work?"

"He's not back to work yet. He took the week off."

"Well, knowing Zane, I'm sure there's a good reason."

"Maybe he doesn't want to see me anymore."

"You think he's ghosting you?"

"Whatever they call it."

"He's not the type. Besides, why would he tell you he loves you and suddenly cut you off? There must be some other explanation."

"What else could it be?"

"Okay, let's back up. Did anything unusual

happen while you were in North Carolina?"

I tried to recall the details of our visit. Zane had seemed delighted to be around his family, and when he saw Cori, he beamed. This made me realize what a good father he would make and wonder what it would be like to have a baby with him. Gama would've been so proud.

"No, nothing I can recall," I said, and then remembered. "Wait, there was this one thing. As we were leaving, I had a warning."

"Oh." Lily paused for a few seconds. "Well, were you able to cover it up?" Her response warmed my heart. She knew I was ashamed of my red warnings and automatically assumed I'd concealed it from Zane. And under normal circumstances, she would've been right.

"I don't believe Zach and Michelle noticed anything, but Zane did. He knows me too well."

"So, what did you do?"

"I decided to tell him."

"Good for you. And how did he react?"

"He was surprisingly understanding. He said he thought my warnings sounded like some sort of post-trauma anxiety."

"So, I guess you talked to him about the wreck then."

"Yes."

"And the blood splatter you saw?"

"I thought he should know everything."

"How did he respond when you told him?"

"Come to think of it, he was a little reticent

afterward. When I asked him if anything was wrong, he said it was just fatigue."

"Well, it is a long trip."

"I shouldn't have told him about the splatter. It was too much at once. Now he thinks I'm nuts."

"No, he's not that kind of guy. It must be something else."

"Like what?"

"I just hope he's okay."

"What do you mean? Do you think something could've happened to him?"

"No need to jump to conclusions."

"What if he had a wreck on the way home, fell asleep at the wheel."

"You would have heard by now if he was in a car accident. But maybe you should drive to his house to make sure he didn't slip in the bathtub or something."

"Why did you have to say that?"

"Well, you never know."

"I'm hanging up and going over there right now."

"Message me when you find out."

On the way to Zane's, I was bombarded with images of him unconscious on his bathroom floor, a puddle of blood beneath his head. As soon as I got there, I pulled into his driveway and bound up to his house. He appeared at the door before I had the chance to knock. He stood on the threshold, seemingly dazed as if he'd wandered there by mistake, then suddenly found himself lost. No smile. No hello. Nothing.

"Zane, are you okay?"

"Yes, I'm fine," he answered in a robotic voice.

"You don't look fine."

He opened the door wider and stepped aside. "Come on in."

"Why didn't you answer my calls? You scared the holy crap out of me. I thought something had happened to you."

"I'm sorry. I needed to gather my thoughts before I faced you."

"Gather your thoughts about what?"

"I was going to call you this afternoon. Addison, there's something I need to tell you."

"I hate when people say that; it's never good."

"You're right; it's not good."

He sat on one of the chairs by the fireplace, and I sat across from him on the couch. We were right back where we started the first time I came to his house. His face was solemn, his head low. Either he was about to break up with me, or he had a terminal illness.

"Zane, what is it?"

"It's regarding what we discussed yesterday on the way home."

"I thought that might be the problem. Look, I know yesterday got weird. My warnings—panic attacks—are enough to spook anybody. The idea of being with someone like me, someone damaged, is scary. But that was the first warning I've had since we've been together. Since I met you, I'm happier and healthier, mentally, than I've ever been."

"No, it's not that at all. There's nothing wrong with you."

"Well, what is it then?"

"I don't know how to begin…where to begin. It's all so…incredible."

"Now you're starting to freak me out."

"Addison…"

"For heaven's sake, Zane, how bad can it be? Just tell me."

"I was on the Snake Shadow Crossing the day of the wreck."

"What? What are you talking about?"

"I was there when it happened."

"What do you mean you were there? No one was *there* besides my parents and me."

"I was there, too; you just didn't know it."

"You mean you were there *after* the wreck."

"Addison, listen to me, please! I was on the crossing before the wreck, and I was there during the wreck, too. I saw the car flip, hit the ditch, the fire —everything."

It occurred to me that Zane could have been on the crossing when the wreck happened. He still lived in Driftwood then. I pictured him as a frightened young boy witnessing something horrifying, not knowing what to do.

"So, what you're trying to tell me is you saw the wreck and didn't do anything to help." I got up and went to him. "Zane, it's okay. What were you, then? Twelve, thirteen? There's nothing you could've done."

"Yes, it's true; I left without trying to help, which was bad enough. But there's more."

"More? Tell me."

"Addison...."

"What?"

"I think I might have killed your parents."

*

When Zane had finished his story, I was even more confused. "No, wait a minute. None of what you said makes sense. It wasn't a water balloon I saw on the windshield; it was a blood splatter."

"Yes, you're right, it was. At least that's what it looked like."

"What? I don't understand."

"I saw the splatter too when the car flipped, and I also thought it was blood, but last night I found out it wasn't. Not real blood anyway."

"What do you mean, *not real blood?*"

"It was fake blood. Zach got it for Halloween and became obsessed with the stuff. That day, before we left for the crossing, he put some inside my balloons as a joke."

"So, what you're telling me is my red warnings are the result of some sort of childish prank?"

"Addison, it kills me to know something stupid like that caused you so much suffering."

"Why don't I already know about this? Why didn't someone tell me? Surely you went to the police and reported what happened."

He looked down. "You weren't told because no

one knew about it but Zach and me...and Ma."

"Your *mother*? I can almost understand why you and Zach didn't tell anyone; you were kids. But your mother, an adult, knew and didn't report it to the authorities?"

"I know it sounds bad, but she was trying to protect us. It's complicated."

"Is this why you were so persistent in getting to know me?" I sprang to my feet. "Are you with me now out of pity? Throw the poor scar-faced orphan girl a bone. Or is it to ease your guilt?"

"No! I had no idea you were the survivor when I met you."

"Oh, *please*. Everybody in this one-horse town knows everything that happens here."

"All I knew was two people from out of town were killed in the wreck and that there was one who lived. I never found out names."

"Hold on. You said you didn't know when we met; but did you ever know?"

He didn't answer.

"Zane?"

"I found out Christmas Eve; Reenie told me."

"So, you've known for over two months, and it didn't occur to you to say anything?"

"I hadn't found out about the fake blood then or that the balloon I'd dropped even hit the car. And I didn't see the point of mentioning something you refused to discuss anyway."

"So, a car flipped into a ditch right after you dropped a water balloon off the crossing, and the thought never entered your mind that the balloon could have caused the wreck?"

"Of course, it entered my mind. But then the investigation confirmed the wreck was because of the road condition, and...I guess I believed what I wanted to be true."

"Were you ever going to tell me, Zane?"

He turned away. "I can't answer that."

I started for the door. "I need to get out of here."

Zane followed me. "Addison, I'm so sorry. Let me take you home. You're too upset to drive."

I backed away from him. "No, I can't be around you right now."

I could barely see the road through my tears, so I pulled over and parked for a while. Zane called my cell phone twice. I didn't answer, but I texted him to tell him I was okay.

When I got home, I went to my bedroom and silenced my phone. For more than thirteen years, not knowing what caused the splatter had gnawed at my well-being and nibbled at my sanity. But now that I'd learned the truth, with all its jagged little edges, I realized that the time I'd spent in the dark had actually been a blessing.

Gama knew I was upset; she knocked on my door to check on me. "I'm fine," I said to appease her. "I need to be alone for a while. Please, Gama, give me some space."

I came out of my room only to go to the bathroom or get bottled water to hydrate myself, so I could continue crying. Gama brought me food, which I couldn't eat, but she didn't pressure me to talk until later that night, around nine.

"Addison, this has gone on long enough," she said through my bedroom door. "I'm coming in." She marched straight to my bedside lamp and turned it on. "Let's talk." There was a tough-love sternness to her usually gentle tone. "Now, tell me why you're so upset. Did you and Zane break up?"

I sat up and squinted at her through the painful light. "No. At least not officially."

"Then what went on earlier while you were at his house?"

"Gama, something terrible has happened," I blubbered.

She sat on my bed and took me into her arms. "Oh, honey; what is it?"

"Zane was there the day of the wreck."

She pulled back and looked at me incredulously. "What do you mean?"

"He was on the Snake Shadow Crossing when it happened. He and his brother Zach were riding their bikes on the river trail."

"That was the twins?"

"You knew?"

"One of the police officers mentioned someone thought they'd seen a couple of kids on the crossing right after the wreck, but they never found out who they were."

"Why didn't you tell me, Gama? Why doesn't anybody tell me anything?"

"There was no reason to. It didn't seem

important then."

"Turns out it was."

"How so?"

"You know the blood splatter I saw on the windshield before the wreck? Zane did that."

"What?"

"He and Zach went to the crossing that day to drop some water balloons off the side. Zane didn't know, but Zach had filled the balloons with some sort of fake blood, and Zane dropped one of them off the crossing as we were driving out from under it."

"Oh, good Lord! You *did* see blood!"

"Fake blood, but it was realistic."

"No wonder you're so upset."

"And that's not even the main reason I'm crying. After I left Zane's house, I started thinking about the wreck, trying to process what he'd told me, and I remembered something, a detail I must've pushed from my memory."

"What did you remember?"

"Gama, I think the wreck was my fault."

"Child, what on earth are you talking about?"

"Early in the trip, I was trying to sleep, but my seatbelt was uncomfortable, so I took it off and put my coat over my lap to keep Mom and Dad from finding out. When I woke up, our favorite song was on the radio, and the three of us started singing."

"Was "Don't Worry Be Happy" the song?"

"Yep, that's the one."

"Irony can be a little twisted sometimes."

"Anyway, Dad was joking around, making faces

at me in the back seat. Once when he looked back, he noticed my seatbelt was unbuckled—I guess my coat had slipped off my lap." A snapshot of Dad's joyful, singing face suddenly distorted by anger and disappointment flashed before me. Tears welled in my eyes, and I had to stop for a minute.

"Take it slow," Gama said gently.

"As he scolded me, the blood splatter appeared on the windshield behind him, and then he lost control of the car. So, I know Zane couldn't have caused the wreck because Dad never even saw the splatter."

"Well, it sure wasn't your fault," Gama said. "Now, you listen to me. I talked to the authorities a lot after the wreck, seeking answers, and they were certain the car slid out of control due to a slick spot caused by the rain. You know they can tell these things by the tire skid marks and all." She pulled me close, and held me for a few minutes, stroking my hair.

"Hey, you want to hear something crazy?" she asked.

"You mean something *else* crazy?"

"For the longest time, I was convinced that *I* was the one responsible for the accident."

"But you weren't even there."

"You probably never knew this, but your mom didn't want to come to Driftwood that day. She suggested we wait until Friday; let the weather clear up. But I wouldn't have it. I was too worried about my dinner when I should've been thinking of my family's safety. What's worse, I kept calling, trying to rush things along. The wreck may have never happened if I'd agreed to wait one more day."

"That's the most ridiculous thing I've ever heard. You know how headstrong Mom was. If she didn't want to come, she wouldn't have."

"My point is that if any of us—Zane, you, me—look hard enough, we can find a way to blame ourselves. But what good would it do?" She took my hands into hers. "Addy, I owe you an apology."

"For what?"

"We should have discussed these things years ago. It's my fault we didn't. I guess I was trying to bypass the pain."

"Gama, you dealt with your emotions the only way you knew how."

"But I should've known that just because you pretend you don't see something doesn't mean it isn't there."

"Well, you aren't the only one who should've talked about the wreck. If Zane had come forward and told someone about the balloons, instead of running, I wouldn't have spent all those years trying to figure out where the blood splatter came from."

"Granted, he shouldn't have been throwing things off the crossing, and he shouldn't have run either," Gama agreed. "But let's remember Zane was only a kid too."

I thought of him on the Snake Shadow Crossing, engulfed in billowy black smoke, frantically looking around, unsure of what to do. "You're right, Gama; he was probably terrified."

"And you know what? As strange as this may sound, in a way, I'm glad Zane dropped that balloon filled with fake blood. I think obsessing over the splatter sidetracked you from the despair of losing your mom and dad."

"That's a possibility," I said. "In fact, it all can be worked out...except one thing."

"Let's hear it."

"Gama, I can't help but wonder if Zane pursued a relationship with me out of pity or guilt."

"Nonsense! That young man is in love with you; anybody can see it."

"He said he had no idea who I was before we met at the clinic, but that's so hard to believe."

"But you need to understand that although the wreck may still be prevalent in our minds, for most folks in town, it's buried history. Honey, you know Zane, his character. Do you honestly think he's the type of man who'd do that and then turn around and tell you what he did? He could've kept it all a secret, and you would've never known."

"That's a good point; he didn't have to say anything. I've been so overwhelmed I haven't even thought of that."

"And rightly so. But now you need to fix this. You need to pull yourself together and go talk to Zane."

"I will." I glanced at the clock on the nightstand. "It's too late tonight, but I'll do it first thing in the morning."

When Gama realized the time, she hugged me and popped to her feet. "I need to start getting ready for bed."

*

When I pulled up to Zane's house, he was standing in the doorway. "I was just leaving," he said. "I need to take care of some things at the clinic."

"Can we talk before you go? I have something important I need to tell you."

"Why haven't you answered my phone calls or texts?"

"I turned off my phone; I had to sort things out in my head."

"I guess I have a few minutes." He motioned for me to come inside, but instead of going to the living room's seating area, he stopped inside the door.

After I'd told him about the seatbelt, I expected a look of relief to come over his face. I expected us to magically go back to the way we were. But that's far from what I got.

"Surely you're not trying to say you were the one responsible for the accident."

"In the beginning, I believe I subconsciously thought I was, but somehow found a way to transfer the blame to the splatter. Maybe it was my mind's way of protecting me. Then, last night Gama told me details about the investigation we'd never discussed before, and now I'm convinced it wasn't my fault or yours. It was a slippery road." I waited several minutes for him to respond, but he didn't. "So, where do we go from here?"

"Addison, I appreciate you telling me this, and

it helps to know the balloon I dropped wasn't responsible for the wreck, but it doesn't change the fact that my actions caused you years of suffering." He raked his fingers through his hair. His guilt was palpable; I could almost see it standing beside him. "I had a choice, and I made the wrong one. The worst part is I knew it was wrong."

"But you were only thirteen. And, as Gama said, if it hadn't been for your actions, I would've had nothing to blame but myself, which probably would've been much worse."

His face softened, and for an instant, I thought I saw an opening in his heart. Then, as quickly as it had appeared, it was gone. "You know that doesn't justify what I did."

Daunted by the reality that nothing I could say would change his mind, I was swallowed into the cavernous silence that formed between us.

"I'm thinking about returning to North Carolina for a while." He looked away from me. "We should take some time apart from each other to digest all this."

"Why can't we digest it together?" I grabbed his forearm and flipped it over. "Do you remember why you got this?"

"Of course, I remember."

"You let go once, and you can do it again."

"I never really let go. Neither did you. And my biggest fear is that we won't be able to. The last thing I want is to be a constant reminder of the worst day of your life."

"Or maybe you're afraid I'll be *your* reminder."

He turned and put his hand on the doorknob. "I really do need to get to the clinic now."

I followed him out, and he walked with me to my car. "How long of a break are we talking about?" I asked. "And don't you dare say as long as it takes."

"Honestly, Addison, I have no idea."

## CHAPTER 24
# ADDISON

I gave him three days before I was in the car on my way to his house again. Beside me, on ribbons tied to the passenger door handle were two shiny, red balloons, their heads bobbling. They were part of my plan to convince Zane we could put the past behind us and start all over. Earlier that afternoon, while I was at the party store buying them, I'd pictured us on his front lawn, releasing them into the sky. We watched them drift up and away, growing smaller and smaller, until a gust of wind whipped them behind a cluster of trees, out of our sight forever.

The first thing I noticed as I pulled up to Zane's house was the For Sale sign was back in the front yard. That should have been enough for me to turn around and go home. But sometimes we want something so much we ignore the reality before us. Holding the balloons, I stepped out of the car and, guided by a tiny flicker of hope, made my way up to the door.

When I knocked, there was no answer; still, I didn't leave because I knew Zane sometimes kept his car in the garage. I pressed my face against the front window and saw the living room was empty. I went back and knocked on the door again. I don't know why; he was clearly not home.

For three pathetic hours, I stood on Zane's front porch like a lonely circus clown until the darkness slowly erased me, and then I tied the balloons to the porch railing and went home.

*

The following morning, Lily stopped by my house to let me know Zane had moved to North Carolina. "Reenie told me when she was in the shop yesterday," she said.

"No, he didn't move; he went to Zach's for another visit. He told me he was going, but only for a while."

"He's selling the house."

"You don't know that. Maybe he's putting out feelers to see if he gets any offers."

"He quit his job."

"Oh, that doesn't mean anything, either. Zane's been planning to resign for a while to start his own practice."

"Addy, I'm so sorry about all this...."

"Sorry about what? We're only taking a break to let everything sink in. He's coming back."

She put her arm around my shoulders. "I feel partly responsible. I pushed you into being with this guy when you didn't want to."

I shrugged her arm off. "Don't be silly. You didn't push me into anything; you only helped me to realize my true feelings. Zane is the best thing that's ever happened to me."

"So, what are you going to do now?"

"I'm going to let him have his space, and when he gets back from North Carolina, we'll figure things out."

*

Denial is the first stage of mourning a loss. For the next two weeks, I drove to Zane's house every day, stalker-like, not knowing what I was hoping to see. Each time I went by, the balloons I'd tied to his porch railing had sunk slightly lower. On Wednesday of week one, they lay on the ground, shriveled and limp. By that weekend, they were gone.

At the end of the second week, the For Sale sign was no longer in his front yard. My heart leaped when I first noticed it was missing. *Was he back? Had he decided not to sell?*

I parked on the side of the road to investigate. As I got out of the car, the house door opened, and a woman appeared. She was thirtyish, petite, attractive. In my head, I began filing through everything I knew about Zane's family and friends. *Maybe she's a cousin? One of Brady's kids?*

"Hello," she called out from the porch. "Are you Addison?"

I'd never seen this woman before, yet she somehow knew my name. "Yes. Have we met?"

"No, I don't think so. My name is Kelly Warner."

*Kelly. Have I heard him mention her before? What*

*was his ex's name?* "Are you a friend of Zane?"

"He's my landlord," she said. "My husband and I recently moved here from Michigan and were lucky to find this place so quickly."

I should've been pleased to learn Zane's ex-girlfriend had not reentered his life, but I was not. The news of a tenant living in his house ripped away the last few threads of hope I'd been clinging to. "Oh," was all I had the will to say.

"Dr. Isaac told us we were to give you access to the back yard whenever you wanted," Kelly said. "It was a stipulation he included in the lease agreement. He said you have a dog buried there."

I nodded.

After I'd stood there a few minutes without saying anything, she asked, "Did you come to visit the gravesite?"

"Yes, if you don't mind," I said, and began walking around to the back of the house.

Standing over Hero's grave, I tried not to think of his decaying body beneath the earth but rather how he'd once been: bounding up the road at the end of a leash, clumsy, curious, and full of life. That was the Hero I needed. I needed him to put his head on my feet while I cried like he'd done after I lost Mom and Dad. I needed to look into his soulful eyes that seemed to absorb my pain and know he understood. He thought he was leaving me in a safe, blissful place. He had no way of knowing that the very person he'd entrusted with my happiness would leave me broken.

If only my hero had been there to rescue me once more.

Being abandoned by someone you love is as brutal as losing them to death, except the finality— the clean cut—is replaced with false hope. Knowing they're wandering around somewhere in the world carrying your happiness with them is nearly unbearable.

I spent several days in isolated bereavement. Gama offered at once a consoling presence and compassionate distance. Lily covered for me at the shop and told me to take all the time I needed. Zane texted me occasionally to say hello, and see how things were going, but his messages seemed obligatory and superficial. The distance between us had become more than physical.

Gama and Lily staged a mini-intervention and gently suggested a counselor might help me cope with all I'd been through. Initially, I dismissed the idea. I'd never believed that paying someone fifty dollars an hour to listen to your problems could make them disappear. However, Zane's theory that my red warnings were panic attacks was still lingering in the back of my mind, and I was curious to see if he was right, so I agreed to give therapy another try.

Choosing a therapist was easy; it had to be Dr. Conway. When I called for an appointment, she got me in right away. Her office was still at the same location, and except for a few gray hairs, some crow's feet, and the new tortoise shell glasses she'd traded in her wireframes, she hadn't changed much since I'd last seen her.

I told Dr. Conway everything I should have when I was nine and brought her up to speed on what had happened since. As part of my therapy, she suggested some uncomfortable exercises, like writing down ten personality traits I admired in myself. She also told me to keep a daily journal to document the things that made me feel grateful. Although I was skeptical, I went along with whatever she asked me to do, and to my surprise, after a few sessions, I began to feel better.

Dr. Conway said my red warnings could've very well been caused by the trauma of losing my parents. "But if you're lucky, now that you know the source of the splatter, your mind may no longer have the need to explain it." Even though I hadn't had a warning since the one in North Carolina, she said only time would tell if they were gone for good.

Dr. Conway helped me to understand that Zane's leaving was not about me but rather his own limitations. While I would always be grateful to him for tearing down the wall I'd built around my heart and helping me discover parts of myself I never knew existed, he had deeply disappointed me. Not his actions as a boy, but how he handled the consequences as an adult. It took tremendous courage to tell me what he'd done on the Snake Shadow Crossing the day of the wreck. What happened to that brave man?

The one thing I'd learned from life—the greatest

therapist of all—was this: It's a coward's way to leap from a tall building and end it all, but stepping back off the ledge and facing what put you there in the first place, now that's courage.

\*

Losing Zane was not the worst thing that had ever happened to me. Fortunately and unfortunately, I'd become well-equipped to bounce back from all the little tragedies thrown into my path. I knew from experience the world didn't stop because I did. Life continued around me—Gama and Lily made sure of that—until one morning, before I knew it, I got caught in the flow, went to the basement, and started working again.

Lily was shocked when I showed up at Kaleidoscope unannounced toward the end of April. She greeted me with a big hug, took my hand, and lifted our arms. "It's Crazy Addy and Bag Lady Lily against the world again!"

She was excited to show me all she had done while I was away. She'd moved the furniture from her apartment above the cleaners into one of the back rooms and set up her sewing station in another. The clothing racks were full of her designs, but she swiftly pointed out that the stained glass inventory was a tad thin.

She also had a big surprise for me she couldn't wait to unveil. She'd created a website for Kaleidoscope with photos of her clothing, and my suncatchers and window panels. She pulled the site up on the shop computer and showed me dozens of inquiries about my art. "You need to get busy making us some money," she said.

That afternoon, we got all my glass staining supplies from Gama's basement and moved them into another room behind the shop.

After a long day, I went home, took a hot shower, and put on some joggers and a sweatshirt. I was in the bathroom when a sharp sound, like breaking glass, cut through the whirring of the blow-dryer. It was almost time for Gama's evening tea, so I figured she'd dropped something in the kitchen. A few seconds later, I thought I heard her calling my name and turned off the dryer.

"Addison! Can you come in here for a minute?" The weakness of her voice told me something was not right.

I rushed to the kitchen and found her standing by the sink, bracing herself with one hand against the counter. On the floor at her feet was a shattered teacup. The cabinet where she kept her medicine was open, and pill bottles were strewn across the countertop. She was facing the window above the sink with a vacant gaze, her mouth open, eyes crinkled as if she was about to sneeze.

"Gama, what's the matter?"

"Well, I don't know for sure, but I believe I might need to go to the hospital."

"The hospital?" I darted to her side. "What happened? Did you cut yourself?"

"No, no, but I think I may be having a heart

attack," she said so calmly I might've thought she was joking if it hadn't been for the grimace on her face.

"A heart attack? What makes you think that?"

"Well, my chest feels tight, and I have a piercing pain running down my arm."

"Oh, no!" I dragged one of the dinette chairs over to her. "Here, sit down." She collapsed into the chair. Her face was ashen and glazed with perspiration. "Were you trying to take some aspirin?"

"Yes, but I couldn't find any."

I went to the medicine cabinet and plowed through pill bottles and boxes until I found the aspirin. "Here, let this dissolve in your mouth."

"Maybe it's indigestion," she said.

"I don't think so. Do you feel like you can walk?"

"Yes, I believe I can."

I ran to my room and got some shoes. When I returned to the kitchen, Gama had scooted to the front of the chair. "Take it slow," I said, helping her to her feet. "Your car's parked behind mine. Where are your keys?"

"On the table, by the front door," she said. "Are you driving?"

"Of course, I am."

"You don't have to, you know. We can call an ambulance."

"I can make it to the emergency room in seven minutes. It would take an ambulance that long to get here."

On the way to the hospital, Gama reached over

and patted my leg. "Honey, I'm beginning to feel much better now. Maybe I don't need to go to the emergency room after all."

"That's probably because of the aspirin."

"Why don't we turn around and go back home? I'll call and make an appointment with my doctor in the morning."

"To be safe, you should still get checked out."

"But what if it wasn't a heart attack after all? What if it was just indigestion? I'll be so embarrassed."

"Better embarrassed than dead."

By the time we made it to the hospital, Gama was well enough to reprimand me for not getting her purse on our way out the door. She still looked pale, and I could feel her trembling while helping her out of the car. "I wish I could at least put on some lipstick," she said. "I must look a mess."

The ER doctor who came out to the waiting area to update me on Gama's condition had slightly bulging eyes that gave her a look of urgency, so I thought the news was bad before she even said anything. "Your grandmother might have had a mild heart attack."

"Is she going to be okay?"

"She'll be fine. There's a possibility the episode could've been brought on by anxiety. Has she been under any stress lately?"

I'd been so wrapped up in myself since my breakup with Zane that I hadn't taken much notice of Gama. "Maybe. It's hard to say; she worries about almost everything."

The doctor touched my arm as if to comfort me. The gesture made me nervous. "We'll know more after the test results," she said.

"How long will that take."

"Not too long. I'll tell you as soon as I know something."

The hospital reminded me of those excruciating days immediately following the wreck. I remember lying in bed, staring at a rusty water stain on the drop ceiling, despising the world. The sun even pissed me off. I hated rainy days too, of course, but something about the morning light slanting through the hospital window blinds stirred my simmering bitterness. *Now the sun decides to show up, all bright and cheerful*, I thought. *Where was the sunshine when I needed it?*

The first person I saw when I woke up in the hospital—a squatty, roundish nurse who waddled when she walked—became the target of my animosity. She stood over me in bed, her moonish face eclipsing the harsh overhead light. "Addison, you were in an accident," she said. "Do you remember?" Everything came rushing back, the blood, the wreck, the fire. "You have some injuries," the nurse said. "But the doctor stitched you all up, and you're going to be fine."

What she said, the flippant way she said it, caused something to snap inside my head. She lied to me. I wouldn't be fine; I would never be fine again. From then on, I refused to talk to the nurse and stared at her contemptuously.

My misplaced anger had waned over the years. Time seems to take care of these things; it gradually decomposes the toxic garbage we carry. But I still hated hospitals. I stepped outside to get some air and call Lily.

I had no more than hung up the phone when she appeared by my side firing questions. "What did the doctor say? Is she going to have to be admitted?"

"The doctor said it could've been a heart attack, but she doesn't know for sure. And I don't know yet if they will admit her."

"What do you mean they don't know for sure?"

"She said it could've been caused by stress."

"What's Gama have to be stressed about?"

"Do you think she could've been worried about this whole thing with Zane and me?"

"Maybe if it had happened a few weeks ago, but you've been doing fine lately."

"I don't know what else it could've been. You know Gama; she tends to hold everything inside."

"Yeah, that must run in the family." Lily lifted the corner of her mouth to let me know she was teasing. "By the way, how did she get here?"

"I drove her."

"*You* drove?"

"I can drive, you know."

"It's not the driving part that surprises me. It's that you drove under the Snake Shadow Crossing."

The hospital was outside the Driftwood city limits, past the vet clinic, going toward Braxton. I had to have gone under the crossing to get there, but I couldn't remember doing it. "I guess I did."

The doctor came out again, and Lily and I pounced on her. "How is Gama?"

"She's fine. The test results show she did have a very mild heart attack."

"What does that mean?" I asked. "She'll be okay, right?"

"With medication and a few lifestyle changes, yes," the doctor said. "But I am going to need to admit her for observation."

"When can we see her?" I asked.

"She needs her rest, but I guess it would be all right if you go in for a few minutes." She glanced at Lily. "Immediate family only."

I locked my arm in Lily's. "We're sisters."

The doctor smiled. "Sisters, huh?"

"Half-sisters. We have different Dads. Hers is Puerto Rican."

When we walked into Gama's hospital room, I was relieved to see her color had returned, though she still seemed weak. "How are you feeling?" I asked.

"Like I just finished doing a big ironing in high-heeled shoes."

Lily and I looked at each other and laughed.

"You sure gave us a scare," I said.

"Scared me, at first. But I'm fine now. I don't know why I have to stay overnight."

"Gama, you had a heart attack; they have to keep you for observation."

"I can't believe I walked off and left my purse."

"No worries," I said. "Lily and I will run home and get everything you need in a few minutes."

Gama adjusted her gown. "I don't like hospitals."

"Me, either." Lily leaned into Gama and whispered, "I'll bust you out of here if you want me to."

Gama giggled. "I know you would, Lily." She cut her eyes over at me. "But I guess I'd better stay."

I sat on the side of her bed. "I'm so sorry if I've made you worry lately."

"Addy, I love you with all my heart, but I'm not worried about you. Why would I worry about you? Heck, you're the strongest person I know." She took my hands. "You didn't cause my heart attack; bacon did. Old habits die hard."

"The doctor said there would have to be a few changes. Your diet, maybe some exercise."

"I need to eat more vegetables anyway," she said. "You know, I miss having a garden. We should plant one this spring." There was a glitter of excitement in her eyes. "We'll put out tomatoes, squash, green beans...."

"Wait a minute, green beans?"

She smiled. "It's time for a change. Surely, I can eat a green bean or two if you can drive under the Snake Shadow Crossing."

"What about the fives, Gama?" Lily asked.

"Baby steps, Lily, baby steps."

## CHAPTER 25

# ZANE

Zane stood on the deck outside his room at the bed and breakfast, looking at the lush wooded mountains around him. He'd been finding himself there often since he'd left Driftwood, searching for answers in Lake Lure's stunning vistas.

He liked being at the B&B as much as possible in his miserable state. Although Zach and Michelle had offered to let him stay in one of the guest rooms free of charge, Zane had insisted on paying the full price. The way he saw it, he was occupying space they could've been renting out to someone else. Plus, he was receiving a monthly income from leasing out the house, and with no mortgage or other bills to speak of, he had the money.

Having somewhere to stay and plenty of cash was a problem for Zane, as it presented him with no urgency to return to work. He had intended to take a short break—a week, maybe two—while he attempted to clear his mind before seriously looking for a location for his practice. But more than a month had slipped by, and he was having trouble summoning the motivation.

He clutched the neck of the Jack Daniels bottle in his hand. He'd never been much of a drinker, except for the occasional glass of wine or beer. Now he was a drinker. A hard drinker. He turned up the bottle; the whiskey burned his throat and sucked the air from his lungs. He wanted to cry, but he couldn't. It was like being nauseated but unable to throw up. He thought if he could only get the poison out, he'd feel better.

Zane wondered what Addison was doing at that very minute. He checked his watch; it was around 6:15 in the afternoon, so it was after 5:00 in Driftwood. Was she still at the shop? In her basement, working on a stained glass project? He pulled his phone from his back pocket and sent her a text. *Just wanted to say Hi.* He waited a few minutes for a response but didn't get one. When he checked the message to make sure he'd pushed *send,* he saw it had not been delivered. He dialed her number and got an automated recording. Addison had blocked his number.

He heard the whine of the screen door and glanced back over his shoulder to see his brother walking out. Zach touched him on the arm with a cold beer. "Let's trade." When Zane took the beer, Zach grabbed the whiskey and put it on a table behind them, out of Zane's reach.

The twins stood side by side, leaning on the deck railing, drinking and admiring the scenery. Usually, there was no need for words because they both already knew what the other was thinking. They'd been known to refrain from conversations for hours while together.

"Tell me, how do you like living in Lake Lure?" Zach finally asked.

"I'd be enjoying it more if the circumstances were better."

They hadn't discussed Zane's breakup, aside from the gist. But now that Zane had brought up the subject, essentially opening the door, Zach jumped all over the opportunity.

"I've got to tell you, brother, this is the damnedest situation you've gotten yourself into. The whole thing is just so unbelievable."

"Well, I certainly didn't plan it."

"Just to clarify, did you say Addison was living in Driftwood when we were kids?"

"Yep."

"Then how is it we never knew about her?"

"She moved in with her grandmother right before we left for Braxton. So, really there were only a few weeks we could've run into her, and remember, we were grounded to the house for dropping balloons off the crossing during that time."

"Yeah, Ma was adamant, straight to school and straight home. No riding bikes, no TV, nothing but homework."

"And remember how much of a hurry she was in to leave Driftwood? We were packed up and gone just like that after she told us we were moving."

Zane chugged his beer. "That must've been when she found out about Addison."

"What makes you think that?"

"If she knew about Sunny, she knew about Addison," Zane said. "I recall asking her who was in the wreck, and she acted like she didn't know anything except that they were some random people from Indy."

"I guess she thought if we found out about Addison—put a face to the survivor—it would've made it more real."

"She figured the less we knew, the easier it would be for us to deal with. She thought she was protecting us."

"She sure did a good job hiding what she knew," said Zach.

"She's not the only one."

"What do you mean by that?"

Zane turned and faced his brother. "Man, what were you thinking when you put that shit in those balloons?"

"I was thinking like a kid. I intended to slip them in the next time we played war. I wanted to see your face when you saw me spattered with blood."

"If the bloody balloons were for playing war, why did you want to drop them off the crossing that day?"

"To be honest, I forgot all about them until I saw that splatter on the car's windshield. I made them right after Halloween and then hid them in the corner of our closet with some clothes piled on top.

Ma must have put them in the bucket with the rest of the water balloons when she was cleaning our room."

"You saw the splatter on the car, too? Why didn't you say something?"

"Why do you think, moron?" Zach said. "Wait a minute. You said *too*, so that means you saw it. The question is, why didn't *you* say anything?"

"Since you didn't bring it up, I was hoping I'd imagined it." Zane drained the last of his beer from the bottle. "I wish there was a way I could somehow *unknow* all of this."

"Not me."

Zane looked at him dumbfounded.

"Even though Ma and the police told us the wreck wasn't our fault, deep down, I always had doubts because of the fake blood I put in those balloons. A water balloon hitting a car probably wouldn't have caused a wreck, but a blood-filled balloon might have. I'd have never known the truth if you hadn't met Addison."

"Glad I could help you out, bro."

"Yeah, sorry about the whole broken heart thing, but sometimes you've got to take one for the team."

"That's not even funny."

"Just trying to lighten things up."

"Not helping."

"So, what did Addison say when you told her about Sunny...I mean, Hero?"

"I haven't told her, and I'm not going to."

"Why not?"

"Hero finding Addison was the one pure thing that happened in this mess. I'm not taking that away from her."

"You're probably making the right call on that one. There's no good reason to add another freakish element to the narrative." Zach held up his empty beer bottle. "I need another one of these. Can I bring you one?"

"Sure. My refrigerator is full."

As soon as Zach returned with the beers, he started talking again. "I don't mean to poke around in your business, but I've got another question. Now that everything's out in the open and Addison knows the wreck wasn't your fault, what's the problem?"

"Just because we didn't cause the wreck doesn't mean we're completely innocent in all this. There was still damage. Did you know that Addison was so traumatized by the blood she started having panic attacks whenever she saw something red?"

"You're joking."

"She had one when we were at your house. Remember when we were leaving to go home, and Michelle gave us those cookies for the road?"

"Yeah?"

"The cookies were in a red container. After Addison saw it, she had a panic attack in the car."

"We thought she was acting kind of strange."

"And do you know why she suffered like that for so long? Because we ran."

"In our defense, how could we have helped?

There's nothing we, or anyone else, could've done for her parents, and the paramedics got to Addison in time to save her."

"Yes, she survived and went on to have a productive life, but I bet it wasn't easy. If we'd come forward and told what we knew, we could have at least given her closure."

"Closure? You should know there's no such thing when it comes to losing family. There's only gaping. A bloody, open wound that never heals."

"You're justifying."

"Maybe, but regret is a futile emotion; we need to start looking ahead."

"If I've learned anything from all this it's that running never gets you anywhere."

Zach turned to Zane, exaggerating a bewildered expression. "Is that so?"

"What?"

"If running gets you nowhere, why are you still doing it?"

"What do you mean?"

"You're running instead of trying to work things out with Addison. And it seems to me you're acting out of guilt. Your problem is you can't forgive yourself for something you did as a thirteen-year-old boy."

"So, how have *you* lived with it all these years?"

"That's the difference between you and me," Zach said. "I know I made some stupid mistakes when I was a kid, but that's not who I am now."

"Can I get some consolation here, brother?"

"Hey, just calling it like I see it."

"Where are you going with all this?"

"I think you should try to reconcile with Addison. There's one important reason to go back to Driftwood and give it all you've got."

"What's that?"

"Do you love her?"

"More than anything."

"Then she's worth the trouble."

"It's not going to happen. I'm not putting that girl through any more hell."

"Come on, Zane, drop the bullshit. You claim you're doing this for her, but who are you really trying to protect?"

"What are you saying?"

"Addison's made her position clear; she wants to try to save the relationship. The bottom line is it's your fault the two of you aren't together. Hope you can live with *that* choice."

"Looks like I'll have to."

Zach glanced at his watch. "Come on, we should head on over to the house now. Michelle's probably got dinner ready."

\*

"How's your steak?" Michelle asked.

Zane knew she had said something; he'd seen her lips move—he was staring right at her from across the table—but her words were drowned out by the storm in his mind. He had chewed the bite of meat in his mouth for so long it had almost disintegrated.

What he was really chewing on was his conversation with Zach.

"Zane? Is your steak tough?" This time her voice cut through the static.

"No, no." He quickly cut off another bite and popped it into his mouth. "Steak's delicious."

I feel awful about you and Addison," Michelle said. "The two of you seemed so in love."

Zane took a gulp of his wine. "I guess, in this case, love wasn't enough."

"So, it's over?"

"It's for the best. Addison must feel the same way because she blocked my number from her phone."

"What did you expect her to do?" Zach asked. "It wasn't right to keep her hanging on like that."

"I only wanted to make sure she was okay."

"You gave up that right when you left."

"Damn, brother. When did you become so brutal?"

The thought of facing the rest of his days without Addison made Zane feel dead inside. He glared down at his food; the salad on his plate made him depressed, taking him back to his first date with Addison when they prepared dinner together at his house. He glanced across the room at Daisy lying on the floor, face between her paws. She'd been eyeing Zane since he returned to North Carolina; he figured she was probably disappointed that he didn't bring Addison with him. He scanned the room in search of something, anything, to look at that would not remind him of what he'd lost. His sight landed on Cori, asleep in her carrier in the chair beside him. Seeing her only worsened things; she represented the little girl named Katy he and Addison would never have. Zane topped off his wine and surrendered to the sad truth: everything would always remind him of Addison because Addison was everything to him.

"Hey, I've got some good news," Zach said. "There's a veterinarian in town planning his retirement and needs someone to take over his practice."

"Oh, yeah?" Zane said, feigning interest.

"I happened to run into him at the grocery store yesterday. How's that for perfect timing? I mentioned you, and he said he'd love to talk. If you're interested, I could put you in contact with him."

The idea of going back to work exhausted Zane to his core. But he knew he needed to be busy again; it was the only thing that could save him now. "Set it up," he said. "As soon as possible."

## CHAPTER 26
# ADDISON

It was Saturday morning, just after nine, and I was standing behind the shop counter setting up a display of stained glass keychains. Lily and Andre were preparing for a road trip to Florida, loading suitcases, straw hats, and beach towels into Andre's car. Every time one of them came in or went out, the annoying doorbell Lily had insisted we install startled me, and I looked up, thinking it was a customer.

Once they were packed, Lily stood before me dressed in a loose army green t-shirt and ripped jeans; her dreads pulled low at the back of her head with a scrunchie. "I guess we're ready to go now," she said lackadaisically. Lily was doing an admirable job of containing her excitement about her first trip with Andre. Since Zane and I had split, she'd put extra effort into downplaying their relationship for my benefit. "Are you sure you're okay to run the shop by yourself for a week?"

I was more than okay. I was eager for the opportunity to give Lily a much-needed vacation. After Zane went to North Carolina, she'd run the shop alone, no questions asked, while I struggled to pull myself together. "Yes, I'm positive."

She glanced out the front door to make sure Andre was in the car, then leaned over the counter toward me. "I'm asking him to marry me while we're in South Beach."

I was not surprised to hear she was ready to become engaged or even that she would be the one doing the asking. Nothing about Lily James was by the book. My immediate reaction was joy. Then, for a selfish split-second, the news wrenched my heart, thinking of what I could've had if circumstances were different.

But this wasn't about me. Putting my self-centeredness aside, I focused on Lily. "Congratulations!" I said with as much effervescence as I could manage, and then walked around the counter to embrace her. "I'm so excited for you both! But don't get any wild ideas and decide to get married while you're in Florida because I want to be standing beside you when it happens."

"I like the notion of a destination wedding," Lily said. "But I would never do it without you." Right then, Andre honked the car horn. "I'd better go; somebody's getting restless. You're sure you'll be all right?"

I took her by the shoulders, turned her around toward the door, then slapped her ample butt. "Get out of here; I've got this!"

"Thanks, Addy!" Before she walked out, she looked back and blew a kiss over her shoulder. "See you next Sunday."

As usual, traffic in the shop was slow. It was, after all, Driftwood—population 3,244. Regulars from town came in sporadically to buy a new outfit for a special occasion or stained glass wind chimes and sun catchers they probably didn't need, but mostly to chit-chat. Luckily, Lily and I had a steady flow of orders from the website to keep us busy and bring in enough profit to sustain the business. I thought it would be a good day to work on some of those orders. Thanks to Lily's doorbell, I could be in the back and still know when a customer came in.

Before I got busy, I called to check on Gama. It had been only a couple of weeks since her heart attack, and I was worried about leaving her alone. That morning, she told me she planned to plant the vegetable garden before noon. About a week earlier, she'd staked off a spot in the back yard, and I turned the ground with a shovel. She bought seeds with intentions of sowing them after Mother's Day —some sort of midwestern rule—but a rainy spell set her back. Now it was May 16, warm and sunny, and she was determined to get those seeds planted before the end of the month.

"Quit fretting over me," Gama said on the phone when I called. "I'm fine."

Really, she was. She took a brisk walk every morning before breakfast and was eating right, lots of fruits and vegetables, no red meat, except for the two slices of bacon once a week on Saturday mornings that she'd negotiated with the doctor.

"So, are you still going to put out the garden today?" I asked.

"I've got my straw hat on, and I'm headed outside now."

"Okay, but please take the phone with you." I'd recently bought her a cell phone that she hated. She never could remember which button to press to answer it.

About half an hour later, while I was in the back of the shop working on the website orders, I heard the doorbell chime. When I got to the front, I saw Kevin Winslow walking toward me.

"I heard you were running the store yourself today, so I brought you something to eat," he said.

"Oh, Kevin, you didn't have to do that."

He held up a white sack. "It's only a deli sandwich."

Kevin stopped by about once a week—the pharmacy was within walking distance—for a friendly visit. We still joked about when we pretended to talk at church to make Gama happy. Now, we were actually talking. Melissa had called off the engagement, so we found common ground because we'd both been dumped.

A few days earlier, I'd mentioned Kevin's visits to Gama, and she'd smiled and winked like she might be getting her hopes up again that he and I would become a couple. Although I enjoyed Kevin's company, and he was better looking than I remembered—his hair had toned down to the color of an old penny—I had no interest in dating him.

He'd suggested we go to dinner once, but we both agreed it would be best if we were not each other's rebound.

"Melissa called last night," Kevin said as soon as we sat at the counter to eat the sandwiches. "She wants to try again."

"Oh, really?" For the second time that day, I felt jealous because someone else had a relationship, and I didn't.

"We talked on the phone until daybreak," he continued.

"Well, that's good news. I'm glad for you." I sensed that he wanted me to ask questions about their conversation, but I just couldn't.

"So, have you heard anything from the handsome vet?"

"Nope."

One of the first things Dr. Conway advised me to do was cut off all contact with Zane. "He's made his decision, and he has that right," she told me. "You're only making your healing process more difficult by clinging to the hope he'll come back." Putting my trust in her guidance, I blocked Zane's phone number so I would no longer receive his token text messages. It had been almost two weeks now, and he'd made no effort to contact me. He could have gotten in touch if he really wanted to—through Gama, Lily, or Reenie—there were ways. I could only assume he was relieved that I'd severed the final thread connecting us.

"Maybe the separation will do you some good,"

Kevin said. "The space between Melissa and me made everything much clearer and...."

I cut him off mid-sentence. "My situation is more complex."

I knew he was only trying to help, but I didn't want to analyze my breakup with Zane—that's what my therapist was for—nor did I want to hear about how elated Kevin was to be reunited with Melissa.

We finished our lunch in polite silence. As I was cleaning off the counter, we chatted for a few minutes about nothing significant—I was beginning to appreciate the value of small talk—then Kevin left to return to the pharmacy.

As I worked on the Internet orders, I tried to stay positive and not dwell on, as Dr. Conway had put it, "matters over which I had no control." Around two, I began planning my journal entry in my head. It had been an outstanding day so far. I'd learned Lily was getting married, got a free lunch and a visit from a friend, finished another order, and found out that Gama—I'd called her twice more—had finally planted the vegetables, five rows, of course, including green beans.

How could I not be grateful?

*

Five o'clock arrived, and I was making my way to the front to lock up for the day when I heard movement outside the shop. At first, I assumed it was a customer, so I waited a few minutes. When no one came in, I opened the door to investigate and a brown and white spotted puppy, no more than three months old, staggered up to me. "Well, hello there," I said. "Are you lost?" I picked up the puppy and walked out onto the porch to look for the owner. As I was about to take the steps, I noticed someone standing on the sidewalk to the right of me, approximately eight feet away. Upon closer inspection, I realized it was Zane.

Suddenly, it no longer mattered that he'd left or hadn't tried to contact me; all that mattered was he'd somehow found the strength to come back. *There's my brave man!* I snuggled the puppy to my face, trying to conceal my spontaneous smile.

*But wait. How do I know he's here to see me?* He could have come to Driftwood to tie up loose ends or tend to his rental property and was merely passing by the shop. I decided it would be best to let him speak first.

"You blocked me," he said. There was a pitiful dejected-little-boy look in his eyes.

"My therapist told me I should."

"Your therapist?"

"Yeah, a lot has happened in the last couple of months." I held up the puppy. "Does she belong to you?"

"Her name is Chance."

I remembered him telling me he planned to get a dog whenever he settled somewhere and I wondered if he'd decided to put down stakes in North Carolina. "Why'd you name her that?"

"I thought it fit." He half-grinned. "I'm taking her

to the riverfront for a walk. I came here to ask you if you'd like to join us."

I wanted to fall into his arms, and be done with it all, but he wasn't getting off that easy. There was something I needed him to know, and talking about the puppy was not going to segue into the subject, so I just said it. "You hurt me when you left, Zane."

"I realize that, and I'm sorry; if it gives you any comfort, I hurt myself even more. I have no excuse for my actions. All I can say is, I thought I was doing what was best for both of us." He took a few cautious steps toward me. I noticed he'd lost about five pounds and his spirit was dim. "Addison, I'm not sure what the future holds, but I don't care if we fight every day. It can't be any worse than the hell I've lived in for the past couple of months. I made a dumb mistake, and if you'll let me, I'll spend the rest of my life making it up to you."

"What changed your mind?"

"Zach set me straight. He let me ruminate for a few weeks, then came to me and was like, 'You love the girl, so go be with her. Life's too short to worry about shit that happened in the past.' He's always had an uncomplicated, pragmatic approach to problems; it's a gift."

"So, did you come here expecting us to pick up where we left off?"

"No. I was hoping we could start all over, knowing what we now know, the way it should've been in the beginning."

"Why did you have to bring a puppy?"

"Guess I felt like I needed some help."

"But a puppy? That's not fair."

"You should know I don't play by the rules when it comes to you. I've been known to utilize all available resources."

"You didn't talk to Lily this time, did you?"

"No, but she was next on my list if the puppy didn't work." He had inched his way closer and was now standing right in front of me, at the bottom of the steps. "Addison, please, come walk with us. If you want to talk everything out, we will, and then we can leave it all behind. But whatever you decide, believe me when I say my love for you has always been genuine and grew organically, uninfluenced by anything other than who you are as a person."

Chance started licking my face. "If I say no, can I keep the puppy?"

"Absolutely not," he said. "But I'd love to share her with you."

"You mean the way we shared Hero?"

It sounded like a simple question, but Zane and I knew it was anything but. He hesitated, aware that what happened next might be contingent upon his response. Then a smile of relief slowly crept across his face. "Yes," he said. "Exactly like we shared Hero."

# THERE'S BEEN AN ACCIDENT

Made in the USA
Las Vegas, NV
01 December 2022

60756374R00207